The Student's Dictionary of Phrasal Verbs

Nigel D. Turton
and
Martin H. Manser

Macmillan

First published 1985

Published by *Macmillan Publishers Ltd*
London and Basingstoke
*Associated companies and representatives in Accra,
Auckland, Delhi, Dublin, Gaborone, Hamburg, Harare,
Hong Kong, Kuala Lumpur, Lagos, Manzini, Melbourne,
Mexico City, Nairobi, New York, Singapore, Tokyo*

Printed in Hong Kong

Turton, Nigel
    The student's dictionary of phrasal verbs.
    1. English language——Verb phrase——Dictionaries
    I. Title   II. Manser, Martin H.
    428.2′4   PE1689

ISBN 0–333–35023–5

Table of Contents

To Patrick and Friedemann

Acknowledgements

We would like to thank Jeremy Clear, Gwyneth Fox and Susie Turton for their assistance in preparing the manuscript.

Preface

To be fluent in English, you have to be able to use phrasal verbs. This dictionary has been written for intermediate and advanced students who want an easy-to-use reference book that deals with this area of the language. The emphasis is on idiomatic phrasal verbs, whose meaning and use are especially difficult for the student

The dictionary is a development of the highly successful *English Verbal Idioms* and *English Prepositional Idioms* by the late F. T. Wood. Great care has been taken to present the meaning and use of each verb clearly, and a system of notation has been devised that shows at a glance how each verb is used in a sentence.

Nigel D. Turton
Martin H. Manser

Introduction

To understand and use the idioms of a language correctly requires a degree of proficiency that is hard for the non-native speaker to acquire. An area of the English language which presents the student with particular difficulty is the idiomatic phrasal verb.

Idiomatic phrasal verbs

A phrasal verb is a verb which consists of two or three separate parts: *come in, run away, look forward to*, etc. With an idiomatic phrasal verb, the meanings of the separate parts tell us little or nothing about the meaning of the whole. For example, the student may be fully familiar with the meanings of *pick* and *up* as individual words, but this knowledge does not help him when he wants to know the idiomatic meaning of *pick up* in, say, 'Business is picking up'. This dictionary has been written to help the learner with this type of idiomatic combination. Non-idiomatic or literal phrasal verbs, which simply combine the meanings of their parts, are excluded.

However, having made the distinction between idiomatic and non-idiomatic phrasal verbs, we must point out that these are merely labels for the opposite ends of a scale: there are many phrasal verbs which are neither fully idiomatic nor fully literal. The guide for selection in these cases has been comprehensibility, so that a verb combination has been included if its meaning is not obvious from its parts. There are two exceptions to this rule: verbs used only in technical or specialised fields are not included, nor are verbs which are no longer in common use. Our intention has been to concentrate on the items likely to be of greatest use to the majority of students.

Grammatical notation

The language learner has to know how to use phrasal verbs correctly in sentences. A very simple guide has therefore been developed, providing the student with a clear visual impression of the grammatical behaviour of a verb without involving him in a long technical description. The basic system is shown in the table below.

1	●●	Suddenly all the lights *went out*.
2	●●○	I *bumped into* one of my old schoolfriends today.
3	●○●	The examiner *caught* everybody *out*.
4	●○●○	He *landed* me *with* the bill.
5	●○●	They're *bringing* a new book *out*.
or	●●○	They're *bringing out* a new book.

6	●●●○	I don't *feel up to* answering their questions.
7	●○●○	The mushrooms *brought* her *out in* spots.

The system employs two symbols: a filled circle and an empty circle. Each filled circle represents one part of the phrasal verb. Each empty circle represents one or more words that the user must add.

1 and 2   Consider the first two sentences in the above table:

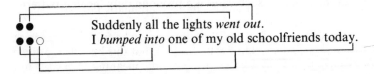

Suddenly all the lights *went out*.
I *bumped into* one of my old schoolfriends today.

Both *go out* and *bump into* have two parts, so both are represented by two filled circles. However, while *go out* does not necessarily have to be followed by anything, *bump into* must be followed by something, and this is shown by the final empty circle.

3   In some cases, it is necessary to insert an object between the parts of a verb. Again, an empty circle shows where the object must be placed:

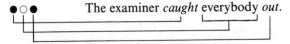

The examiner *caught* everybody *out*.

Note that when the object is a single word or short phrase, no other pattern may be used. But if the object is of some length, it is also possible to use pattern 2:

●●○   The examiner *caught out* everybody who took the exam.

If a long object contains a moveable part, as in the above example, this may follow the second part of the verb:

●○●   The examiner *caught* everybody *out* who took the exam.

To reduce the possibility of incorrect usage, only the basic pattern (●○●) is shown in the notation.

4   In other cases, it is necessary to insert something between the parts of a verb **and** to follow the last part with something:

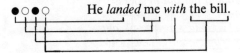

He *landed* me *with* the bill.

5 With many phrasal verbs, the user has a choice of word order:

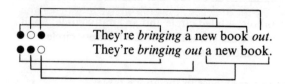

However, when the object in such cases is a pronoun only the first pattern may be used:

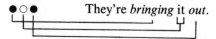

On the other hand, if the object is rather lengthy, it is typically the second pattern that is used:

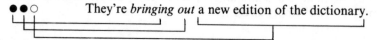

unless the object contains a movable part, such as a relative clause, when either pattern may be used:

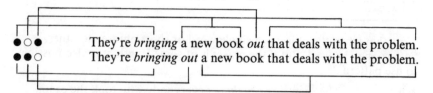

6 and 7 There are just two basic patterns for the three-part verbs:

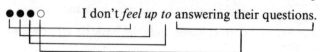

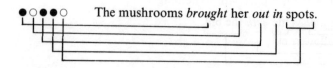

The following points about the notation system should also be noted:

1   Word order is not necessarily the same for each meaning of a phrasal verb. Compare the pattern of *draw up* when it means 'arrive at a place and stop':

●●   A car *drew up* and two men jumped out.

with the patterns used when it means 'compose and write down something in a formal way':

●○●   They've *drawn* the contract *up*.
●●○   We've *drawn up* the list of names you asked for.

In such cases, there is a separate entry for each meaning:

●●   **draw up¹**

●○●   **draw up²**
●●○

2   Some phrasal verbs may be used with two parts **or** three parts:

●●   I *called in* and saw John instead of going straight home.
●●●○   I *called in on* John instead of going straight home.

Verbs of this type are shown by the use of round brackets:

●●(●○)   **call in (on)**

3   A slash mark (/) is used to show alternatives. For example, '*Come on! I'm in a hurry!*' and '*Come along! I'm in a hurry!*' mean the same. Instead of having two separate entries, pairs of this type are therefore shown in the following way:

●●   **come along/on**

Sometimes the alternatives behave differently. This is true of, for example, *break in* and *break into*:

●●   Thieves *broke in* and stole the jewels.
●●○   Thieves *broke into* the house and stole the jewels.

The pattern of the first combination is therefore shown first, followed by a slash mark and then, beneath, the pattern of the second combination:

●●/   **break in/into**
●●○

Similarly, when the first combination has two or more patterns, these are shown first, followed by a slash mark and, beneath, the pattern(s) of

the second combination. Consider, for example, the notation for
get in/into²:

●●   **get in/into²**
●○●/
●●○
●○●○

This notation expresses the following possibilities:

●●   She's lucky to *get in* without the right qualifications.
●○●   Her father must have *got* her *in*: he knows the headmaster.
●●○   How did she manage to *get into* the school?
●○●○   Somehow her father *got* her *into* the school.

4   Nouns derived from the verbs shown in the dictionary have been
included, and are signalled by the letter **N** in heavy type in the notation
column alongside an example:

N   ☐ The first goal came just two minutes after the *kick-off*.

5   Usage is reflected in the examples. For instance, a single example of a
passive construction indicates that the verb is typically used in this way:

●●○   **get at** . . . . .
        4 influence or persuade somebody, especially with a bribe or
        threat:
        ☐ The witness had obviously been *got at*. He refused to tell
        the jury what he had seen.

Style

Most idiomatic phrasal verbs are used by native speakers in everyday
conversation, and these have been left unmarked. Occasionally, however,
the style-markers *Formal* and *Informal* are used.

Formal is shown against verbs which belong to formal written English,
such as business correspondence or to unusually formal spoken English.
These verbs will not form part of the spoken vocabulary of the average
learner. (It might be helpful to point out here that, in the case of **on/upon**
alternatives, the use of **upon** is generally more formal.)

The style marker *Informal* is shown alongside verbs which are used, for
example, between close friends or to express the speaker's anger or
irritation. Since many of these verbs could cause offence if used
inappropriately, the student is advised to treat them with caution.

A, a

●●○ **abide by** 1 accept something without argument, especially a decision or ruling:
□ Both sides in the dispute agreed to *abide by* the findings of the court.
2 obey a rule, regulation, law, etc:
□ If a member fails to *abide by* the rules of the club, he has to leave.

●●○ **account for** 1 provide an explanation for something:
□ Not one of the girl's teachers could *account for* her poor examination results.
□ The librarian was asked to *account for* all the books that were missing.
2 provide or be the source of something, especially of a geographical area:
□ The region *accounts for* almost two-thirds of the world's oil.
3 consume or be the reason for spending something:
□ The gas and electricity bills *account for* a quarter of my salary.
4 beat, defeat or destroy somebody or something:
□ By the end of the third day of fighting, over a half of the enemy's planes had been *accounted for*.

●○●○ **acquaint with** make somebody familiar with something:
□ New students spend the first few days *acquainting* themselves *with* the layout of the university.

●●○ **act as** perform the function of somebody or something:
□ Dr Smith will be *acting as* head of department for as long as the professor is away.
□ The new baby *acts as* a rather noisy alarm clock.

●○●
●●○ **act out** perform in real life something that you have thought or felt:
□ The dream of becoming a famous footballer is one that few boys ever manage to *act out*.

●● **act up** behave or perform badly:
□ Of course, it's always right in the middle of a good programme that the television set starts to *act up*.

●● **add up** seem probable or logical, or make sense; usually used in the negative:
□ She spent a whole year learning French and then went off to work in China! It just doesn't *add up*.

●●●○   **add up to**   mean or indicate something, especially after all points or details have been considered:
    ☐ What the report *adds up to* is that the company is spending far too much on advertising.

●●○   **adhere to**   continue to support or behave according to an idea, rule, plan, etc:
    ☐ Unless we are all prepared to *adhere to* the same set of principles, the project cannot succeed.

●●○   **agree with**   **1** suit somebody's health, digestion, character, etc: usually used in the negative:
    ☐ I can't eat peanuts. They just don't *agree with* me.
    2 be in favour of something, especially a principle or habit:
    ☐ I don't *agree with* allowing young children to buy cigarettes.
    3 be the same as something, or support something logically:
    ☐ I'm afraid that your calculations don't *agree with* mine.
    ☐ Except for one minor detail, the defendant's account of what happened *agreed* exactly *with* the evidence.
    4 correspond grammatically with something:
    ☐ I keep forgetting that a verb has to *agree with* its subject.

●●○   **allow for**   take something into consideration when making a decision, doing a calculation, etc:
    ☐ It would be wise to add another ten pounds to the total to *allow for* price increases.

●●○   **amount to**   may be interpreted as something, especially after all details have been considered:
    ☐ Their behaviour *amounts to* a complete refusal to co-operate.

●●○   **angle for**   try to obtain something, especially a compliment, invitation, piece of information, etc, in an indirect or cunning way:
    ☐ I think that she was probably *angling for* compliments.

●●
 ●○●   **answer back**   **1** reply rudely, especially of a child to an adult:
    ☐ *Answer back* once more and you'll go straight to bed!
    2 defend yourself by replying to a criticism:
    ☐ It's wrong to accuse him when he's not here and can't *answer* you *back*.

●●○   **answer for**   **1** accept the blame or responsibility for something:
    ☐ Who is going to *answer for* all the damage that's been done?

☐ Both governments have a great deal of human suffering to *answer for*.

2 guarantee the truth, accuracy, quality, etc, of something:

☐ Knowing very little about art, I obviously cannot *answer for* the originality of these paintings.

3 accept responsibility for speaking on behalf of somebody:

☐ I know how I feel about the proposal, although I can't *answer for* the other members of the team.

4 suffer or pay for your mistakes, sins, etc:

☐ One of these days you'll have to *answer for* the way you've treated me!

● ● ○   **answer to**   **1** give an explanation of your actions or behaviour to somebody; often used as part of a warning or threat:

☐ If you are caught with the stolen watches, you'll have the police to *answer to*.

2 match or correspond to something:

☐ A man *answering to* the description in the paper was seen in the park.

● ○ ●
● ● ○   **argue out**   continue to discuss an issue until a solution or conclusion is reached:

☐ The whole question of responsibility is by no means clear and if the pair of you wish to *argue* it *out*, I suggest that you wait until after this meeting is over.

● ● ○   **ask after**   ask for news about somebody:

☐ You must go and visit your aunt one of these days. She always *asks after* you.

● ● ○   **ask for**   invite or encourage something unpleasant to happen to you by your behaviour; often used as part of a warning:

☐ You're *asking for* trouble if you drink all that whisky.

● ○ ●   **ask in**   invite somebody to enter your home, especially for a short visit and without previous arrangement:

☐ They were kind enough to drive us home, so naturally we *asked* them *in* for a cup of coffee.

● ○ ●   **ask out**   invite somebody to accompany you somewhere, especially for a meal or entertainment:

☐ If you really like her, perhaps you should *ask* her *out*.

☐ You can imagine how we felt when they *asked* us *out* to an expensive restaurant and then left us to pay the bill!

● ○ ●   **ask over/round**   invite somebody to come to your home for a meal, visit, etc:

☐ We suddenly realised that we're free tomorrow night, so we thought we'd *ask* you and John *over* for a drink.

●●○   **attend to**   give somebody or something your time and attention:
    ☐ For the last two months, both doctors have had far too many patients to *attend to*.
    ☐ I suggest that you *attend to* the most urgent matters and let the rest wait.

B, b

●●   **back down**   withdraw or partly withdraw a demand or claim, usually ending a quarrel or confrontation:
  □ Union leaders are still refusing to *back down* in the dispute with the government over pay.

●●(●○)   **back out (of)**   withdraw from a plan or arrangement, often breaking a promise:
  □ Once you've paid a deposit, it's too late to *back out*.
  □ Her father will be furious if you try to *back out of* the marriage now.

●○●
●●○   **back up**   **1** give your support to somebody, especially in a discussion, or confirm that somebody's claim or statement is true:
  □ Before you go and complain to the headmaster, are you sure that the rest of the class will *back* you *up*?
  2 support something, especially a commercial product, by providing service or additional materials:
  □ The more expensive models are *backed up* by a guarantee.

N   □ Is there a tape as *back-up* for the course-book?

●●○   **bank on**   have confidence in somebody or something, or expect confidently that something will happen:
  □ You certainly can't *bank on* her help if she is about to leave the country.

●●○   **bargain for/on**   expect and be prepared for something; often used in the negative or preceded by *more than*:
  □ We certainly didn't *bargain for* all this rain when we booked the holiday.
  □ Giving birth to twins was more than she had *bargained for*.

●●/
●●○   **barge in/into**   *Informal* enter a room or interrupt a conversation in a rude way:
  □ Must you always *barge in* without knocking?
  □ He has a bad habit of *barging into* private conversations.

●●●○   **bear down on/upon**   *Formal* approach somebody or something quickly or purposefully, especially in a threatening way:
  □ Enemy tanks *bore down on* us so swiftly that there was no time to withdraw.

●●○   **bear on/upon**   be relevant to something:
  □ Everything that was said yesterday *bears* directly *upon* what we decide to do.

5

●○●
●●○   **bear out**   agree with somebody or confirm a story, account, etc:
     □ I'm sure you will all *bear* me *out* that far too much money has been spent on this project already.
     □ Her account of what happened is simply not *borne out* by the facts.

●●   **bear up**   not despair, despite misfortune or suffering:
     □ In view of the death of her husband, she's *bearing up* as well as can be expected.

●●○   **bear upon**   see **bear on/upon**.

●●○   **bear with**   be patient with or tolerate somebody or something:
     □ If you will just *bear with* me for a few moments, I'll explain the reasons behind the decision.

●○●
●●○   **beat down**   make somebody reduce the price of something by bargaining:
     □ If you think he is asking too much for the car, why not try to *beat* him *down*?

●●(●○)   **beaver away (at)**   work busily and steadily:
     □ The organisers have been *beavering away* all week preparing for the exhibition.

●●○   **become of**   happen to somebody or something; usually preceded by *what* or *whatever*:
     □ She was worried about what would *become of* her son if he couldn't get a job.
     □ Whatever *became of* old John Carmichael? I haven't seen him for years.

●○●
●●○   **beef up**   *Informal* strengthen or improve something by making a useful or valuable addition:
     □ The first two chapters need *beefing up* a bit with more facts and background details.

●●○   **believe in**   **1** feel certain that something which cannot be seen or heard nevertheless exists:
     □ Do you *believe in* ghosts?
     2 support or favour a principle, practice, etc:
     □ They *believe in* going to bed before ten o'clock and getting up at six.
     3 have confidence, trust or faith in somebody or something:
     □ We stopped *believing in* the football team after they lost twelve matches in a row.

●●   **belt up**   **1** *Informal* stop talking or making a noise; often used in the imperative to express anger or irritation:
     □ For heaven's sake, *belt up!*

2 fasten yourself into a car seat by using a safety belt:

☐ He always got his passengers to *belt up*.

●○●
●●○

bite back   stop yourself from saying something that you are just about to say:

☐ Knowing that she would misunderstand if he told her the truth, he *bit back* the words.

●●

black out¹   suffer a temporary loss of consciousness:

☐ I felt so faint, I thought I was going to *black out*.

N

☐ If he has another *blackout*, you really must call the doctor.

●○●
●●○

black out²   **1** prevent light from showing or being seen somewhere:

☐ You could use the kitchen as a darkroom if you *blacked out* the windows.

N

☐ They hoped that the *blackout* would reduce the number of night attacks by enemy aircraft.

2 stop television or radio programmes or the release of information:

☐ Both channels have been *blacked out* all week due to a strike by engineers.

N

☐ The military government imposed a complete news *blackout*.

●○●
●●○

block out   **1** draw a plan or outline of something without using details:

☐ Having *blocked out* the ground floor, they realised that there was no room for a kitchen!

2 cover or mask something, especially part of a picture or page so that it will not be printed:

☐ The photograph could be improved by *blocking out* one of the trees.

●○●
●●○

blot out   **1** kill or destroy a large number of people, especially in wartime:

☐ During the first hour of the engagement, almost a third of the naval force was *blotted out*.

2 hide or partly hide something from view:

☐ The top of the mountain was completely *blotted out* by a layer of mist.

●●

blow in   *Informal* arrive unexpectedly, especially in a casual way:

☐ You can't just *blow in* when you feel like it. You need an appointment.

●●

blow over   pass, especially of a storm or quarrel:

☐ The dispute soon *blew over* and everyone was happy again.

●● **blow up¹** **1** explode:
□ The terrorists hoped that the car would *blow up* just as the officer drove off.
2 *Informal* lose your temper:
□ He *blows up* nowadays whenever the slightest thing goes wrong.
3 arise or develop:
□ I shouldn't go sailing today if a storm's *blowing up*.
□ The present crisis *blew up* when the question of ownership was raised.

●○● **blow up²** **1** destroy something by the use of explosives:
●●○ □ They *blew up* the bridge just as the train was about to come across.
2 scold or reprimand somebody severely:
□ Her boss *blew* her *up* for losing the contract.
3 enlarge a photograph:
□ If you really like the picture, why don't you have it *blown up*?

N □ There's a lot more detail in the *blow-up*.
4 make something seem bigger or more important than it really is:
□ The incident was *blown up* by the press.

●● **bob up** appear or reappear suddenly:
□ Say hello to Susan for me if she *bobs up* while I'm away.

●○● **bog down** *Informal* overload somebody with work, difficulties, complications, etc:
□ Please don't *bog* me *down* with any more of your problems.
□ If you get *bogged down*, ask Paul to help you.

●●●○ **boil down to** may be reduced to something:
●○●○ □ His reasons for not wanting to go all *boil down to* the fact that he doesn't have enough money.

●● **boil over** **1** reach a crisis and become violent or uncontrollable:
□ The government is afraid that the growing political unrest will *boil over* unless something is done quickly.
2 *Informal* lose your temper or be very angry:
□ He *boiled over* when his wife drove their new car into the wall.

●● **boil up** arise or develop, especially of quarrels and arguments:
□ The latest row to *boil up* is over the train-drivers' refusal to work overtime.

●● **book in¹** register your name, address, etc, especially at a hotel:

☐ Always insist upon seeing your room before *booking in.*

●○●   **book in²**   reserve a room for somebody at a hotel:
●●○   ☐ If they're only staying for two nights, I suggest that you *book* them *in* at the Palm Beach.

●○●(●○)   **boot out (of)**   *Informal* make somebody leave a house,
●●○   job, club, etc, often because of bad behaviour or bad work:
     ☐ Now that they've decided to build a shopping centre, nearly a hundred local people are going to be *booted out of* their homes.

●○●   **bottle up**   hold back or refuse to give expression to a
●●○   strong feeling, especially sorrow or anger:
     ☐ If only she would allow herself to cry, instead of *bottling* everything *up*!

●●   **bottom out**   reach the lowest point of a slope, descent or scale:
     ☐ Sales *bottomed out* between June and August at approximately forty-five per cent of the January figure.
     ☐ Inflation has at last *bottomed out.*

●●   **bounce back**   recover quickly from a defeat or setback:
     ☐ Not many players could *bounce back* into the first team after such a serious leg injury.

●●(●○)   **bow down (to)**   yield or show a respectful attitude to somebody or something: often used in the negative:
     ☐ They won't *bow down to* you just because you're rich, you know.

●●   **bow out**   resign or retire, especially from an important position:
     ☐ After twelve years of faithful service, he has decided to *bow out* as chairman of the committee.

●●○   **bow to**   accept and act in accordance with a wish, decision, judgement, etc:
     ☐ After some hesitation, she *bowed to* the will of the majority.

●○●   **bowl over**   overwhelm or take control of somebody's
●●○   feelings or impress somebody greatly:
     ☐ She was completely *bowled over* by his good looks.
     ☐ The news of the air disaster *bowled over* the entire population.

●○●   **box in**   **1** limit the movement of somebody or something:
●●○   ☐ The American is running on the outside of the track after being cleverly *boxed in* by his opponents earlier in the race.

2 build an enclosure around an object in order to hide it from view:
□ The bathroom would look much nicer if the pipes were *boxed in*.

●●   **branch off**   leave a road, path, etc, and go onto a different, usually smaller one:
□ Remember to *branch off* at the next junction, unless you want to go straight on to London.

●●(●○)   **branch out (into)**   start or expand something, especially a business:
□ He should have stayed with his father's company instead of *branching out* on his own.
□ Several clothing manufacturers have *branched out into* sportswear in recent years.

●●(●○)   **break away (from)**   **1** leave or escape from somebody:
□ One of the prisoners *broke away from* the police escort and jumped out of the train.
2 end an association or political dependence:
□ At least three members have decided to *break away from* the party on account of the change in leadership.
□ It was exactly a hundred years ago today that the island *broke away from* colonial rule.

●●   **break down¹**   **1** suddenly develop a fault and stop working, especially of machines:
□ If the car *breaks down* just once more, I'm going to get a new one.

N   □ The technicians are responsible for maintenance and *breakdowns*.
2 be overcome by great emotion:
□ Both parents *broke down* and wept when the doctor said that the child would be blind.
3 fail and come to a halt:
□ The talks have again *broken down* over the issue of pay.

N   □ Friends of the couple feel very sad about the *breakdown* of their marriage.
4 collapse or fail, especially of somebody's mental health:

N   □ After the second *breakdown*, he spent six months in a private nursing home.

●○●
●●○   **break down²**   **1** overcome or suppress something; be overcome or defeated:
●●   □ Gifts of food and clothing soon *broke down* the hostility and suspicion with which we were greeted.
□ Local opposition to the scheme has *broken down* under government pressure.
2 separate something into different parts or categories:

□ Since the bill was unusually high, I asked the waiter to *break* it *down*.

N   □ Without a *breakdown* of these figures, they are meaningless.

3 change the chemical composition of something or experience a chemical change:

□ Fats are *broken down* in the body before they can be digested.

●○●   **break in**   **1** help somebody get used to a new job:

●●○   □ During the first two weeks we'll be *breaking* you *in* with some very simple drawings.

2 tame a horse so that it can be ridden:

□ Never buy a horse that hasn't been properly *broken in*.

3 make new clothes or equipment less stiff by wear or use:

□ The boots won't hurt so much once you've *broken* them *in*.

●●(●○)   **break in (on/upon)**   interrupt a conversation, meeting, etc:

□ She kept *breaking in* with the most ridiculous questions.

□ The operator *broke in on* our conversation to ask me if I wanted to pay for more time.

●●/   **break in/into**   force your way into a room or building,

●●○   often with a criminal purpose:

□ Thieves *broke in* last night and stole jewellery valued at thousands of pounds.

N   □ There has been an increasing number of *break-ins* in the area recently.

●●○   **break into**   **1** start using an amount of money, supply of food, etc:

□ So far I've managed not to *break into* the hundred pounds that my father gave me.

□ If there aren't enough biscuits, we can *break into* a new packet.

2 suddenly start to do something, especially sing, laugh, cry, run, etc:

□ She *broke into* tears when she heard the news.

□ The rider fell off when the horse unexpectedly *broke into* a gallop.

●○●   **break off¹**   unexpectedly end or discontinue something,

●●○   especially a relationship or association:

□ She threatened to *break* the engagement *off* unless he promised to take her on a long honeymoon.

□ Following two days of shooting along their borders, the two countries have *broken off* diplomatic relations.

●●   **break off²**   **1** stop speaking, suddenly or abruptly:

□ Feeling the gun in his back, he *broke off* and slowly raised his hands above his head.

2 stop work, especially for a short rest or pause:

□ I suggest that we *break off* now and meet back here at three o'clock when the lorry is supposed to arrive.

●● **break out**   **1** start or arise suddenly, especially of fire, disease or war:

□ It is believed that the fire *broke out* in the basement.

N □ There have been further *outbreaks* of fighting in the region.

2 exclaim, especially in anger or impatience: usually used for reporting speech:

□ 'I refuse to listen to any more of this nonsense!' he *broke out*, crashing his fist down upon the desk.

●●●○ **break out in/into**   **1** suddenly develop or become covered with spots, a rash, etc:

□ One of the baby's legs has *broken out in* little red spots.

2 suddenly utter or express something, often in a loud manner:

□ The audience *broke out in* peals of laughter when his trousers fell down.

●●(●○) **break out (of)**   escape, especially from a prison:

□ They planned to *break out* in the middle of the night, when the guards were asleep.

N □ Following the improvement of security measures, there have been fewer *break-outs*.

●●●○ **break out of**   stop doing something that you do regularly:

□ He promised to buy her anything she wanted, if only she would *break out of* the habit of smoking in bed.

●● **break through**   force a way through a wall, defence or
●●○ other barrier:

□ After six days of fierce fighting, our troops finally *broke through* the enemy line.

□ The sun keeps trying to *break through*.

●● **break up¹**   **1** dissolve or come to an end, especially of a marriage, friendship, partnership, etc:

□ The relationship began to *break up* when he realised that she didn't really want children.

N □ We didn't know about the *break-up* of their marriage until you told us.

2 separate or end a relationship:

□ Did you hear that John and Sue have *broken up* and that she's now living in Paris?

3 reach the end of a school term and start a holiday period:

☐ When do you *break up* for your summer holidays?

4 disperse or depart in different directions, especially after a meeting or other gathering:

☐ The demonstration *broke up* peacefully, so the police were not needed.

● ○ ●
● ● ○

break up² **1** bring a relationship or association to an end, especially without argument or conflict:

☐ After working together for thirty years, they *broke up* the partnership so that George could retire.

2 cause a crowd to disperse:

☐ The police used tear-gas to *break up* the rioters.

● ● ○

break with cease to have relations or dealings with a person, group, tradition, etc, especially following a disagreement:

☐ He *broke with* his family over their refusal to pay their share of his university fees.

● ○ ●
● ● ○

bring about **1** cause something to happen:

☐ Nobody knows what *brought about* the change in his political thinking.

2 reverse the direction of a ship or other vessel:

☐ Seeing the storm ahead, they *brought* the little fishing boat *about* and set course for the safety of the harbour.

● ○ ●
● ● ○

bring along/on **1** help somebody to develop a skill, especially by coaching:

☐ Instead of buying new players, several clubs are attempting to *bring on* their juniors in the hope that one day they will win a place in the first team.

2 help or encourage the growth of a plant, crop, etc:

☐ A bag or two of fertiliser should *bring* the tomatoes *on* nicely.

● ○ ●(● ○)

bring around/round (to) persuade somebody to accept an opinion, belief, etc:

☐ We're sure that she can be *brought round to* adopting the proposal, especially when she learns how little it will cost.

● ○ ●
● ● ○

bring back **1** cause the memory of something to return:

☐ This song *brings back* the evening we had dinner together, when the waiter upset wine over your new jacket.

2 restore or reintroduce a rule, law, custom, etc:

☐ The discussion has revealed that most of us are against *bringing back* the death penalty.

● ○ ●
● ● ○

bring down **1** reduce or persuade somebody to reduce the price of something:

☐ Many shops are having to *bring down* their prices in order to attract more custom.

☐ I tried to *bring* her *down*, but she wouldn't accept less than £10.

2 cause the defeat of a political body, authority, etc:

☐ Such a disastrous mistake could be enough to *bring* the Government *down* at the next election.

3 shoot at and hit an aircraft, bird or animal, so that it falls to the ground:

☐ The plane was *brought down* over northern France just one week before the war ended.

☐ He *brought down* the elephant just as it was about to charge.

4 cause an opponent on a sports field to fall to the ground by a tackle, foul, etc:

☐ The team demanded a penalty when their forward was *brought down* on the edge of the penalty area.

● ○ ●
● ● ○
bring forward **1** advance a meeting to an earlier time; advance a watch, clock or similar instrument:

☐ If you want everybody to come, you'll just have to *bring* the party *forward* a few days.

☐ Passengers are reminded to *bring* their watches *forward* before disembarking.

2 raise a topic for discussion:

☐ It was most surprising that, during the whole meeting, nobody *brought forward* the question of funds.

3 transfer a figure from one page to the next, or from one period of time to the next:

☐ Don't forget to *bring forward* the £30 from July.

● ○ ●
● ● ○
bring in **1** earn or yield money:

☐ In her new job she *brings in* an extra twenty pounds a month.

☐ The six hours a week that I work *bring in* enough to pay the gas and electricity bills.

2 employ somebody, especially a specialist, for a particular purpose:

☐ A consultant has been *brought in* to advise on suitable areas for company expansion.

3 introduce something, especially a new law or fashion:

☐ The Government has *brought in* several reforms aimed at improving conditions for old people.

4 take a criminal or suspected criminal to a police-station:

☐ The police have *brought* the two suspects *in* for questioning.

5 gather a harvest:
□ Most farmers managed to *bring in* their crops during the dry spell.

bring in on involve somebody in a plan, discussion, etc:
□ They refuse to *bring* him *in on* the project because he's too unreliable.

bring off win or accomplish something in spite of great difficulty or strong opposition:
□ Nobody dreamt that, with half their players sick, the team could *bring off* such an amazing victory.

bring on **1** be the cause of something, especially illness or physical discomfort:
□ The first cigarette she smokes each morning always *brings on* a fit of coughing.
2 see **bring along/on**.

bring on/upon cause trouble, worry, etc, especially for yourself:
□ She has *brought* all these problems *on* herself by marrying the wrong man.

bring out **1** reveal, express or show something clearly:
□ It is impossible to *bring out* the full meaning of the poem in a translation.
□ The sunlight *brought out* the gold in her hair.
2 publish a book, magazine, etc; release a new product to the public:
□ Have you tried the chocolate-flavoured toothpaste that has just been *brought out*?
3 cause something to emerge, especially a human quality or characteristic:
□ She believes that money *brings out* the worst in some people, especially their greed.
4 cause a group of workers to go on strike:
□ The new union leader is quite capable of *bringing out* the entire work force.
5 help somebody become less shy:
□ We tried to *bring* her *out* by sending her to a drama school, but she's still very quiet and nervous.
6 cause a blossom or flower to open:
□ The long hot spell has *brought* the roses *out*.
7 introduce your daughter to society as a debutante:
□ Caroline's parents are *bringing* her *out* this summer.

bring out in cause spots or marks to appear on a body:
□ I mustn't eat bananas. They *bring* me *out in* a rash.

●○●(●○)   **bring over (to)**   persuade somebody to change their
●●○(●○)   loyalty:
        ☐ As long as the salary is attractive, I'm sure he can be
        brought over to our side.

●○●(●○)   **bring round (to)**   see **bring around/round (to)**.
●○●   **bring round/to**   cause somebody to revive or regain
        consciousness:
        ☐ It was such a hard punch that it needed a cold sponge
        to *bring* him *round*.

●○●●○   **bring round to**   lead a conversation or discussion to a
        particular topic:
        ☐ No matter what we start talking about, she always
        manages to *bring* the conversation *round to* her family
        problems.

●○●   **bring through**   lead somebody safely through a crisis or
●○●○   ordeal:
        ☐ He was *brought through* the operation by an
        experienced team of surgeons, working round the clock.

●○●   **bring to**[1]   see **bring round/to**.
●○●○   **bring to**[2]   cause something, especially a bill or calculation,
        to reach a particular amount:
        ☐ Five times eleven, less twenty per cent discount, *brings*
        the total *to* £44 exactly.

●○●   **bring together**   introduce or reconcile people or parties:
●●○   ☐ The more they talk about divorce, the more her father
        tries to *bring* them *together* again.

●○●   **bring up**   **1** provide a home, care and education for a child
●●○   until it becomes an adult:
        ☐ Sally spent most of her childhood with her
        grandparents, who *brought* her *up* in a little village by the
        sea.

N   ☐ The poor girl has had a very sad *upbringing*.
        2 teach a child over many years to do or believe
        something; usually followed by a *to-* infinitive:
        ☐ We were *brought up* to respect the elderly.
        3 raise a point or topic during a conversation or
        discussion:
        ☐ Several matters of interest were *brought up* during the
        course of the interview.
        4 vomit:
        ☐ For a whole week he couldn't eat anything without
        bringing it *up* again.
        5 make somebody appear at a court of law for trial:
        ☐ His younger brother has been *brought up* before the
        magistrate on a charge of disturbing the peace.

● ○ ● ● ○   **bring up against**   make somebody realise or confront something, especially something unpleasant:
□ Having spent the last of their money, they were suddenly *brought up against* the reality of their situation.

● ○ ● ○   **bring upon**   see **bring on/upon**.

● ○ ● ● ○   **bring up to**   **1** increase a figure to a particular sum:
□ Your uncle's five pounds *brings* the amount we've been given *up to* £42.50.
2 cause somebody or something to reach a particular standard:
□ With a good service, the efficiency of the engine can be *brought up to* that of a new one.

● ● ○   **bristle with**   **1** display strong emotion, especially anger or hatred:
□ The mere mention of his name would make her *bristle with* rage.
2 display a great number or quantity of something:
□ The letter simply *bristled with* the most awful spelling mistakes.

● ○ ●   **brown off**   *Informal* bore or annoy somebody:
□ Addressing envelopes all day is enough to *brown* anybody *off*.
□ What really *browns* me *off* is the way she wakes the whole household in the middle of the night.

● ○ ●
● ● ○   **brush aside**   **1** dismiss or disregard something, especially a comment, suggestion, etc:
□ The chairman tended to *brush aside* any objections he didn't agree with.
2 remove something, especially a barrier or obstacle, very easily:
□ The advancing flood waters *brushed* houses and cars *aside* like matchsticks.

● ○ ●
● ● ○   **brush off**   end a conversation or relationship, especially in an abrupt way:
□ She *brushed* us *off* with the excuse that she had another appointment.
□ How can you just *brush* me *off* like this after all the years we've been together?

N   □ Henry is afraid to invite the new typist to dinner, in case he gets the *brush-off*.

● ●
● ● ○   **brush past**   move past somebody or something, touching them lightly:
□ When they *brushed past* each other in the corridor, he noticed that she was wearing a new perfume.

●●○   **brush up**   improve or regain a skill or area of knowledge by practice or revision:
     □ You'll need to *brush up* your German if you get the job in Austria.

●●   **buck up¹**   *Informal*   **1** become more cheerful or lively; often used in the imperative:
     □ *Buck up!* You're making me feel miserable too.
     2 hurry; often used in or with the force of the imperative:
     □ Richard! If you don't *buck up*, we're going to miss the start of the film.

●○●   **buck up²**   make somebody more cheerful or energetic:
●●○   □ I'm sure that the news of the new baby will *buck* your father *up* a bit.

●●   **bucket down**   *Informal* fall in great quantity, especially of rain:
     □ It's been *bucketing down* all morning.

●●(●○)   **buckle down (to)**   begin to apply yourself diligently to a task:
     □ You're going to fail the exam unless you *buckle down* and do some serious work.

●○●   **build in**   **1** construct something, especially a cupboard, so
●●○   that it is fixed to or forms a part of a structure:
     □ The wardrobe in the front bedroom has been *built in*.
     2 include a statement in a written agreement as a necessary part of it:
     □ The new owner wants to *build in* a clause which will prevent the public from using the footpath.

●●○   **build on/upon**   use something as a basis for further effort:
     □ The sales figures are pretty miserable, I suppose, but at least they give us something to *build on*.

●●   **build up¹**   increase in size, strength or intensity:
     □ Several jams have been *building up* on roads out of London due to holiday traffic.

N   □ Many people are worried about the *build-up* of tension in the Middle East.

●○●   **build up²**   **1** develop or increase something gradually:
●●○   □ It took him twenty years to *build up* the business.
     □ A good reputation cannot be *built up* overnight.
     2 develop or cover an area with buildings, roads, etc:
     □ Most of the city centre had already been *built up* by the time my father arrived here in the 1960s.

●○●   **build up³**   **1** improve somebody's physical condition:
     □ After six weeks in hospital he needs *building up*.

☐ With just one month to go, they've started to *build* him *up* for the fight.
2 develop the image or reputation of somebody or something, often by excessive praise:
☐ He's been *built up* by the media as one of the heroes of our time.

N
☐ After the big *build-up* we've given her, I hope she doesn't disappoint everybody.

●●○ **build upon**   see **build on/upon**.

●● **bum around**   *Informal* spend your time lazily and aimlessly; often used in a derogatory way:
☐ It's about time you stopped *bumming around* and started to look for a job.

●●○ **bump into**   meet somebody by chance:
☐ Guess who I *bumped into* in the market today?

●○● **bump off**   *Informal* kill or murder somebody; often used
●●○ in a light-hearted way:
☐ People say that the old doctor had managed to *bump off* half his patients by the time he finally decided to retire.

●○● **bump up**   increase an amount:
●●○ ☐ Don't let him know that you like the car, or he'll *bump* the price *up*.

●○● **bung up**   block a narrow opening, especially in a pipe or
●●○ tube, often by accident:
☐ You'll *bung* the sink *up* if you pour that hot fat down it.

●○● **buoy up**   **1** make somebody more cheerful; encourage
●●○ somebody:
☐ It was the thought of one day finishing the book that *buoyed* him *up* during the long lonely hours he spent at his desk.
2 stop a price, value, etc, from falling:
☐ The country's increasing share of the oil market has been *buoying up* its currency overseas.

●○● **burn out**   **1** exhaust or over-exert yourself:
☐ By the end of the third set, the older player had obviously *burnt* himself *out*.
2 ruin your health, especially by neglect or maltreatment:
☐ The actress *burnt* herself *out* on pills and alcohol.

●●○ **burn with**   experience emotion very strongly:
☐ She was *burning with* the desire to have children.
☐ If he only wants to see her once a fortnight, I'd hardly say that he's *burning with* passion.

●●(●○)   **burst in (on/upon)**   **1** interrupt somebody speaking:
           ☐ 'And who's going to pay for it?' she *burst in*, right in
           the middle of his opening remarks.
           2 disturb somebody by entering suddenly and
           unexpectedly:
           ☐ It's very rude to *burst in on* somebody without
           knocking! You should know better at your age.

●●/   **burst in/into**   enter somewhere in a great hurry:
●●○   ☐ Breathless, the little girl *burst into* the bedroom,
           grabbed her doll, and rushed out again.

●●○   **burst into**   **1** do something suddenly, especially laugh, cry,
           sing, etc:
           ☐ As the final curtain fell, the audience *burst into* loud
           applause.
           2 develop buds, leaves or flowers:
           ☐ You know that spring has arrived when you see the
           trees *bursting into* blossom.

●●   **burst out**   **1** utter something suddenly and with emotion:
           usually used for reporting speech:
           ☐ 'I just wish that all of you would leave me alone!' he
           burst out.

N   ☐ His sudden *outburst* was very much out of character.
           2 suddenly sing, laugh or cry; followed by *-ing*:
           ☐ She *burst out* laughing at the expression on his face.

●●(●○)   **burst out (of)**   leave or escape from a building, room,
           yard, etc, especially using force:
           ☐ Eventually the wall collapsed, and the men *burst out of*
           the prison.

●●(●○)   **butt in (on)**   interfere or interrupt a conversation: often
           used as part of an apology:
           ☐ Excuse me for *butting in*, but there's a telephone call
           for you, Mr Harrison.

●○●   **butter up**   *Informal* be nice to somebody, especially with
●●○   the intention of gaining a favour:
           ☐ She spent the evening *buttering up* the professor in the
           hope that he would give her a good reference.

●○●   **buy in**   buy a large quantity of something as a reserve or
           stock:
           ☐ She's *buying in* all the sugar she can, in case there's
           another shortage.

●○●   **buy off**   bribe somebody not to do something:
●●○   ☐ They know that I could give their names to the police,
           so now they're trying to *buy* me *off*.

●○●
●●○   **buy out¹**   buy all of somebody's share or interest in a business:
□ *Buying* him *out* is going to be difficult as long as his profits keep rising.

●○●   **buy out²**   obtain the release of somebody from the army, navy, etc, by paying a sum of money:
□ He hates the army but he can't afford to *buy* himself *out*.

●●   **buzz off**   *Informal* leave: often used in the imperative:
□ Just *buzz off* and stop annoying me, will you?

C, c

●○●   **call away**   cause somebody to leave their home, office, etc:
●●○   □ Her husband is always being *called away* on business.

●●(●○)   **call by (at)**   visit or stop somewhere for a short time, especially on your way to somewhere else:
□ If I have enough time, I'll *call by* and see you tonight on the way home.

●●○   **call for**   **1** come or go somewhere, especially to somebody's home, to collect somebody or something:
□ The train leaves at half-past ten, so she's *calling for* me at a quarter to.
2 require or deserve somebody or something:
□ These wonderful results *call for* a celebration.
□ The job *calls for* a man who can accept responsibility.
□ That unkind remark certainly wasn't *called for*.

●○●   **call in**   **1** ask a doctor, builder, expert, etc, to come to your
●●○   home or office:
□ If you think that the repair is going to be a difficult job, we'll just have to *call in* a builder.
2 request or order somebody to return something:
□ All library books are being *called in* this week for the annual inspection.

●●(●○)   **call in (at)**   visit or stop somewhere for a short time, especially on your way to somewhere else:
□ If I remember, I'll *call in at* the chemist's on my way back to collect your pills.

●●(●○)   **call in (on)**   pay somebody a short casual visit, especially when this does not require a long journey:
□ It's only ten o'clock. Why don't we *call in on* John instead of going straight home?

●○●   **call off**   **1** abandon or cancel something:
●●○   □ The strike which was planned to begin on Tuesday has been *called off*.
□ After six days the search for the missing climbers was *called off*.
2 give an order for somebody or something to stop a search or attack:
□ *Call* your dog *off*! I'm the new gardener.

●●○   **call on**   visit somebody:
□ I always try to *call on* friends when they're ill.

●●○   **call on/upon**   **1** invite or request somebody to do something, especially to speak to a group of people:
□ If I were you, I'd make a few notes just in case you are *called upon* to make a speech.
2 ask somebody for help, support, etc:
□ Parents are being *called upon* to help raise funds for the new swimming pool.

●○●
●●○   **call out**   **1** summon somebody, especially to help in an emergency:
□ Don't *call out* the fire brigade unless the smoke gets worse.
2 order workers to go on strike:
□ Steel workers stopped work today after being *called out* by their union leaders.

●●   **call over/round**   pay a short visit to somebody's home, office, etc:
□ She said she would *call round* at about half-past three to collect the children.

●○●
●●○   **call up**   **1** telephone somebody:
□ I can give you his number if you want to *call* him *up*.
2 order somebody to join the army, navy, etc:
□ Her husband was *called up* right at the beginning of the war, and was away for six years.

●●○   **call upon**   see **call on/upon**.

●○●
●●○
●●   **calm down**   become or cause somebody to become quiet, relaxed, etc, especially after being excited or worried:
□ If you don't *calm down*, you're going to have a heart attack.

●●○   **care for**   **1** like somebody or something; often used in the negative:
□ I certainly don't *care for* the way he treats his wife.
2 like to have something; usually used to make an offer:
□ Would you *care for* a cigar?
3 nurse or be responsible for somebody:
□ Who's *caring for* the children since his wife went away?

●○●
●●○   **carry away**   inspire somebody; cause somebody to be overcome with emotion or excitement; usually used in the passive:
□ She refused to let herself be *carried away* by his good looks.

●○●(●○)   **carry back (to)**   cause somebody to remember something which happened much earlier:
□ The old photograph *carried* her *back to* the days before the war.

●○● 　**carry forward/over**　transfer a figure from one page to the
●●○ 　next, or from one period of time to the next:
　　□ Don't forget the £30 to be *carried forward* from July.
●●○ 　**carry off¹**　win something, especially in a competition:
　　□ She's playing so well this year that people expect her to
　　carry off all the big prizes again.
●○● 　**carry off²**　**1** perform a role successfully, especially of an
●●○ 　actor or actress:
　　□ Considering that he had never played the part of an
　　old man before, he *carried* it *off* remarkably well.
　　2 manage or handle a difficult situation successfully:
　　□ She postponed the press conference several times,
　　afraid that she would never be able to *carry* it *off*.
●● 　**carry on¹**　**1** continue to do something:
　　□ Despite all the noise, the girl *carried on* reading.
　　□ Just *carry on* with your work as if I wasn't here.
　　□ Most of these machines will *carry on* without an
　　operator.
　　2 continue to live or survive:
　　□ The poor man doesn't really want to *carry on* since his
　　wife died.
　　3 *Informal* keep complaining or making a fuss; often used
　　in a derogatory way:
　　□ That woman is always *carrying on* about the price of
　　food.
N 　　□ I've never heard such a *carry-on* about nothing!
　　4 *Informal* have a sexual relationship; often used in a
　　derogatory way:
　　□ It seems that they'd been *carrying on* for at least six
　　months before his wife found out.
●●○ 　**carry on²**　**1** cause a conversation, discussion, etc, to⁻
　　continue:
　　□ Some of the students were able to *carry on* fairly long
　　conversations in English after just ten lessons.
　　2 cause something to continue to happen or exist,
　　especially a business or tradition:
　　□ Despite the fire, we're *carrying on* business as usual.
　　□ If you want to *carry on* the family name, you'll have to
　　have a son.
●●○ 　**carry out**　**1** execute an order, plan, duty, etc; fulfil a threat
　　or promise:
　　□ Unless you *carry out* his instructions, you'll soon be
　　looking for a new job.
　　□ The workers are worried that the owner will *carry out*
　　his threat to close the factory.

2 do or conduct an experiment, operation, study, etc:
□ Doctors are *carrying out* tests to discover the nature of the new disease.

●○●
●●○
carry over **1** postpone something to a later time:
□ Other business will be *carried over* to the next meeting.
2 see **carry forward/over.**

●○●
●○●○
carry through **1** enable somebody to endure a period of difficulty or suffering:
□ What *carried* him *through* the long years of imprisonment was the hope that he would one day return to his wife and family.
2 continue to work at something until it is completed:
□ The building programme was the idea of the previous government, but it was the present one that *carried* it *through.*

●○●
●●○
carve up *Informal* **1** divide something into parts or shares:
□ How are you going to *carve up* the winnings? Half each?
2 beat somebody easily in a competition, race, etc:
□ He always thought that he was good at chess until he was *carved up* by a beginner.
3 inflict injuries on somebody with a knife:
□ Unless you want one of the gang to *carve* you *up,* you'd better keep quiet about the robbery.

●●(●○)
cash in (on) *Informal* benefit or make a profit for yourself from something:
□ Dozens of news photographers *cashed in on* the tragedy with their pictures of the young widows.
□ Whenever I have a good idea, he always wants to *cash in.*

●●(●○)
cast about/around/round (for) try to find or acquire something, especially by looking in different places:
□ The boss has been *casting about for* suggestions as to how business might be improved next year.

●○●
●●○
cast aside reject, abandon or get rid of somebody or something:
□ *Cast* all your cares *aside.*
□ She refused to be *cast aside* for another woman.

●●
cast off¹ untie the rope which stops a boat or ship from moving:
□ Once everybody's on board, we'll *cast off.*

●○●
●●○
cast off² **1** stop wearing something:
□ It's time you *cast off* that old suit and bought yourself a new one.

N □ She's too proud to wear other people's *cast-offs*.
2 reject, abandon or get rid of somebody or something:
□ Her mother was rather annoyed with her for *casting off* such a nice young man.

N □ Tomorrow you'll be just another one of his *cast-offs*.

●●
●●○ **cast off³** finish a piece of knitting by removing the last row of stitches from the needle to make a finished edge:
□ I'm almost ready to *cast off*, and then I can sew the jumper together.

●●
●●○ **cast on** begin a piece of knitting by making the first row of stitches:
□ It tells you to *cast on* fifty-eight stitches for a thirty-six-inch chest.

●○●
●●○ **cast out** reject or dismiss somebody or something:
□ The immigrants were *cast out* by the rest of the community.

N □ Homeless, friendless and without a job, he began to feel more and more like an *outcast* from society.

●●(●○) **cast round (for)** see **cast about/around/round (for)**.

●● **catch on** **1** understand something:
□ Some children take much longer to *catch on*, and it's these slow learners that I feel sorry for.
□ I kept looking at my watch and yawning, but she didn't *catch on*.
2 become popular or fashionable:
□ We thought that the idea of making clothes from old newspapers was a good one, but it didn't *catch on*.

●○● **catch out** **1** cause somebody to make a mistake or be unable to give a correct answer; discover somebody doing something wrong:
□ There was one question in the examination paper that *caught* everybody *out*.
2 reveal somebody's guilt, lies, etc:
□ It was the blood on his jacket that *caught* him *out*.

●●(●○) **catch up (on)** **1** bring yourself up to date with news, gossip, etc:
□ He loves to *catch up on* the news after a trip abroad.
2 reduce the amount that one is behind in something, especially by making an extra effort:
□ Why not try and go to bed a bit earlier tonight, and *catch up on* some of the sleep you've lost?

●○●
●●(●○) **catch up (with)** **1** reach, find or draw level with somebody you are following, chasing or in competition with:
□ The traffic wasn't so bad when I left, so I drove fast and *caught* the others *up* quickly.

2 reach a level that others have already reached by making an extra effort:
 □ If you miss too many lessons, you'll never be able to *catch up*.

●●●○ **catch up on** have an effect on somebody's health, work, behaviour, etc, especially a damaging effect:
 □ Don't be surprised if all these cigarettes you are smoking *catch up on* you one day.

●●○ **cater for** **1** provide somebody or something with what is wanted or liked:
 □ Only two of the newspapers *cater for* people who are interested in golf.
 □ It's impossible to *cater for* all tastes.
 2 be prepared for something:
 □ We knew that the husband and wife were coming to look at the house, but we hadn't *catered for* them bringing a dozen relatives, too. .

●●○ **cater to** provide what is required to satisfy a particular appetite or demand:
 □ Films that *cater to* the desire for violence on the screen seem to be as popular as ever.

●● **cave in** **1** collapse, especially of a roof:
 □ Luckily, most of the men were able to get out of the tunnel before it *caved in*.

N   □ Wives of the trapped miners wept uncontrollably when they heard about the *cave-in*.
 2 collapse, fail or be ruined:
 □ His business suddenly *caved in* when a competitor opened a new supermarket just across the street.

●○● **chalk up** add something to a list or score, especially a
●●○ success:
 □ The boys *chalked up* a fine victory on Saturday with a win against strong opposition.

●●○ **chance on/upon** meet somebody by chance:
 □ The two couples just happened to *chance upon* each other while on holiday in France.

●● **change down** change to a lower gear in a vehicle:
 □ You'll have to *change down* to get up the next hill.

●● **change over/round** exchange places, activities, roles, etc:
 □ Tell me if you get tired of driving and we'll *change over*.

N   □ Both sides played much better after the *change-over* at half time.

●● **change up** change to a higher gear in a vehicle:
 □ *Change up* as soon as you can if you want to save petrol.

●●○   **chase after**   pay a lot of attention to a member of the opposite sex in order to win the person's love, admiration, etc; usually used in a derogatory way:
□ She's been *chasing after* him for years, but with little success.

●○●   **chase up**   **1** search for something, especially information:
●●○   □ If you know the name of the author, I can easily *chase up* the title for you.
2 urge somebody to do something quickly:
□ If they haven't paid the bill by the end of the month, we'll have to start *chasing* them *up*.

●○●   **chat up**   *Informal* talk to somebody in a way that is
●●○   intended to win their friendship or gain an advantage:
□ I wouldn't try *chatting* her *up* if I were you. She's married to a former world heavyweight champion!
□ She *chatted up* the producer in the hope of getting a part in his next film.

●●(●○)   **check in (at)**   **1** register, your name, address, etc, especially at the reception desk of a hotel:
□ You go and *check in* while I pay the taxi driver.
2 report your arrival at an airline desk before the departure of your flight:
□ What time do we have to *check in*?

N   □ Somebody had lost his ticket, so there was a long queue at the *check-in*.

●●/   **check out/out of**   pay the bill and return the room key
●●●○   before leaving a hotel:
□ We'll need at least an hour to *check out* and get to the airport.

N   □ We'd like to remind our guests that *check-out* is no later than twelve o'clock.

●○●   **check off**   put a mark against a name or item on a list,
●●○   especially to show that the person or item is present, correct, etc:
□ A polite young lady came round *checking off* the guests one by one.

●●   **cheer up**   become or cause somebody to become happier;
●○●   often used in the imperative:
●●○   □ *Cheer up*, John! It can't be as bad as all that.

●○●   **cheese off**   *Informal* bore and depress somebody:
●●○   □ Hearing the same joke three times in one evening is enough to *cheese* anybody *off*.
□ I'm really *cheesed off* with this bad weather.

●○●   **chew over**   *Informal* consider something carefully,
●●○   especially before reaching a decision:

□ It's an interesting suggestion, but we need a bit longer to *chew* it *over*.

●●/
●●●○ **chicken out/out of** *Informal* withdraw from something because of anxiety or fear; usually used in a derogatory way:

□ Having seen how far it was to swim to the other side of the lake, he *chickened out*.

●●(●○) **chime in (with)** interrupt a conversation or discussion:

□ 'And about time too, if you ask me!' a voice at the back *chimed in*.

●●(●○)
●●○ **chip in (with)** **1** interrupt, especially to contribute ideas, facts, etc, to a discussion:

□ I'd like to remind you all that you are free to *chip in* at any time.

2 give money to a collection, especially to buy a gift for a colleague:

□ If we're going to give Henry something special for his retirement, each member of staff will have to *chip in* at least five pounds.

●○●●○ **chisel out of** *Informal* get something from somebody, especially money, by cheating or deceiving them:

□ Surely she wasn't stupid enough to let him *chisel* her *out of* her savings, was she?

□ He's not going to *chisel* another penny *out of* me.

●○●
●●○ **choke back** prevent yourself from expressing anger or sadness:

□ She tried her best to *choke back* the tears, but the sight of his thin white hand on the sheet was too much for her.

●● **chop about** *Informal* keep changing your plans, opinions, etc:

□ I wish they'd stop *chopping about* and decide whether they want to sell the house or not.

●○●
●●○ **chuck in/up** *Informal* resign from a job; abandon a course, etc:

□ He stayed with the firm for just six weeks and then *chucked* it *in*.

●○●(●○)
●●○ **chuck out (of)** *Informal* **1** dismiss or expel somebody from a company, school, club, etc, especially because of bad work or behaviour:

□ They *chuck* you *out* if you fail your first-year exams more than once.

2 make a person leave a club, bar, restaurant, etc, especially by using physical force:

□ The last time he tried dancing on the table, they *chucked* him *out*.

●●●○   **chum up with**   become friendly with somebody:
□ He was lonely for several weeks until he *chummed up with* one of the other new boys.

●○●   **churn out**   produce something quickly or in great
●●○   quantities, like a machine:
□ Some of these journalists *churn out* stories faster than people can read them!

●●   **clam up**   become silent or refuse to talk about something:
□ As soon as I mentioned his research, he immediately *clammed up*.

●●(●○)   **clamp down (on)**   make an effort to restrict or prevent something, especially criminal or undesirable behaviour:
□ Her husband's firm is beginning to *clamp down on* time-wasting.

●○●(●○)   **clean out (of)**   *Informal*   **1** take all somebody's money,
●●○(●○)   especially by winning or stealing it:
□ Of course they *cleaned* you *out*: they're professional gamblers.
2 take all the money or an entire stock of something from a bank, shop, etc, especially by stealing it:
□ Another jeweller's was *cleaned out* of all its stock on Saturday night.

●●   **clear off**   *Informal*   go away; often used in a derogatory way:
□ She *cleared off* after lunch without even saying goodbye.
□ *Clear off* or I'll call the police!

●●(●○)   **clear out (of)**   leave somewhere, especially quickly, or
●○●(●○)   cause somebody or something to do this:
□ We all *cleared out* as soon as we heard the alarm.

●●   **clear up¹**   become fine, especially of weather:
□ They're lucky that the weather has *cleared up* in time for the tennis match.

●○●   **clear up²**   disappear or cause something to disappear,
●●○   especially a problem, mystery or disagreement:
●●   □ All it needed was a little explanation to *clear up* the misunderstanding.

●●(●○)   **climb down (over)**   stop pursuing a claim, argument, etc, especially while admitting your weakness or mistake:
□ There is little possibility of the newspaper's owner *climbing down* once he has threatened to sell it.
N   □ They must have hated having to admit that they were wrong. What a *climb-down*!

●●   **clock in/on**   record your time of arrival at work, especially by using a machine made for this purpose:

        ☐ What time do you have to *clock in* in the morning?

●●   **clock out/off**   record the time of your departure from work, especially by using a machine made for this purpose:
        ☐ Don't forget to remind the new girl to *clock out* before she goes home.

●●   **close down¹**   stop operating, or cause something to stop
●●○   operating:
●○●   ☐ The factory *closes down* for two weeks in August.
        ☐ We're losing so much money that I think we'll have to *close* the business *down*.

●●   **close down²**   stop broadcasting for the day:
        ☐ They normally play the National Anthem before *closing down*.
N   ☐ *Close-down* is at midnight after the late news summary.

●●   **close in**   become shorter, especially of days:
        ☐ As the days gradually *closed in*, we began to stay at home more in the evenings.

●●(●○)   **close in (on/upon)**   approach or surround somebody or something, especially in a threatening way:
        ☐ The police quietly *closed in on* the house where the escaped prisoners were hiding.

●●   **club together**   combine to do something, especially to share the cost of something:
        ☐ Let's *club together* to buy them something they really need, like a washing machine.

●○●   **cock up** *Informal* spoil something or do something badly;
●●○   usually used in a derogatory way:
        ☐ He really wanted the job, but was so nervous that he *cocked up* the interview.
N   ☐ She's made a complete *cock-up* of the translation.

●●   **come about**   happen or occur:
        ☐ I just don't understand how it *came about* that you weren't informed.

●●○   **come across¹**   find something or meet somebody by chance:
        ☐ If you *come across* any records by French singers in that pile, would you keep them for me?

●●○   **come across²** **1** be communicated effectively:
●●   ☐ It doesn't matter how good your ideas may be if they don't *come across* clearly in the book.
    2 make an impression, especially at a first meeting:
        ☐ If you want to be given the job, it's vital that you *come across* well when you meet the directors.

●●●○   **come across with** *Informal* provide something, especially money, on demand or request:
□ You can rely on John to *come across with* the cash whenever you need it.

●●○   **come after** pursue somebody, often in a threatening way:
□ You'll have the police *coming after* you if you start taking things that don't belong to you.

●●   **come along/on** **1** improve or progress, especially in connection with work, growth or health:
□ How's your piano-playing *coming along* these days?
□ The vegetables are *coming on* nicely, thanks to all the rain we've been having.
□ The doctors are pleased with the way he's been *coming along* since the operation.
2 hurry, make more effort; often used in the imperative:
□ *Come on!* We're going to be late again.
□ *Come along*, Mary! You can do better than that.

●●   **come apart** **1** fall or break into pieces:
□ He says that the cup *came apart* in his hands, but I think he must have dropped it.
2 be separated into parts or be opened:
□ How does the watch *come apart* when it needs a new battery?

●●   **come around/round** **1** happen or arrive, especially in the case of a yearly event:
□ Birthdays *come round* all too quickly once you're past thirty.
2 stop being angry, annoyed, etc, and return to your normal mood:
□ It usually takes about an hour for him to *come round* after an argument.

●●○   **come at** attack somebody:
□ I keep having this nightmare about a madman *coming at* me with a knife.

●●(●○)   **come away (from)** become detached from something, especially unexpectedly:
□ I reached down to open the door, but the handle *came away* in my hand.

●●   **come back** **1** become popular or fashionable again:
□ I never thought I'd see high heels *come back* again.
N   □ The pop group failed to make the *come-back* that they'd been hoping for.
2 be remembered or recalled:
□ For weeks I couldn't remember her name, and then suddenly it *came back* to me.

3 be reintroduced or restored:
☐ I wonder how many of us would like to see the death penalty *come back*?

●●●○ **come back at**   reply to something somebody has said, especially critically:
☐ Those of you who don't like my suggestion will have the chance to *come back at* me later on.

●●●○(●○) **come back to (on)**   talk again to somebody on a particular matter:
☐ I can't answer your question immediately, I'm afraid. Can I *come back to* you *on* that in half an hour?
☐ I'll need to *come back to* you later with the name of our representative.

●●○ **come before**   **1** be of more importance than something else:
☐ The child's education *comes before* summer holidays abroad.
2 be brought in front of a court or committee for consideration:
☐ The accused *came before* the judge.
☐ The plan will *come before* next week's council meeting.

●●○ **come between**   interfere with a relationship or cause two people or animals to separate:
☐ She didn't accept her daughter's choice of husband, and for a long time tried to *come between* them.

●●○ **come by**   obtain or receive something:
☐ How did you *come by* all that dirt on your sleeve?
☐ Good jobs were hard to *come by* in those days.

●● **come down¹**   **1** be reduced, especially of prices:
☐ Did you know that sugar's *coming down* next week?
2 collapse or be demolished:
☐ The town council has said that all these lovely old buildings have got to *come down* by the end of the year.
☐ Of all the tents I've erected, only one has ever *come down*.
3 be passed from one generation to the next:
☐ The writing desk must be antique by now if it has *come down* through all those generations.
4 be hit by gunfire, etc, and fall to the ground, especially of aircraft:
☐ The aeroplane *came down* over France.
5 lose your wealth or status:
☐ Since he left the company, he's really *come down* in the world.

N   ☐ She was a top pop star once, so playing in night-clubs must be quite a *come-down*.

●●○   **come down²**   reach a decision about who or what to support:
     □ After several hours of discussion, the union leaders *came down* in favour of a return to work.
     □ The court *came down* on the side of the defendant.

●●●○   **come down on/upon**   **1** scold or criticise somebody:
     □ The headmaster *came down* heavily *on* them for not wearing their uniforms to school.
     2 demand money from somebody:
     □ What will you do if the tax people suddenly *come down on* you?

●●●○   **come down to**   **1** amount to something, especially of a question, argument, etc:
     □ The whole issue *comes down to* whether we are prepared to fight for our freedom or not.
     2 be forced to lower your standards:
     □ Since her husband lost his job, they've *come down to* accepting any work the pair of them can get.

N
     □ I can't believe he's gone bankrupt. What a *come-down*!

●●●○   **come down with**   catch or develop an illness:
     □ Her younger daughter has *come down with* measles.

●●   **come forward**   **1** present yourself, especially to provide information:
     □ The police would like anybody who saw the accident to *come forward.*
     2 give or offer something, especially money, in response to a public request:
     □ Several members of the public have *come forward* with large sums in answer to the appeal.

●●○   **come from**   **1** originate from somewhere:
     □ Where do you *come from*?
     □ You can tell he *comes from* Scotland by listening to his accent.
     2 have a particular family background:
     □ She's a pleasant girl and *comes from* a good family.

●●   **come in**   **1** arrive:
     □ I hope the train *comes in* on time.
     2 be received, especially of a communication:
     □ A lot of letters have *come in* asking us to repeat the programme.
     □ News has just *come in* of a shooting in the centre of London.
     3 be introduced, especially of a new law or fashion:
     □ The law on wearing seat belts *came in* in 1983.
     □ Long hair *came in* with the Beatles.

4 become available in the shops, especially of fresh foods:
□ She waits for the strawberries to *come in* before she starts her jam-making.
5 finish a race:
□ Poor old Henry! His horse always *comes in* last.
6 be earned or received by a family, community, etc, especially of money:
□ There's a bit more *coming in* now that his wife has found herself a part-time job.
7 gain power or be elected:
□ How many of its promises has the government kept since it *came in* three years ago?
8 take part; have a role or serve a purpose:
□ It sounds like an interesting project, but I'd like to know where I *come in*?
9 approach and cover the shore, of the sea or tide:
□ Why don't we stay on the beach until the tide *comes in*, and then go for a drive?
10 take a turn in a game, especially of a batsman:
□ The last player to *come in* was hit by the first ball he received, and had to retire hurt.

●●●○ **come in for**   receive or attract something, especially criticism:
□ Some of the violent scenes in the film *came in for* angry comments from the mothers in the audience.

●●●○ **come in on**   take part in a project, scheme, etc:
□ I'm very honoured that you've invited me to *come in on* such an interesting project.

●●●○ **come in with**   become the business partner of somebody or share the cost of something with somebody:
□ I'm looking for somebody with sales experience and a bit of spare cash to *come in with* me.

●●○ **come into**   receive or inherit something:
□ If I *came into* a fortune, I'd spend it all on travel.

●●○ **come of**   **1** result from something:
□ I'm afraid that nothing will *come of* your application, because you don't have the right qualifications.
2 happen to somebody; usually used in a question:
□ Do you know what *came of* that young man you used to play tennis with at university?

●● **come off¹**   **1** succeed, especially of a plan, business deal, etc:
□ The attempt to shoot the President would almost certainly have *come off*, if it hadn't been for one of his bodyguards.

2 happen or take place:

☐ They argue so much these days that it will be a miracle if the wedding ever *comes off*.

3 cease to be shown or performed, especially of a film, play, etc:

☐ The show you've been wanting to see *comes off* at the end of the month.

● ● ○ **come off²** emerge from a situation, especially a conflict, with a level of failure or success:

☐ The other boxer was stronger and had a longer reach, so everybody knew who was going to *come off* worse.

● ●
● ● ○ **come off³** become detached from something:

☐ The last time I bought a cheap shirt, all the buttons *came off* in the wash.

☐ The mirror *comes off* the wall very easily, if you just undo those screws.

2 be removable from something, especially by cleaning or erasing:

☐ If you spill glue on the carpet, it will never *come off*.

3 fall from something:

☐ He wants to paint the house himself, but is worried about *coming off* the ladder.

4 leave a motorway:

☐ Remember that you *come off* just after the second service station.

5 stop taking a medicine:

☐ I didn't know that you'd *come off* these pills.

● ● **come on** **1** see **come along/on**.

2 begin; develop:

☐ If you keep sneezing, perhaps you have a cold *coming on*.

☐ His work is *coming on* well.

3 stop worrying, crying, etc; used only in the imperative:

☐ *Come on*, Ann! Dry your eyes!

4 appear on stage, at a sports ground, etc, in order to perform:

☐ After each act a comedian *came on* and told a few jokes.

☐ The crowd cheered as the teams *came on* again after half-time.

5 be shown at the cinema, on television, etc:

☐ What time does the news *come on*?

6 fall, especially of rain:

☐ The rain *came on* before they could get to any shelter.

● ● ○   **come on/upon**   meet or find somebody or something by chance:

   □ I *came upon* the necklace in a tiny little shop on the outskirts of Paris. I was looking for a ring at the time.

● ●   **come out**   **1** appear, especially of the sun, moon, etc:

   □ On holiday he likes to sip a cold drink on his balcony, and watch the stars *come out*.

2 bloom or flower:

   □ It's been too cold recently for the blossom to *come out*.

3 be published or produced, and become available to the public:

   □ His new novel *comes out* in the autumn.

   □ Why don't you wait for the new model to *come out*?

4 become known or public, especially of a secret, truth, set of facts, etc:

   □ Eventually it *came out* that not one word of his story to the police was true.

5 go on strike:

   □ I see that the railwaymen are *coming out* again.

6 be announced, released or broadcast:

   □ The news has just *come out* that there is to be another royal wedding in the autumn.

7 produce a clear picture; used of camera film:

   □ She was very disappointed that her holiday photographs didn't *come out*.

8 produce an answer, especially of a calculation, problem, etc:

   □ I spent at least an hour adding, dividing, and subtracting, and then the whole thing *came out* wrong!

9 emerge or become evident, especially of a human quality or characteristic:

   □ You'll often find that a person's courage *comes out* in a crisis.

10 be conveyed or shown:

   □ The artist's true feelings about women don't *come out* in this painting.

   □ You always *come out* well in photographs.

● ● ● ○   **come out against**   declare your opposition to something, especially by criticising it:

   □ Our advisers *came out against* the plan, saying that it would be too costly.

● ● ● ○   **come out at**   have as a final cost or result:

   □ With the fitting costs, the carpet *comes out at* ten pounds a square metre.

●●●○   **come out in**   develop spots, marks, etc, on your skin, especially as a sign of illness:

□ If the child has *come out in* a rash, you'd better call the doctor.

●●(●○)   **come out (of)**   be removable from something, especially by cleaning:

□ I'm worried that these ink stains won't *come out of* the tablecloth.

●●●○   **come out with**   say something, especially something that causes surprise or shock:

□ You just can't imagine the hurtful things she *came out with* when we said we were going to live abroad.

●●   **come over¹**   travel from another country, especially to visit somebody:

□ Our American friends are *coming over* in July for three weeks.

●●○   **come over²**   **1** take hold of somebody, especially of an unpleasant feeling:

□ A sudden wave of sickness *came over* me, and I had to rush out of the room.

□ I really don't know what *came over* me. I'm not usually aggressive.

2 experience a feeling of sickness, dizziness, etc:

□ At the top of the stairs she suddenly *came over* very faint, and had to sit down.

●●(●○)   **come over/round (to)**   **1** pay somebody a short visit, especially for pleasure:

□ We've got a few friends *coming over* on Saturday night and we thought you might like to *come round* as well.

2 change your belief, opinion, loyalty, etc, and agree with or join the side of somebody:

□ With just a little more persuasion, I'm sure she'll *come round to* our way of thinking.

●●   **come round**   see **come around/round**

●●   **come round/to**   regain consciousness:

□ The driver of the car didn't *come round* until two days after the accident.

●●
 ●●○   **come through¹**   survive a serious illness, operation or dangerous situation:

□ He became so weak from loss of blood that at one time we started to think that he wouldn't *come through*.

●●   **come through²**   reach or arrive somewhere, especially of a message, telephone call, etc:

□ Have your instructions *come through* from London yet?

●●○   **come to¹** **1** make a total:
    ☐ How much does the bill *come to*?
    2 concern, involve or be a matter of something; always preceded by *it*:
    ☐ When it *comes to* cameras, you really can't beat the Japanese.
    3 enter somebody's mind, especially of a thought, idea, etc:
    ☐ While I was sitting there working, it suddenly *came to* me that what I was doing was a complete waste of time.

●●   **come to²** see **come round/to**.

●●   **come together** form a relationship with somebody:
    ☐ David and I would never have *come together* if it hadn't been for your introduction.

●●○   **come under** **1** belong in a particular category or under a particular heading:
    ☐ What does 'language testing' *come under*? 'Language' or 'testing'?
    2 be controlled or managed by somebody or something:
    ☐ All these schools *come under* the regional education authority.
    3 become the target or victim of something:
    ☐ The report *came under* heavy criticism.

●●   **come up** **1** happen or arise, especially unexpectedly:
    ☐ I'll see you tonight at seven, unless something important *comes up* and I have to work late.
    ☐ Let me know if any interesting jobs *come up* while I'm away.
    2 be mentioned, discussed or considered:
    ☐ Your name *came up* several times during the meeting, so they obviously haven't forgotten your application for the job.
    3 be selected, especially of a lottery ticket:
    ☐ She's convinced that this is going to be the lucky week when her number *comes up*.
    4 become clean, bright, etc, especially as a result of being polished:
    ☐ Look how well these silver spoons have *come up*. Just like new!
    5 be vomited:
    ☐ Everything she eats *comes up* again five minutes later. We'd better get the doctor.
    6 appear above the horizon:
    ☐ The coldest moment of the day is just before the sun *comes up*.

●●●○ **come up against** encounter a problem, obstacle, etc:
□ We were making fairly good progress until we suddenly *came up against* a lack of funds.

●●●○ **come up to** reach a particular standard:
□ This new book doesn't *come up to* his previous writing.

●●●○ **come up with** discover, invent or provide something:
□ Is it true that the professor has *come up with* a way of getting chickens to lay hard-boiled eggs?
□ She's always *coming up with* interesting suggestions.

●●○ **come upon** see **come on/upon**.

●●○ **conjure up** 1 cause somebody to imagine or form a mental picture of something:
□ The holiday brochure *conjured up* a very false impression of the hotel.
2 cause something to be remembered:
□ This music *conjures up* the time we spent together in Hong Kong.

●● **conk out** *Informal* stop functioning, especially of a mechanism; die:
□ The last time I flew in this plane, one of the engines *conked out*.

●○●
●●○ **cook up** invent an excuse, story, etc:
□ It's amazing how she's always able to *cook up* a reason for being late.

●●
●○●
●●○ **cool down** become, or cause somebody to become, calmer:
□ He *cooled down* as soon as I offered to pay for the damage.

●● **cool off** 1 become less excited or angry:
□ After exchanging so many insults, they're going to take a long time to *cool off*.
2 become less enthusiastic:
□ Her new boyfriend soon *cooled off* when he discovered that she wore false teeth.

●●(●○) **cotton on (to)** *Informal* understand the point of something or how to do something:
□ He'd never been shown how to fish before, but he soon *cottoned on*.

●●
●○●
●●○ **cough up** *Informal* provide or hand over, especially money or information:
□ How are we going to get our deposit back if they refuse to *cough up*?

●●○ **count against** cause people to judge or regard somebody unsympathetically:
□ His years in prison *counted against* him when he tried to get a job.

●○●   **count in**   include somebody or something, especially when
●●○   doing a calculation:
      □ There's a coach trip to London on Tuesday. Can we
      count you *in*?

●●○   **count on/upon**   **1** rely or trust somebody to do something:
      □ You can always *count on* John to be there on time.
      2 expect or anticipate something; usually used in the
      negative:
      □ We certainly hadn't *counted on* the house falling down
      two weeks after we moved in!

●○●   **count out**   **1** exclude or disregard somebody or something:
●●○   □ If there aren't enough seats for all of us to go, you can
      count me *out*.
      2 declare that a boxer has lost a fight when he fails to get
      up from the ground within ten seconds:
      □ The former champion was *counted out* at the end of
      the seventh round.

●○●   **cover up**   prevent something from becoming known or
●●○   being noticed:
●●   □ Her parents tried to *cover up* the scandal, but somehow
      the story got into the newspapers.
N   □ It was such a clever *cover-up* that the truth wasn't
      discovered until twenty years later.

●●●○   **cover up for**   prevent something from becoming known in
      order to protect somebody:
      □ Naturally his wife will try to *cover up for* him, so we
      can't believe everything she says.

●●(●○)   **crack down (on)**   become more strict with somebody:
      □ The police are really beginning to *crack down on*
      drivers who park their cars just where they like.

●●   **crack up**   *Informal* become mentally or emotionally ill:
      □ Stop talking to yourself, or people will think you're
      cracking up!

●○●   **cream off**   choose and take the best:
●●○   □ The students with the highest marks are being *creamed
      off* and sent to overseas universities.

●●   **crop up**   occur or appear, especially unexpectedly:
      □ We should be finished by September, as long as no
      more difficulties *crop up*.

●○●   **cross off**   remove something from a list by drawing a line
●●○   through it:
●○●○   □ When you said that you didn't want to go on the trip
      after all, I *crossed* your name *off*.

●○●   **cross out**   draw a line through something, especially to
●●○   show a mistake, cancellation, etc:

☐ If you've made a spelling mistake, I suggest that you *cross* the word *out* and write it again.

●● **cry off**   withdraw from an arrangement; usually used in a derogatory way:
☐ I do get annoyed with people who accept an invitation and then *cry off* at the last minute.

●●(●○) **cry out (for)**   be in urgent need of something:
☐ The whole house is *crying out for* a good coat of paint.

●● **cut across**   cross an area in order to shorten your journey:
●●○ ☐ The gardener used to hate it when we *cut across* his beautiful lawn.

●●(●○) **cut back (on)**   reduce something especially because of
●○● economic circumstances:
●●○ ☐ In these difficult times, even the universities have had to *cut back on* their staff.

N ☐ The government is planning several major *cutbacks* in national spending over the next twelve months.

●●(●○) **cut down (on)**   reduce something, especially to save
●○● money or promote health:
●●○ ☐ He has managed to *cut down* his cigarettes to ten a day.
☐ She'd rather stay fat than have to *cut down on* chocolate.

●●(●○) **cut in (on)**   move suddenly in front of a person or moving vehicle:
☐ If I hadn't braked when he *cut in*, there would have been an accident.
☐ That stupid fool suddenly *cut in on* me.

●●(●○) **cut in (with)**   interrupt a conversation:
☐ We got more and more annoyed with her for the way she kept *cutting in with* silly comments.

●○● **cut off¹**   **1** disconnect somebody who is having a telephone
●●○ conversation, usually by accident:
☐ No sooner had she answered than we were suddenly *cut off*.
2 cause somebody or something to be isolated or separated:
☐ The sea comes in very quickly along this stretch of the beach, and can easily *cut* you *off* if you're not careful.
☐ She feels very *cut off* in that village in the middle of nowhere.
3 disconnect a supply of gas, electricity, water, etc:
☐ The telephone company have *cut* us *off* for not paying our last bill.
4 disinherit somebody:

☐ His father has *cut* him *off* without a penny for marrying without his permission.

●●○ **cut off²** block the route or passage of somebody or something to prevent escape:

☐ We *cut off* their retreat by destroying the bridge.

●○● **cut out¹** **1** stop eating or drinking a particular food or
●●○ drink; discontinue a habit:

☐ The doctor told me that if I didn't start *cutting out* potatoes, I'd soon look like one.

☐ *Cut out* the smoking and you'll live for another ten years.

2 delete or exclude something:

☐ The story reads much better with some of the long descriptive passages *cut out*.

3 stop doing something; often used in the imperative:

☐ Either *cut out* the talking or leave the examination hall.

☐ *Cut* it *out*, will you!

●● **cut out²** **1** fail to function, especially of an engine:

☐ Each time I stop at the traffic lights, the car *cuts out*.

2 stop automatically:

☐ As soon as the water reaches the temperature you want, the boiler *cuts out*.

D, d

● ○ ●   **damp down**   cause a fire to burn less quickly:
● ● ○   □ She usually *damps* the fire *down* before going to bed.
● ○ ●   **dash off**   produce something very quickly:
● ● ○   □ Could you *dash off* these letters before lunch?
● ● ● ○   **date back to**   be known to have existed since a certain time in the past:
          □ The university *dates back to* the seventeenth century.

● ● ○   **dawn on/upon**   be realised by somebody:
          □ It suddenly *dawned on* me that she didn't want to go.

          □ The extent of the damage slowly *dawned on* them.

● ● ○   **deal in**   buy and sell certain goods regularly to earn money:
          □ His company *deals in* tobacco.

● ● ○   **deal with**   **1** be concerned with something:
          □ Her new book *deals with* the subject of childbirth.
          2 be responsible for handling somebody or something, especially an enquiry, problem, complaint, etc:
          □ She's never had to *deal with* an emergency before.
          3 do business with a person or company:
          □ We only *deal with* firms that are well known.

● ○ ● ○   **debar from**   *Formal* prevent somebody from doing something, usually by law:
          □ Foreigners are *debarred from* buying property here.

● ○ ●(● ○) **deck out (in)**   dress somebody in or decorate something with something bright or attractive:
          □ Her father has *decked* himself *out in* a new suit for the wedding.

● ○ ● ○   **deck with**   decorate a place or thing with something, especially for a celebration:
          □ The whole of the city centre had been *decked with* flags and banners to welcome the team home.

● ● ○   **delight in**   receive pleasure from doing something:
          □ Some students think that their teachers *delight in* finding mistakes.

● ○ ●(● ○) **deliver over/up (to)**   pass or surrender somebody or
● ● ○(● ○) something, especially to somebody in authority:
          □ The two suspects were *delivered over to* the police for questioning.
          □ After the battle the last of the enemy soldiers *delivered* themselves *up*.

● ● ○   **depend on/upon**   **1** rely or be dependent on somebody or something:
          □ You can *depend on* John. He never misses a game.

☐ All the major banks can be *depended upon* nowadays.

2 be influenced or determined by something:

☐ Where we go for our holiday *depends upon* how much money we have to spend.

3 expect confidently that something will happen:

☐ The farmers are beginning to say that we can *depend upon* a very good harvest this year.

●●○
●○●○ **derive from** come from or get something from a source:

☐ A lot of English words *derive from* Latin.

☐ She *derives* a great deal of pleasure *from* writing stories for children.

●●○ **descend on/upon** **1** visit somewhere or somebody unexpectedly, especially in large numbers:

☐ Every summer thousands of holidaymakers *descend on* the town.

☐ The whole family *descended on* me last Christmas.

2 attack somebody or something in large numbers:

☐ Most of the crew were killed when five enemy aircraft suddenly *descended upon* the ship.

●●○ **descend to** do something which reduces your status, dignity, etc:

☐ He's proud and won't *descend* to accepting charity.

☐ People say that he even *descended to* robbing his own family.

●●○ **detract from** reduce the quality, value, attractiveness, etc, of something:

☐ The thought of having to return to work *detracted from* the pleasure of their holiday.

●● **die away** become weaker or fainter until no longer heard, felt, etc:

☐ The sound of their footsteps eventually *died away* in the distance.

●● **die down** become less violent or intense:

☐ All the passengers will be seasick if this storm doesn't *die down*.

☐ Wait until all the fuss has *died down*.

☐ The applause gradually *died down*.

●●○ **die for** need or want something very much:

☐ I'm *dying for* a cigarette.

●●○ **die of/with** have an intense feeling of something, especially curiosity, hunger or thirst:

☐ Is dinner nearly ready? I'm absolutely *dying of* hunger.

●● **die out** gradually cease to exist or be practised, especially in the case of a race, species, tradition, etc:

☐ Is the elephant really in danger of *dying out*?

☐ That old custom *died out* a long time ago.

●●   **dig in¹**   begin to do something with a great deal of energy, especially to eat:
      □ Come on! *Dig in* before the food goes cold.
      □ The job won't take long if we all *dig in*.

●●
●○●   **dig in²**   **1** dig a hole or trench in the ground for protection against enemy fire:
      □ Our soldiers have landed and are now *digging* themselves *in*.
      2 establish a secure position for yourself:
      □ The more the boss tries to get rid of her, the more she *digs in*.

●○●(●○)
●●○   **dig out (of)**   find or obtain something, especially information, by searching:
      □ He's gone to the library to *dig out* a few facts and figures for the report.
      □ The headmaster finally *dug* the truth *out of* the boy – he'd stolen the watch.

●○●
●●○   **dig up**   reveal or discover something that has been secret or hidden for a long time:
      □ He's worried about what the police might *dig up* if they start asking too many questions.

●●   **dine in**   have dinner at home:
      □ I'd better see what there is to eat if we're *dining in* tonight.

●●   **dine out**   have dinner at a restaurant:
      □ Tom prefers to *dine out* because then he avoids the washing-up.

●●   **dip in**   take a share of something that is offered:
      □ An enormous tin of biscuits was passed round and everybody except Helen *dipped in*.

●●○   **dip into**   **1** read or glance at something in a casual way:
      □ I've *dipped into* the report but haven't had time to read it properly yet.
      2 make a brief or casual study of a subject:
      □ He enjoys *dipping into* branches of science that he knows nothing about.
      3 use part of a stock or supply of something, especially money:
      □ If we're having a holiday abroad this year, we'll have to *dip into* our savings.

●●○   **disagree with**   have a bad effect on your health or physical comfort, especially of food and weather:
      □ He used to love onions until they started to *disagree with* him.

● ○ ● **dish out** **1** serve food, especially to a group:
● ● ○ □ Shall I *dish out* the potatoes, or do you want to help
yourselves?
2 *Informal* distribute or hand out something:
□ Don't *dish out* the question papers until all the
students are in their seats.
3 *Informal* give or inflict something, especially advice,
criticism, punishment, etc, in a careless way:
□ She's always eager to *dish out* the blame when
something goes wrong.
□ The manager doesn't seem to be happy unless he's
dishing out orders to somebody.

● ● **dish up¹** put cooked food onto plates ready for people to
● ○ ● eat:
● ● ○ □ I'm not going to *dish up* until you're all ready to sit
down at the table.

● ○ ● **dish up²** present something, especially information,
● ● ○ opinions, etc, in a lazy, boring or repetitive way:
□ Every night you get the same old rubbish *dished up* on
the television.

● ● ○ **dispense with** **1** get rid of something or somebody:
□ We won't ever make a profit unless we *dispense with*
some of the staff.
2 make something unnecessary:
□ I'm not convinced that buying a sunlamp would
dispense with the need for a holiday.

● ● ○ **dispose of** **1** remove, sell or get rid of something:
□ Before buying a new piano, we'd better *dispose of* the
old one.
2 remove a complaint, problem, etc, by finding an answer
or explanation for it:
□ *Disposing of* these objections isn't going to be easy.

● ● **dive in** do something without hesitation, especially eat:
□ *Dive in*, everybody, before the ice cream melts!

● ○ ● ○ **divest of** **1** take something, especially clothing, away from
somebody:
□ At the end of the ceremony, they were glad to *divest*
themselves *of* the heavy robes.
2 take a power, right, title, etc, away from somebody:
□ The prisoners who tried to escape were *divested of* all
their privileges.

● ● ○ **do as/for** be able to be used as something:
□ These empty beer cans will *do as* ashtrays.

●●●○   **do away with**   **1** discontinue, abolish or get rid of something, especially a law, institution, etc:
      ☐ Slavery was *done away with* a long time ago.
      2 kill somebody or yourself:
      ☐ When his wife left him, the poor fellow *did away with* himself.

●○●   **do down**   speak about somebody in an unkind way:
      ☐ It's unforgivable that you should *do* your own children *down*.

●●○   **do for**   see **do as/for**.

●○●   **do in**   *Informal* murder somebody:
●●○   ☐ She threatened to *do* him *in* if she caught him stealing from her purse again.
      ☐ I wonder how many more of us are going to be *done in* before the police catch him?

●○●   **do out**   **1** clean or tidy something, especially a room or
●●○   cupboard:
      ☐ I've got to *do out* the bedroom before I go shopping.
      2 decorate a room:
      ☐ It won't take more than two days to *do out* the kitchen if we're only going to paint it.

●○●○   **do out of**   deprive or cheat somebody of something:
      ☐ Don't let them *do* you *out of* your travelling expenses.
      ☐ He's been *done out of* the opportunity of a week in Paris.

●○●   **do over**   *Informal* attack and beat somebody in a planned attack, especially of a gang:
      ☐ He had to spend a week in hospital after being *done over* for talking to the police.

●○●   **do up**¹   **1** repair, modernise or decorate something:
●●○   ☐ The house is very cheap because it needs *doing up*.
      ☐ You should have seen the state of the place before it was *done up*.
      2 fasten something, especially something which has to be buttoned, knotted or zipped:
      ☐ Not many children of his age can *do up* a shoe-lace without help.
      3 make a parcel of something:
      ☐ I can't *do* the books *up* without any string.

●●   **do up**²   be able to be fastened together:
      ☐ None of your trousers will *do up* if you continue to eat so much.

●○●   **do up**³   make yourself look particularly attractive:
      ☐ She *did* herself *up* for the office party.

●●○   **do with**   **1** need or want something; used after *can* or *could*:

□ I could *do with* something to eat. How about you?

□ We can always *do with* a bit more help.

2 tolerate something which annoys or irritates; used in the negative and with *can* or *could*:

□ I just can't *do with* all this noise when I'm trying to concentrate.

●●○ **do without¹** be better or happier without something; used after *can* or *could*:

□ We could *do without* his interference all the time.

□ I could have *done without* her arriving just as I was about to start work.

●● **do without²** manage without something:

●●○ □ On holiday he prefers to *do without* a watch.

□ You simply can't *do without* a phone if you're in business.

●○● **dole out** distribute something, especially in a routine way:

●●○ □ Their government has started *doling out* food coupons again.

●○● **doll up** *Informal* use a lot of cosmetics or dress yourself in unusually elaborate or colourful clothes; often used in a derogatory way:

□ Isn't she a bit too old for *dolling* herself *up* like that?

●● **doss down** *Informal* find yourself somewhere free or cheap to lie down and sleep, especially a floor or a public place:

□ It's surprising how many homeless people *doss down* on railway platforms at night.

●●○ **dote on/upon** have exaggerated love or affection for somebody:

□ I've never seen parents *dote on* a child as much as they do.

●● **double back** return along the same route, especially in a hurry:

□ If you've forgotten your wallet, you'd better *double back* and get it.

●● **double up¹** bend or cause somebody to bend at the waist,

●○● especially because of laughter or pain:

□ The whole audience *doubled up* at some of the jokes.

□ The blow to his stomach *doubled* him *up*.

●● **double up²** share a flat, room, etc, with somebody:

□ Would you mind *doubling up* just for one night?

●● **doze off** fall asleep unintentionally:

□ You must have *dozed off* while you were watching the television.

●● **drag behind** be unable to stay level with somebody or

●●○ something:

☐ You know when the child is getting tired by the way he starts *dragging behind*.

☐ Her results were quite good last term, but this term she's *dragging behind* the others.

●○●
●●○

drag down　cause somebody or something to deteriorate, especially in health, behaviour or rank:

☐ I warned you that she would *drag* you *down* if you married her!

☐ To open another betting shop would really *drag down* the whole area.

●○●
●●○/
●○●○

drag in/into　1 introduce a topic into a conversation, discussion, etc, especially one which is not directly relevant:

☐ Why do you have to *drag in* the question of money all the time?

2 cause or force somebody to become involved in an argument, activity, etc:

☐ Don't try *dragging* me *into* your family rows.

●●

drag on　continue, especially with the effect of making people bored, impatient or unhappy:

☐ How much longer is this ridiculous meeting going to *drag on*?

●○●
●●○

drag out　cause something to continue for longer than usual or necessary, especially with the effect of making people bored or irritated:

☐ He *dragged* the speech *out* so much that we almost fell asleep.

●○●
●●○

drag up　1 *Informal* fail to bring up a child properly:

☐ It's obvious from the way he talks to you that he's been *dragged up*.

2 cause something, especially something unpleasant or embarrassing, to be remembered or talked about:

☐ I'm worried about what her lawyer might be able to *drag up*.

●●

draw in　grow dark progressively earlier, especially of days during autumn:

☐ You won't be able to play tennis in the evening once the days start *drawing in*.

●●/
●●○

draw in/into[1]　slow down and stop at a platform or at the side of the road:

☐ Carriage doors began to open as the train *drew in*.

☐ The car in front of us *drew into* a petrol station.

●○●
●●○/

draw in/into[2]　attract or persuade somebody to enter or join something:

●○●○   □ The football club isn't *drawing in* as big a crowd as it used to do.

□ I refuse to be *drawn into* other people's arguments.

●●   **draw on**   approach, especially of a time, season, etc:

□ It's important that we feed the birds now that winter is *drawing on.*

●●○   **draw on/upon**   make use of something:

□ He doesn't want to *draw upon* his savings if he can possibly avoid it.

□ You can *draw on* my advice as much as you like, as long as you pay me for it!

●○●   **draw out¹**   make somebody feel less shy:

□ He still feels very awkward in company, although we've done all we can to *draw* him *out.*

●●   **draw out²**   stay light for longer, especially of days or evenings:

□ As soon as the evenings begin to *draw out,* we have our dinner in the garden.

●●(●○)   **draw out (of)¹**   move away from a station or from the side of the road:

□ A whistle sounded and the train *drew out of* the station.

□ Always look in the mirror before you *draw out.*

●○●(●○)   **draw out (of)²**   **1** extract a secret, confession, piece of
●●○   information, etc, from somebody:

□ I hope you managed to *draw* all the details we need *out of* him.

2 take money from an account:

□ I'll need to *draw out* some more money if we've got to buy petrol too.

●●   **draw up¹**   arrive at a place and stop, especially of a driver or vehicle:

□ A black car *drew up* in front of the gates.

●○●   **draw up²**   **1** compose and write down something in a
●●○   formal way, especially an agreement, contract, list, etc:

□ The contract has been *drawn up,* but it hasn't been signed yet.

2 move something near or next to a particular place:

□ She *drew* a chair *up* and sat down right in front of my desk.

●●○   **draw upon**   see **draw on/upon.**

●●○   **dream of**   *Informal* consider the possibility of something; used in the negative and with *would* or *should*:

□ I wouldn't *dream of* smoking inside a church.

●○●   **dream up**   invent or imagine something:

●●○   ☐ He's always *dreaming up* new ways of making a fortune.

●●   **dress up¹**   **1** dress somebody or yourself in smart clothes:

●○●   ☐ Do we have to *dress up* for tonight's dinner party?

●●○   **2** dress somebody or yourself in the clothes of another person or well-known character, usually for fun:
☐ The children love to see him *dressed up* as Father Christmas.

●○●   **dress up²**   make something seem more attractive or

●●○   acceptable, especially by making small additions to it:
☐ I like the story that you've written, but now you need to *dress* it *up* a bit with a few details.

●○●   **drink in**   watch, listen to or experience something with

●●○   great enjoyment or interest:
☐ The audience sat right to the end of the show, *drinking in* every word their hero sang.

●●○   **drive at**   suggest, mean or try to express something; used after *what*:
☐ What exactly are you *driving at*?

●○●   **drive in/into**   cause something to be learnt, understood or

●●○/   remembered, especially by using a lot of repetition:

●○●○   ☐ The point I'm trying to *drive in* is that you won't pass the examination unless you start doing some work.

●●   **drop back**   **1** reduce speed in order to move behind somebody or something:
☐ The American runner has decided to *drop back* and let somebody else take the lead.
2 fail to maintain speed and be left behind:
☐ The car that had been in second position *dropped back* with engine trouble.

●●   **drop behind**   be overtaken or left behind by somebody or

●●○   something:
☐ Our team *dropped behind* in the league when a third of the players went on holiday.
☐ In terms of annual production, the country has *dropped behind* the rest of Europe.

●●(●○)   **drop by/in (on)**   pay somebody a short casual visit, especially when this does not require a long journey:
☐ I thought I'd *drop in* to see if you needed any shopping.
☐ Since we're going almost past her house, why don't we *drop in on* Mary?

●○●   **drop in/off**   bring or take something to somebody's house, place of work, etc, and leave it there:
☐ If you still need the book, I could *drop* it *in* tonight.

●●   **drop off¹**   fall asleep unintentionally:
            □ The film was so boring that Sharon kept *dropping off*.

●○●   **drop off²**   let somebody out of a vehicle or deliver
●●○   something:
            □ I wonder if you could *drop* me *off* at the bank?
            □ Can you *drop off* my coat at the dry cleaner's on your way?

●●   **drop out**   leave a college, university, etc, before the end of a course:
            □ Students who discover that they don't like engineering soon *drop out*.

N   □ Quite a few teenagers become *drop-outs* at college.

●●(●○)   **drop out (of)**   cease to belong to or take part in something:
            □ Several countries *dropped out of* the competition for political reasons.
            □ Three members have *dropped out* already since the club's new manager arrived.

●●   **drop round**   pay a short casual visit, especially when this does not require a long journey:
            □ Can I *drop round* to see you later?

●○●   **drum in/into**   cause something to be learnt or
●●○/   remembered, especially by using a lot of effort and
●○●○   repetition:
            □ I've tried *drumming in* the fact that we can't afford another holiday, but she won't listen.

●●○   **drum up**   obtain interest in a cause by publicity:
●○●   □ We've managed to *drum up* a lot more support for the plan.

●●   **dry up**   **1** be completely used, exhausted or finished:
            □ If the funds *dry up*, we'll have to ask for a loan.
            2 be unable to continue speaking, especially in public:
            □ The poor man had only just started his speech when he suddenly became very nervous and *dried up*.
            3 *Informal* stop talking; usually used in the imperative in anger or irritation:
            □ If you can only make stupid comments, just *dry up*!

●●(●○)   **duck out (of)**   avoid doing or being involved in something:
            □ Her little boy always tries to *duck out of* going to see the dentist.

●●○   **dwell on/upon**   spend a long time thinking, talking or writing about something:
            □ Why do news programmes *dwell on* death and violence all the time?

E, e

●●   **ease off/up** become slower, less intense or less violent:
      ☐ It was an hour before her headache began to *ease off*.
      ☐ I'm not going out until this rain *eases up* a bit.

●●(●○)   **ease off/up (on)** use something with less force or in less quantity:
      ☐ He *eased off on* the accelerator the minute he saw the police car.
      ☐ *Ease up on* the shampoo, will you! I want to wash my hair too.

●○●   **eat away** reduce, remove or destroy something, especially
●●○   of moving water, fire or acid:
      ☐ The river is *eating* the bank *away* in several places.

●●   **eat in** have a meal at home:
      ☐ Of course I don't mind *eating in* again, as long as you do the cooking.

●●○   **eat into** **1** attack and destroy or make a hole in something, especially of chemical action:
      ☐ Can you see where the rust has begun *eating into* the bottom of the driver's door?
      2 use part of a reserve of money, stocks, etc:
      ☐ The money they spent on the washing machine *ate into* their holiday savings.

●●   **eat out** have a meal at a restaurant instead of at home:
      ☐ They're always complaining that they can't afford to *eat out* nowadays.

●●○   **eat up** consume something, especially fuel or money, quickly or in great quantities:
      ☐ It's true it's a comfortable car, but it *eats up* the petrol.

●○●(●○)   **edge out (of)** cause somebody to resign or be removed
●●○   from a job or position of authority:
      ☐ The other directors have been trying to *edge* him *out* ever since he lost our best customer.
      ☐ The previous government was *edged out of* office by just a handful of votes.

●○●(●○)   **egg on (to)** *Informal* encourage or urge somebody to do
●●○   something:
      ☐ Her mother kept *egging* her *on to* enter the song contest.

●●○   **eke out** **1** cause a small amount of something to be sufficient, either by using it carefully or by adding something to it:

□ In those days we had to *eke out* my husband's small salary to feed the whole family, his parents as well.

□ If necessary, you could always *eke out* the meal with a little rice.

2 struggle to earn or produce enough to live:

□ In the south of the country it's much harder to *eke out* a living from the land. The soil is so poor and there is little rain.

●●○ **embark on/upon** begin a new project, pastime, occupation, etc:

□ At your age I would think very carefully before *embarking upon* a career in journalism.

●●○ **end up** **1** conclude a series of actions, processes, etc, in a certain state, place or condition:

□ Did you know that Andrew has *ended up* working for his father after all?

□ After doing the shopping and then seeing a film, we *ended up* at Alan's for coffee.

□ Most of the white liquid running out of these trees *ends up* as rubber tyres.

2 do something or be somewhere as a result of a previous action:

□ If you don't watch the road more carefully, you'll *end up* having an accident.

●●○ **enlarge on/upon** expand or explain something in more detail:

□ The speaker proceeded to *enlarge upon* his initial statement.

●●○ **enquire/inquire after** ask for news or information, especially about somebody's health or activities:

□ Of course he still remembers you. In fact, he *enquired after* you the last time I saw him.

●●○ **enquire/inquire into** seek information by asking questions, especially about something mysterious or unpleasant:

□ The police are now *enquiring into* the events which led up to his disappearance.

●●○ **enter for** register or enrol somebody for a competition:

●○●○ □ They've *entered* me *for* the beauty contest, but I'm sure I won't win.

●●○ **enter into** **1** take part or become involved in a conversation, discussion, written agreement, etc:

□ The Prime Minister refuses to *enter into* further negotiations with the railwaymen until they have all returned to work.

2 begin to report or discuss something at length or in detail:
□ Before we could stop her, she had *entered into* a long and boring account of how the deputy mayor's wife had invited her to tea.
□ There won't be enough time at today's meeting to *enter into* the question of overseas aid.
3 be included in a discussion, plan, calculation, etc; usually used in the negative:
□ The fact that the office already has a good accountant simply didn't *enter into* the decision.

●●○ **enter on/upon**   *Formal* begin something, especially a new stage of your life or work:
□ Next month the President will *enter upon* his second term of office, knowing that there is much work to be done.

●● **even out¹**   become level or steady, especially of ground, prices, etc:
□ At the end of the first year the repayments *even out* at thirty pounds a month.

●○●
●●○ **even out²**   **1** make a surface flat:
□ Naturally, you'll have to *even out* the ground before planting anything.
2 make two or more things equal:
□ Unless the company *evens out* the rates of pay, those on a low wage are going to complain.

●○●
●●○ **even up**   make two or more things equal:
□ Let me pay for the meal this time, just to *even* things *up* a bit.
□ The visitors *evened up* the score with an unexpected goal two minutes before half-time.

●○●
●●○ **explain away**   remove or dismiss an objection, criticism, piece of evidence, etc, by giving a reasonable explanation:
□ Professor Jones, how do you *explain away* the fact that nine times out of ten your theory simply doesn't work?
□ At the police station he tried to *explain* the gold watches *away* by saying that they were birthday presents from his rich uncles.

F, f

●●●○ **face up to**   accept or confront something, especially responsibility, danger or an unpleasant fact:
□ He *faced up to* the fact that he would never walk again with remarkable bravery.

●○● **fag out**   *Informal* tire or exhaust somebody:
□ Swimming is good fun, but it can really *fag* you *out* if you're not fit.
□ After a hard day's work, I'm utterly *fagged out*!

●● **fall about**   laugh uncontrollably:
□ The whole class *fell about* when they saw what the teacher had drawn on the blackboard.

●● **fall apart**   break into pieces, fail or disintegrate:
□ Cheap clothes tend to *fall apart* when you wash them.
□ Both his business and his marriage were *falling apart* during those years.

●●(●○) **fall away (to)**   **1** slope downwards towards somewhere:
□ Just beyond the trees the ground *falls away* very sharply, so we use it for grazing.
2 drop to a lower level:
□ The number of people who go to the cinema is steadily *falling away* these days.

●● **fall back**   move back or retreat, especially in a war or battle:
□ So many of the troops were getting killed that they had to *fall back*.

●●●○ **fall back on/upon**   use or go to a reliable source of help, especially after other sources have been tried unsuccessfully:
□ If we run out of cash, we can always *fall back on* our savings in the bank.
□ It's wonderful to have a friend like John to *fall back on*.

●●
●●○ **fall behind**   be overtaken or left behind by somebody or something, especially by a competitor:
□ A long illness caused him to *fall behind* the rest of the class.
□ Why have all these industrial countries *fallen behind* Japan?

●●(●○) **fall behind (with)**   fail to do or complete something by a particular time:
□ She's very worried about *falling behind with* the rent.

●●   **fall down**   fail or be unsatisfactory:
□ The plan *falls down* by relying too much on the co-operation of the work force.
□ Her test results were very good, but she *fell down* at the interview.

●●○   **fall for**   **1** be strongly attracted to or charmed by somebody or something:
□ She *fell for* his good looks.
2 be easily deceived by a story, argument, suggestion, etc:
□ You didn't *fall for* his story about being a prince, did you?
□ If you tell him that it will make him a lot of money, he's bound to *fall for* the idea.

●●●○   **fall in with**   **1** become friendly or associate with somebody, especially after a chance meeting:
□ On holiday she *fell in with* another visitor staying at the same hotel.
2 accept or agree to something, especially a plan, proposal, etc:
□ She said that she would *fall in with* our arrangements for the outing.

●●○   **fall into**   have a particular number of divisions:
□ The book *falls into* three sections.
□ How many categories do English nouns *fall into*?

●●   **fall off**   **1** become less or fewer:
□ The product was selling well in the first three months of the year, but since April sales have *fallen off*.
□ Attendances tend to *fall off* during the cold weather.
2 become worse:
□ The food was very good when the restaurant first opened, but recently it's been *falling off*.

●●○   **fall on**   be on a particular day of the week, especially of an anniversary, public holiday, etc:
□ Your birthday *falls on* a Tuesday this year.

●●○   **fall on/upon**   **1** attack somebody or something:
□ The children *fell upon* the trapped animal with sticks.
2 seize something eagerly, especially food:
□ After five days without supplies, they *fell on* the food that the rescue team had brought.
3 become the responsibility of somebody:
□ I know that somebody has to pay for these things, but why does it always *fall on* the parents?
□ Meeting visitors at the airport usually *falls upon* a member of staff.

●●   **fall out**   cease to be involved or active in an organisation, project, etc:
□ Two members of the original team *fell out* when they realised how long the project would take.

●●(●○)   **fall out (with)**   quarrel and cease to be friendly with somebody:
□ The young couple next door seem to have *fallen out with* each other. She never speaks to him.

●●   **fall through**   fail or be discontinued:
□ The whole scheme *fell through* because there weren't enough funds.

●●   **fall to**   begin to do something, especially with energy and enthusiasm:
□ When we realised that she had nobody to help her, we all *fell to.*

●●○   **fall under**   be classified as something:
□ Do our fares to work every day *fall under* travelling expenses?
□ The advertisement *fell under* the heading of 'Property for Sale'.

●●○   **fall upon**   see **fall on/upon.**

●●   **fan out**   spread out in the shape of a fan while going forwards, especially of a search party, group of soldiers, etc:
□ The team of police and volunteers *fanned out* across the hillside in their hunt for the murder weapon.

●○●
●●○   **farm out**   pass something for which you are responsible to somebody else, especially a piece of work or the care of a child:
□ If you don't have enough men and machines to complete the order in time, you'll just have to *farm* some of it *out.*
□ She's thinking about *farming out* the youngest boy so that she can go to work.

●●○   **fasten on/onto/upon**   **1** accept or adopt an idea, proposal, etc:
□ The local people took a long time to *fasten onto* the idea of forming queues.
2 seize a particular point or remark, especially to use in a debate or conflict:
□ His lawyer was quick to *fasten upon* this piece of new evidence.

●●○   **feel for**   have sympathy for somebody:
□ I really *feel for* all the parents whose children were in the crash.

●○●
●●○   **feel out**   discover somebody's attitude or opinion in a careful and tactful manner:
□ I suggest that you *feel out* the Prime Minister to make sure that you have his support, before you make a public statement.

●●●○   **feel up to**   **1** feel well or energetic enough to do something:
□ Do you *feel up to* going out tonight, or are you too tired?
2 feel capable of doing something, especially because of having the necessary skill, experience, etc:
□ You'd better resign if you don't *feel up to* the job.

●●○
●○●   **fend off**   protect yourself, somebody or something from a blow, insult, accusation or attack by turning it aside:
□ He managed to *fend off* most of the blows with his arms.
□ She's very skilled at *fending off* difficult questions.

●○●
●●○   **ferret out**   find or reveal something by searching for it in a busy and determined way:
□ The librarian sometimes offers to *ferret out* the information you need.

●●   **fight back¹**   recover, especially with a struggle:
□ It's amazing how she has *fought back* since the operation.
□ He was almost bankrupt just a year ago, but look how he has *fought back*.

●○●
●●○   **fight back²**   struggle to control a strong emotion:
□ It became increasingly difficult for her to *fight back* the tears.

●●○
●○●   **fight off**   struggle to overcome an attack, criticism, illness, etc:
□ He's been *fighting off* a cold for the last three days.
□ She bravely tried to *fight off* her depression.

●●○   **figure on**   expect or forecast something, often used in the negative:
□ We certainly didn't *figure on* the new computer being so popular.

●○●
●●○   **figure out**   **1** calculate or produce the answer to something:
□ It was a very complicated question, but she eventually *figured* it *out*.
2 understand somebody or something; often used in the negative:
□ I just couldn't *figure out* how she could be in two places at the same time.
□ It took me ten years of married life to *figure* him *out*.

●○● **fill in** 1 complete a form with the information required:
●●○ □ It took only five minutes to *fill in* the questionnaire.
2 write the details that are required:
□ If you *fill in* your name and address on this card, I'll send it to you as soon as the book is returned.

●●(●○) **fill in (for)** do the work or take the place of a person during their absence:
□ We need somebody to *fill in for* Alan while he's on holiday.

●○●(●○) **fill in (on)** give somebody information about something, especially recent developments:
□ Could you *fill* John *in on* what was said at yesterday's meeting?

●● **fill out¹** become fatter:
□ Her face has *filled out* a lot since we saw her in hospital.

●○● **fill out²** give something more detail, content, body, etc:
●●○ □ Having finalised the structure of the report, they proceeded to *fill* it *out*.
□ It's a good book, except that one or two of the characters need *filling out*.

●● **find out¹** learn or discover something, especially by
●●○ making enquiries:
□ We were about to buy the house until we *found out* that it was next door to a pub.
□ See if you can *find out* her name and address.

●○● **find out²** discover somebody is guilty of a dishonest or criminal act:
□ He'd been stealing from the company for several years before they *found* him *out*.

●○● **finish off** *Informal* 1 kill somebody or something,
●●○ especially a person or animal that is injured or wounded:
□ He was in such pain that he asked the doctors to *finish* him *off*.
2 completely exhaust somebody:
□ The row we had last night just *finished* me *off*.

●●○ **finish with** 1 end a relationship:
□ Is it true that she's *finished with* her new boyfriend already?
2 no longer require or need to use something or somebody:
□ Have you *finished with* my dictionary yet?
3 finish scolding, criticising or punishing somebody:
□ By the time I've *finished with* them, they'll wish they hadn't tried to cheat me.

●●   **fire away**   begin to do something, especially to ask questions; often used in the imperative:
□ I don't have very long to answer your questions, so *fire away*!

●●○   **fish for**   try to obtain something, especially information or compliments, in an indirect or cunning way:
□ When she tells you how awful she looks, she's only *fishing for* compliments.
□ It became quite obvious that he was *fishing for* an invitation.

●○●(●○)   **fish out (of)**   bring something from a place, especially
●●○   after searching:
□ I know that there is a copy of the report somewhere in the building. I'll try to *fish* it *out* for you.
□ The child suddenly *fished* a mouse *out of* his pocket.

●●(●○)   **fit in (with)**   be in agreement or harmony with somebody or something:
□ He's never had to work in a busy office before, so I hope he *fits in*.
□ How does this decision to buy a big house *fit in with* what you were saying about avoiding responsibilities?
□ Do you think that the green carpet *fits in with* the yellow walls?

●○●   **fit in/into**   **1** have, find or make enough space for
●●○/   somebody or something:
●○●○   □ It's a big car but, even so, I can't *fit* you all *in*.
□ You can't *fit* a piano *into* that little room!
2 have or make time for something, especially to see, treat or examine somebody:
□ Mrs Smith has broken a front tooth, and she wonders if you can *fit* her *in* this afternoon.
□ I can't *fit* more than three interviews *into* one hour!

●○●(●○)   **fit out/up (with)**   provide somebody or something with
●●○(●○)   necessary equipment, clothes, etc:
□ The kitchen has been *fitted out* with new cupboards and shelves.
□ We just can't afford to *fit* him *out with* a new uniform.

N   □ Is that a new *outfit* she's wearing?

 ●○●(●○) **fit up (with)**   supply somebody with a piece of equipment:
●●○(●○)   □ Where can I go to be *fitted up with* a new pair of glasses?

●●○   **fix on**   decide on a date, time, etc:
□ Have you *fixed on* a date for the wedding yet?

●○●(●○)   **fix up (with)**   supply or provide somebody with something
●●○(●○)   they want, especially by making the necessary arrangements:

□ If you need work in London, I know somebody who can *fix* you *up*.
□ He asked me if I could *fix* him *up* with a girlfriend.

●● **fizzle out**   end in a disappointing way:
□ Their relationship got worse and worse and eventually just *fizzled out*.
□ Nobody is interested in his new project after the last one *fizzled out*.

●○●
●●○ **flag down**   stop a moving vehicle by waving your arm or a flag:
□ We tried *flagging down* at least a dozen taxis, but not one of them stopped.

●● **flake out**   *Informal* faint or collapse:
□ I'm going to *flake out* if I don't get some fresh air soon.

●● **flare up**   suddenly become angry, fierce or violent, especially of a fire, temper, battle, etc:
□ The fighting in the Middle East *flared up* again over the weekend with heavy losses on both sides.
□ You can't speak to him about anything these days without him *flaring up*.

N □ The government is deciding what to do about the recent *flare-up* of violence in our cities.

●○● **flash about/around**   display something, especially to gain admiration; usually used in a derogatory way:
□ I hate the way he's always *flashing* his money *about*.

●●(●○) **flash back (to)**   return to an earlier point in time, especially during a film, story, etc:
□ Just before she died, we *flashed back to* the beginning of the film, to the time when she was a child.

N □ The whole story was arranged as a series of *flashbacks*.

●●○
●○● **flesh out**   give something more content, body or support:
□ The government's second defence document, due out this weekend, will *flesh out* its case for independence.

●●○ **flick through**   look at a book, magazine, newspaper, etc, while quickly turning the pages:
□ He *flicked through* the paper looking for the sports page.

●●○ **flinch from**   try to avoid something painful or unpleasant:
□ She *flinched from* telling her husband that she'd smashed their new car up.

●●/
●●○ **flood in/into**   arrive somewhere in great quantities, especially of letters, telephone calls, complaints, etc:
□ Applications *flooded into* the office in response to the advertisement.

● ● ○
● ○ ●
flood out   force somebody to leave their home, place of work, etc, because of floods:
☐ All of the families in the valley were *flooded out* when the river broke its banks.

● ○ ●(● ○)
● ● ○
flush out (of)   force somebody, especially a criminal, to leave or emerge from a hiding place:
☐ Police *flushed* the four men *out of* the bank with the help of smoke bombs.
☐ One of the men in this photograph is a spy, and it's your job to *flush* him *out*.

● ● ○
fly at   suddenly attack somebody, either physically or verbally:
☐ I've never seen her *fly at* him like that before. She must have been very annoyed.

● ○ ●(● ○)
fob off (with)   get somebody to buy, accept or believe something, especially faulty goods, an excuse, a lie, etc:
☐ The salesman tried to *fob* the old lady *off with* a packet that was half empty.
☐ She refused to be *fobbed off with* such an absurd explanation.

● ○ ● ● ○
fob off on/onto   get rid of something worthless by selling it:
☐ That shop will try to *fob* any old rubbish *off onto* you.

● ○(●)● ○
●(●)○ ● ○
foist (off) on/onto   get somebody to buy, accept or take responsibility for something, especially something damaged, inferior or unpleasant:
☐ She's always trying to *foist* her unwanted furniture *off onto* people.

● ●
fold up   **1** bend with pain or laughter:
☐ The goalkeeper *folded up* when a knee hit him in the stomach.
2 collapse or fail, especially of a business, project or a person's spirits:
☐ The company *folded up* when people stopped buying plastic furniture.
☐ He completely *folded up* when his wife left him after twenty years of marriage.

● ○ ●(● ○)
follow through (to)   continue to develop or work on something, especially until it is finished, put into operation, etc:
☐ If you *follow* the argument *through to* its logical conclusion, you'll discover that it is absolute nonsense.
☐ Once you've started on a project, you should *follow* it *through*.

●○●
●●○   **follow up**   **1** investigate something, especially a rumour, story, new piece of information, etc:
□ The police are now *following up* new evidence in connection with the case.
2 pursue, develop or exploit something:
□ The boss seems to like the idea, so I think you should *follow* it *up*.
□ The series of programmes was so successful that it is surprising nobody has *followed* it *up*.

N
●○●○   □ His new book is a *follow-up* to the last one.
force on/upon   press or compel somebody to accept or buy something:
□ She didn't really want the money, but her uncle *forced* it *upon* her.
□ Don't let the sales assistant *force* the perfume *on* you if you don't like it.

●●(●○)
●●○(●○)   **fork out (for)**   *Informal* pay for something, especially unwillingly:
□ Do you realise how much I have to *fork out for* a television licence nowadays?

●●○
●○●   **foul up**   *Informal* spoil or ruin something:
□ Unless you do well in the exam, you'll *foul up* your chances of getting into university.
□ He blames his mother for *fouling up* his marriage.

●●   **freak out**   *Informal* behave in an excited, detached or uncontrolled way:
□ The girls at the front of the crowd *freaked out* when the film star held out his hand.
□ He enjoys *freaking out* on the dance floor from time to time.

●●
●○●   **freshen up**   have a wash and comb your hair, etc, especially when feeling tired and dirty after a journey:
□ Would you like me to show you the bathroom so that you can *freshen up* before we eat?
□ I'd love a quick shower to *freshen* myself *up*.

●○●(●○)
●●○(●○)   **fritter away (on)**   spend your time or money on something in a wasteful way:
□ She *frittered away* all the money he earned *on* new dresses.

●●   **frost over**   become covered with frost:
□ How will you see out of the windscreen if it *frosts over*?

●●○   **frown at/on/upon**   disapprove of something:
□ A lot of people still *frown upon* the idea of ending a sentence with a preposition.

G, g

●●
●●○
gad about/around   keep moving from place to place, especially for fun or pleasure; often used in a derogatory way:
□ Our son is never at home for more than five minutes these days. He's always *gadding about* on his new motorbike.

●●○
gain on/upon   move faster than somebody or something you are following, chasing, or in competition with, etc:
□ I couldn't go any faster, even though the car behind was *gaining on* us.
□ Many Japanese industries are continuing to *gain upon* the rest of the world.

●○●
●●○
gamble away   lose something, especially money, by betting, speculation, etc:
□ His father left him a fortune, but he *gambled* it all *away*.

●●○
gamble on   rely upon something happening; often used in the negative:
□ He may accept the invitation, but I wouldn't *gamble on* it.

●●(●○)
gang up (on/against)   unite in opposition to somebody or something:
□ The head of the department is worried that some of his senior staff are *ganging up against* him.

●○●○
gear to   organize or adapt something so that it suits a particular purpose:
□ He thinks that university courses should be more *geared to* the needs of society.

●●
●○●
●●○
gear up   prepare somebody or something for an important event:
□ The major political parties have begun to *gear* themselves *up* for an autumn election.

●●(●○)
●○●(●○)
gen up (on)   learn or give somebody all the facts about something:
□ None of us will know how to use the new machine unless you *gen* us *up on* how it works.

●●
●●○
get about/around/round   **1** travel or visit many places:
□ I suppose that you *get around* quite a lot in your job.
2 walk or move about after an illness, in old age, etc:
□ It wasn't until six weeks after the operation that she started to *get about* again.
□ Even at ninety-four she still *gets around*.

3 spread or circulate somewhere, especially of news, gossip, etc:
☐ It's surprising how fast the news *got about*.
☐ *News got round* the college quickly.

●●(●○) **get across (to)**   communicate with somebody:
●○●(●○) ☐ It took him a whole hour to *get* the message *across to* the audience.
☐ I just can't *get across to* him nowadays. We seem to speak completely different languages.

●● **get ahead**   progress or succeed:
☐ He told his daughter to choose a career in which there were good opportunities for *getting ahead*.

●●(●○) **get ahead (of)**   progress or advance more than somebody else, especially by working hard:
☐ By spending every evening in the library, he managed to *get ahead of* the rest of his class.

●● **get along**   continue on your way after stopping to speak to somebody; usually used to close a conversation:
☐ I must be *getting along* now, I'm afraid. I'm meeting my husband in ten minutes.

●●(●○) **get along/on (with)**   **1** be on friendly terms with somebody:
☐ Apart from the occasional quarrel, we *get along* very well.
☐ How's John *getting on with* his new girlfriend?
2 progress or advance with something:
☐ She was *getting on* wonderfully until they moved her to a new school.
☐ How are you *getting on with* the French lessons?

●●(●○) **get along (without)**   continue to live or work, especially in spite of a difficulty, setback or tragedy:
☐ Since he died, she's been learning how to *get along without* him.

●● **get around**   see **get about/around/round**.
●●○

●●○ **get around/round**   **1** persuade somebody by using flattery:
☐ She's going to see if she can *get round* her boss to give her the afternoon off.
2 overcome or avoid a problem, obstacle, etc:
☐ There must be some way of *getting round* our money difficulties.

●●●○ **get around/round to**   manage to find enough time for something, especially after a long delay:
☐ So you finally *got round to* answering my letter!

●●○   **get at**   **1** reach or gain access to somebody or something:
     □ The cat climbed to the top of the tree, and none of us could *get at* it.
     □ He's a very busy man, and extremely hard to *get at*, even on the telephone.
     □ After two hours in the library, she finally *got at* the information she wanted.
     2 suggest or insinuate something:
     □ If I had known what she was *getting at*, I would have complained to the chairman.
     □ What are you *getting at*?
     3 criticise somebody, especially repeatedly:
     □ He's always *getting at* me for smoking in the kitchen.
     4 influence or persuade somebody, especially with a bribe or threat:
     □ The witness had obviously been *got at*. He refused to tell the jury what he had seen.

●●   **get away**   **1** leave or escape:
     □ It was impossible to *get away* from the meeting.
     □ The thief *got away* by running into a busy store.
N   □ The bank robbers made a quick *getaway*.
     2 go on a trip, holiday, etc:
     □ We'd love to *get away* for a few days, but we're just too busy.

●●●○   **get away with**   **1** escape punishment for something:
     □ I wonder how many criminals actually *get away with* the crimes they commit?
     2 succeed in doing something, especially against expectation:
     □ We knew he was applying for an extra week's leave, but we never thought he'd *get away with* it.
     3 receive only a light punishment:
     □ He *got away with* a fine.

●●   **get back**   **1** return to the place that you left, especially your home or country:
     □ He leaves school at four o'clock and *gets back* here by five.
     □ I thought you were still in Indonesia. When did you *get back*?
     2 return to a previously held office or position:
     □ The team will have to play much better if they want to *get back* into the first division.
     3 move away, especially when ordered:
     □ The police told the crowd to *get back* to give the firemen more room.

● ● ● ○   **get back at**   retaliate or take revenge on somebody:
☐ She has promised that she will *get back at* him for the things he said about her poems.

● ● ● ○   **get back to**   **1** return to something:
☐ I wonder if we could *get back to* the original question of cost.
2 return to somebody in order to communicate or discuss something:
☐ I'll *get* straight *back to* head office and inform them of your decision.

● ●(● ○)   **get behind (with)**   fail to do or complete something by a particular time:
☐ Try not to *get behind with* your reading during the first term.
☐ If you *get* too far *behind,* you'll never be able to pass the exam.

● ●
● ● ○   **get by¹**   pass through or along somewhere, especially with difficulty:
☐ The boxes had been left right in the doorway, so that it was impossible to *get by.*

● ●   **get by²**   manage to do or pass something; just manage to be approved or accepted:
☐ I don't care if I don't do well in the exam. I just want to *get by,* that's all.
☐ Do you think I'll *get by* without a tie, or will they stop me from entering?

● ●(● ○)   **get by (on/with)**   manage to live, survive or continue in spite of difficulty or hardship:
☐ How does she *get by on* such a small salary? It's amazing.
☐ We've just enough money to *get by* till pay day.

● ●   **get down¹**   leave the table after a meal, especially of children:
☐ Can I *get down* now, Mummy?

● ○ ●
● ● ○   **get down²**   **1** record a talk, announcement, etc, in writing:
☐ Why don't you just listen to the lecture instead of trying to *get* every word *down*?
2 swallow something, especially with difficulty:
☐ The meat was so tough that I simply couldn't *get* it *down.*

● ○ ●   **get down³**   make somebody feel depressed:
☐ All this rain every day is really *getting me down.*

● ● ● ○   **get down to**   start to concentrate on something, especially a job or task:
☐ It's about time you *got down to* some serious work. The exams are next month.

69

●○●   **get in¹**   **1** ask a doctor, builder, electrician, etc, to come to
●●○   your home or office:
□ We'll have to *get* the doctor *in* if she gets any worse.
2 buy, collect or harvest something:
□ She always *gets* her shopping *in* on Tuesday.
□ The manager wants me to *get* all the rents *in* before the
end of the month.
□ We want to *get* the hay *in* before the weekend.
3 manage to do or say something, especially in difficult
circumstances:
□ I was hoping that I might *get in* an hour's reading
before they all arrive.
□ She talks so much that you can't *get* a word *in*.

●●   **get in²**   benefit from being among the first people to do
something:
□ The shirts are so cheap that they'll all be sold unless
you *get in* quickly.

●●●○   **get in on**   take or cause somebody to take part in
●○●●○   something:
□ If it means a free holiday, everybody will want to *get
in on* it.

●●/   **get in/into¹**   **1** arrive home; arrive, especially of a train,
●●○   plane, passenger, etc:
□ She usually *gets in* from work at about six o'clock.
□ Her flight was delayed and eventually *got into* Gatwick
three hours late.
2 be elected or admitted to a committee, the government,
etc:
□ The opposition has very little chance of *getting in* at
the next election in October.

●●   **get in/into²**   be admitted or cause somebody to be
●○●/   admitted to a school, college, hospital, etc:
●●○   □ With such poor examination results, she's very lucky
●○●○   to *get in*.
□ We want to *get* him *into* a private hospital.

●●○   **get into¹**   **1** fasten a piece of clothing after putting it on:
●○●○   □ He'd eaten so much that he couldn't *get into* his
trousers.
2 develop or cause somebody to develop a feeling, mood,
habit, etc:
□ She suddenly *got into* a temper when I told her that the
baby was crying.
□ Whatever *got* you *into* the habit of eating with just a
fork?
3 learn or teach somebody how to do something:

☐ The job is a bit difficult at first, but you'll soon *get into* it.

4 become or cause somebody to become involved in something, especially an unpleasant situation:
☐ He spent more than he was earning, and soon *got into* debt.
☐ Don't expect me to help you if your behaviour *gets* you *into* trouble.

5 become or cause somebody to become interested in something:
☐ I found the first chapter a bit slow, but I've really *got into* the book now.

●●○ **get into²**   **1** take control of somebody or something's behaviour:
☐ I don't know what *got into* me yesterday! I'm sorry!
2 interfere or play with something:
☐ Our baby *gets into* everything these days.

●●●○ **get in with**   become friendly with somebody, especially because you want to help them:
☐ She hopes that by *getting in with* the professor, she'll be given more time for her research.

●● **get off¹**   **1** leave; start a journey:
☐ We had planned to *get off* early and arrive before lunch.
2 escape from an accident, especially without serious injury:
☐ You're lucky to *get off* with just a few bruises. The other driver broke his leg!

●● **get off²**   be released from work:
●●○ ☐ What time do you *get off* tonight?

●● **get off³**   **1** escape or save somebody from punishment:
●○● ☐ A good lawyer should be able to *get* you *off* with just a warning.
2 be sent, posted, cabled, etc; send something or somebody:
☐ Make sure that these letters *get off* today, will you?
☐ I have to *get* the children *off* to school before I can go back to bed.

●●○ **get off⁴**   stop or cause somebody to stop discussing or
●○●○ talking about a particular subject:
☐ Let's *get off* the question of who is to blame for these low figures, and think about how we can improve them.
☐ It's not easy to *get* a cat-lover *off* the subject of cats.

●●●○ **get off with**   *Informal* have or cause somebody to have
●○●○ sexual relationship with somebody:

□ If she didn't already have a boyfriend, I might try to *get off with* her.

●● **get on** 1 become late or have little time left:
□ Since the time is *getting on*, perhaps we should leave discussion of this new problem until tomorrow's meeting.
2 become old:
□ She's *getting on* a bit. She must be at least sixty.
3 be successful in life or in a career:
□ Most parents want their children to *get on*.
4 manage, fare or perform, especially in a new or difficult situation:
□ How did you *get on* when your husband's boss came to dinner?
□ I'm afraid that I didn't *get on* very well in the exam.

●●(●○) **get on (with)** 1 see **get along/on (with)**
2 continue after an interruption or pause:
□ As soon as the rain stopped, we *got on with* our game of tennis.

●●●○ **get on at** criticise, nag or urge somebody to do something:
□ For the last six months she's been *getting on at* me to paint the house.

●●●○ **get on for** be almost a certain age, time, price, amount, etc:
□ It was *getting on for* midnight by the time she arrived.
□ She must be *getting on for* thirty.

●●●○ **get on to** 1 contact somebody:
□ When the shop refused to refund my money, I *got on to* my lawyer straightaway.
2 detect or discover a criminal or criminal activities:
□ He'd managed to cheat four old ladies of their savings by the time the police *got on to* him.
3 proceed to a new topic, activity, etc:
□ Let us now *get on to* the main point of today's meeting: the election of a new chairman.

●● **get out¹** 1 become known, especially of secret information:
□ Nobody would fly in the aircraft after the news of the design fault *got out*.
2 leave your home or office for a while and go somewhere for pleasure:
□ We like to *get out* at the weekend and enjoy some fresh air.

●○●
●●○ **get out²** manage to say something, especially with difficulty:

☐ He was so nervous about having to read aloud, that he could hardly *get* the words *out*.

● ○ ●　　**get out³** **1** publish or produce something for inspection:
☐ The publishers hope to *get* the new edition *out* before Christmas.
☐ How long will it take you to *get* the figures *out*?
2 find the answer to a problem, calculation, etc:
☐ It looked like an easy calculation, but it took the child a whole hour to *get* it *out*.

● ○ ●(● ○)　**get out (of)** **1** cause somebody to leave or abandon a room, building, job, etc:
☐ You can't *get* a tenant *out* if the accommodation is unfurnished.

2 borrow something from a library:
☐ I wonder if you would *get* a book *out* for me if you're going to the library.

● ● ● ○　　**get out of¹** avoid doing something:
☐ He's always trying to *get out of* making decisions.

● ○ ● ○　　**get out of²** **1** gain or derive pleasure, profit, satisfaction, etc, from something:
☐ It's a fairly elementary course, so advanced learners won't *get* much *out of* it.
☐ All we *got out of* the holiday was an empty bank account!
2 obtain or extract something from somebody, especially by force or strong persuasion:
☐ Somehow we have to *get* the information *out of* him.
☐ You could always use blackmail to *get* the money *out of* her.

● ● ● ○
● ○ ● ○　　**get out of³** abandon or cause somebody to abandon a habit:
☐ I can't *get out of* the habit of waking up at six o'clock.
☐ You'll have to *get* her *out of* biting her nails. They look awful.

● ● ○　　　**get over** **1** recover from an illness, shock, bad experience, etc:
☐ It took him six months to *get over* the heart attack.
☐ I don't think she'll ever *get over* the death of her father.
☐ It took him a long time to *get over* Cathy, but he eventually found a new girlfriend.
2 overcome or deal successfully with a problem, difficulty, etc:
☐ It will be a miracle if the country manages to *get over* its present financial difficulties.

3 continue to be surprised or shocked at something; used in the negative:

□ I just can't *get over* the way she married again only six weeks after her first husband died.

4 cease to be worried or troubled by something:

□ Do you think that she'll ever *get over* her shyness?

●○●(●○) **get over (to)** make yourself or something understood by somebody:

□ If you try to *get* too many points *over* in the lecture, you'll only confuse the students.

●○●(●) **get over (with)** do or finish doing something unpleasant so that you don't have to worry about it any more:

□ We have to pay the bill at some time, so why not pay it now and *get* it *over with*?

□ She'll be happier once she's *got* her exams *over*.

●●○ **get round¹** see **get around/round**.

●● **get round²** see **get about/around/round**.
●●○

●●●○ **get round to** see **get around/round to**.

●● **get through¹** **1** pass or be responsible for somebody
●●○ passing a test, examination, etc:
●○● □ Just over half the students who took the exam *got*
●○●○ *through*.

□ I'm very grateful to John for *getting* me *through* my driving test.

2 be approved or cause something to be approved by a group of officials:

□ We were pleased to *get* our application *through* the committee.

●●○ **get through²** **1** spend or consume something; use something until it is no longer usable:

□ When he's hungry, he can *get through* a three-course meal in less than twenty minutes!

□ I wonder how many pairs of shoes you *get through* in a year.

2 manage to do or complete something:

□ How long will it take you to *get through* the whole book?

●●(●○) **get through (to)** **1** contact a person by telephone; connect
●○●(●○) somebody with the person they are telephoning:

□ I've been ringing all morning, but I can't *get through*.

□ The operator will *get* you *through* if you ask her.

□ What's the number you're trying to *get through to*?

2 reach or cause something to reach somebody, especially after a difficult journey:

☐ Not enough food is *getting through to* the earthquake victims.

3 make somebody understand something; communicate with somebody:

☐ I can't *get through to* my son nowadays. He seems to be living in a different world.

☐ You'll have to *get* it *through to* her that she will fail the examination unless her work improves.

●●●○
●○●○ **get through to**   reach or cause somebody to reach a particular stage in a competition:

☐ The team did very well to *get through to* the final round.

●●●○ **get through with**   **1** finish a task:

☐ Once I *get through with* the housework, I'll be free for the afternoon.

2 finish scolding or attacking somebody:

☐ He'll wish he hadn't tried to cheat me when I *get through with* him!

●● **get together**   meet informally for a discussion or pleasure:

☐ It's an interesting idea. Why don't we *get together* and discuss it further?

N ☐ Are you going to the Spanish Society's *get-together* on Tuesday?

●●
●○● **get up**[1]   rise or cause somebody to rise out of bed, especially in the morning:

☐ I usually *get up* a bit later on holiday.

●● **get up**[2]   develop or increase in strength, especially of a wind or storm:

☐ In Singapore you know that it's going to rain if the wind suddenly *gets up*.

●○● **get up**[3]   make yourself look unusually smart or attractive, especially for a party, wedding, interview, etc:

☐ She spent hours *getting* herself *up* for the dinner party.

N ☐ That's an outrageous *get-up* you're wearing, Sarah!

●○●
●●○ **get up**[4]   organise something, especially a party, petition, group activity, etc:

☐ We're *getting up* a coach trip to Scotland and thought you might like to join us.

●●●○ **get up to**   **1** do or get involved in something, especially something naughty or mischievous:

☐ Don't think I don't know what you're *getting up to* behind that armchair!

☐ The things these children *get up to*!

2 reach a particular place or standard:

☐ I only *got up to* the third page, I'm afraid. Your writing is so hard to read.

●○●   **ginger up**   make somebody or something more lively or
●●○   interesting:
         □ The courtesy campaign needs *gingering up* a bit.
         People seem to have forgotten it.

●○●   **give away**   **1** betray somebody or reveal a secret:
●●○   □ He said that unless I shared the money with him, he
         would *give* me *away* to the police.
         □ She assured me that they had enough money, but the
         holes in her shoes *gave* her *away*.
         □ I promised never to *give* her secret *away*.
N   □ The answer to the question was very obvious. It was a
         real *give-away*.
         2 lose or fail to make use of something:
         □ When he lost the fight, he *gave away* his last chance of
         regaining the world title.
         3 formally present a bride to her husband at their
         wedding ceremony:
         □ It's usually the bride's father who *gives* her *away*.

●○●(●○)   **give in (to)**[1]   pass or submit something to somebody,
●●○(●○)   especially something you have written:
         □ Don't forget to *give in* your homework before you
         leave the classroom.

●●(●○)   **give in (to)**[2]   yield or surrender to somebody or
         something:
         □ Although the smaller child was obviously losing the
         fight he refused to *give in*.
         □ I was forced to *give in to* the opinion of the majority.

●●○   **give off**   emit or release something into the air, especially
         a smell, gas, heat, etc:
         □ That old gas fire doesn't *give off* much heat. I'm
         freezing.
         □ The market was full of dried fish, *giving off* the worst
         smell that you can imagine.

●○●   **give out**[1]   **1** distribute something:
●●○   □ It shouldn't take more than five minutes to *give out* the
         question papers and answer books.
         2 announce or broadcast something:
         □ This morning the headmaster *gave out* that the school
         is going to have a new science laboratory.
         □ It was *given out* on the news that there are to be
         heavier penalties for dangerous driving.

●●   **give out**[2]   **1** cease to function, especially because of a fault:
         □ You can imagine how concerned I became when I saw
         one of the plane's engines *give out*.

2 come to an end, especially of a supply that has been consumed, used or spent:

□ The expedition had very few problems, except for the time when the water *gave out*.

●● **give over** *Informal* stop doing something; usually used in the imperative to express annoyance or irritation.

□ *Give over*, you lot! How can I work when you're so noisy?

●○●○ **give over to** **1** resign yourself to live in a certain way:

□ By his early twenties he had *given* himself *over to* a life of crime.

2 transfer the care of a child to somebody:

□ She was forced to *give* the girl *over to* foster parents.

●●○ **give up¹** **1** stop doing something, especially something habitual:

□ I wish I could *give up* smoking.

□ She's *given up* playing tennis since she finished with John.

2 abandon an attempt, pursuit or other activity, especially as a sign of defeat:

□ Yorkshire police today *gave up* their search for the missing Leeds girl.

□ I *gave up* trying to play the violin when I listened to one of my recordings.

●○● **give up²** **1** leave or resign from a job, course, profession,
●●○ etc:

□ His doctor has advised him to *give* the job *up* and find something less strenuous.

□ Why did you decide to *give up* medicine, Dr Green?

2 let somebody have something that is yours:

□ He *gave up* his seat to the old lady.

□ They were told that unless they *gave up* their guns, they would all be killed.

□ He's had to *give up* his house in order to pay his debts.

3 present a wanted person, especially yourself, to the police, army, etc:

□ He was frightened of what they would do to him if he *gave* himself *up*.

4 end a relationship with somebody, especially a boyfriend or girlfriend:

□ She *gave up* her last boyfriend because he used to drive too fast.

5 devote time to something:

□ I'm certainly not prepared to *give up* all my weekends to cleaning the house.

6 renounce or abandon an idea, belief, principle, etc:
□ She said that she wouldn't marry him unless he *gave up* his religion.

● ○ ● **give up³** **1** stop expecting somebody to arrive:
□ We'd just *given* her *up* when the doorbell rang.
2 stop expecting somebody to recover from an illness, operation, misfortune, etc:
□ The expression on the doctor's face told her that he had *given* her husband *up*.

● ● **give up⁴** acknowledge defeat or stop trying:
□ Will you tell me the answer if I *give up*?
□ Some of the players had *given up* and stopped running.

● ●
● ● ○ **glance off** strike something lightly and be deflected:
□ Fortunately the stone *glanced off* the windscreen without shattering it.

● ● ○ **glance over/through** look very briefly at a magazine, report, letter, etc:
□ I won't even have time to *glance through* the manuscript until next week, I'm afraid.

● ● ○ **glory in** obtain great pleasure from something:
□ I hate the way she seems to *glory in* other people's misfortunes.
□ We left both parents still *glorying in* the birth of their baby boy.

● ● ○ **gloss over** try to hide or ignore a fault, mistake, criticism, etc:
□ We are tired of the management's habit of *glossing over* our complaints instead of giving them proper attention.

● ● ○ **go about** **1** approach or start work on a job, problem, etc:
□ It's an easy job if you *go about* it the right way.
□ How do you *go about* getting a passport these days?
2 perform or keep busy with a task or activity:
□ You could see that the illness had affected him from the way he now *went about* his exercises.

● ● **go about/around/round** circulate or be passed from person to person:
□ There's a rumour *going about* that the price of petrol is going to double by September.
□ Apparently there's a lot of illness *going around* at the moment.

● ●(● ○) **go about/around/round (with)** spend time regularly with somebody, especially for pleasure:
□ How do you like your daughter *going around with* the son of a millionaire?

●●○   **go after**   pursue or try to get somebody or something:
    □ I *went after* her to stop her from posting the letter, but it was too late.
    □ She's decided to *go after* a job she saw in yesterday's newspaper.

●●○   **go against**   **1** be or act in opposition to something:
    □ Working on a Sunday would *go against* his principles.
    □ She *went against* her parents' expressed wishes by marrying him.
    □ What will happen to him if the court's decision *goes against* him?
    3 reduce or weaken something, especially a person's chances of doing something:
    □ This new injury will certainly *go against* his chances of winning the championship.

●●   **go ahead**   **1** permit or encourage somebody to do something:
    □ *Go ahead* and buy it if you really like it.

N   □ They won't start building until they get the *go-ahead*.
    2 proceed or progress:
    □ The work on the new airport is *going ahead* as planned, and so far there have been no major setbacks.

●●   **go along**   proceed or continue to do something:
    □ The job will be easier if you clean up as you *go along*.

●●(●○)   **go along (with)**   accompany somebody:
    □ They want me to *go along with* them to see the manager.

●●●○   **go along with**   be or act in agreement with somebody or something:
    □ I knew that she would never *go along with* sending the child to a boarding school.
    □ There are several points in the report that I can't *go along with*, I'm afraid.

●●   **go around**   see **go about/around/round**.
●●(●○)   **go around (with)**   see **go about/around/round (with)**.
●●○   **go at**   **1** attack someone or something fiercely:
    □ The two women *went at* each other like wild cats.
    2 do something with great energy or effort:
    □ With only an afternoon to complete the job, they really *went at* it.

●●(●○)
●●○(●○)   **go back (to)**   be known to have existed since a certain time in the past:
    □ The custom *goes back* to my great-grandfather's generation.

●●●○   **go back on**   fail to keep a promise or change your mind about something you said before:

        □ He never *goes back on* his word.

        □ You seem to be *going back on* what you said earlier about the importance of discipline.

●●●○   **go back to**   resume an old habit, especially a bad one:

        □ It's a pity he's *gone back to* smoking again.

●●   **go by**[1]   pass or elapse, especially of time or an opportunity:

        □ Several years *went by* before they met again, this time in Poland.

        □ You'd be silly to let this chance of improving your qualifications *go by*.

●●○   **go by**[2]   **1** form a judgement on the basis of something:

        □ *Going by* the way she speaks, she must have had a good education.

        2 be guided by something:

        □ Don't *go by* my watch. It's slow.

●●   **go down**   **1** sink to the bottom of the sea, especially of a ship:

        □ The ship *went down* so quickly that it is surprising that anyone survived.

        2 disappear beneath the horizon:

        □ It's surprising how cold it gets when the sun *goes down*.

        3 be swallowed or digested, especially of food:

        □ Most meals *go down* more easily with a glass of wine.

        4 be reduced, especially of prices, etc:

        □ If the society could attract more members, the fees might *go down*.

        5 fall to the ground:

        □ She tripped over the carpet and *went down* with a crash.

        6 decrease in size, level, pressure, etc:

        □ I'm glad that your temperature has *gone down*.

        □ One of my tyres keeps *going down*.

        7 decrease in value or quality:

        □ The value of the property *went down* the day they started to build a factory opposite it.

        □ The service in this restaurant has *gone down* a lot since it opened last year.

        8 become less violent:

        □ You'd better hold onto your hat until the wind *goes down* a bit.

●●(●○)   **go down (in)**   **1** be recorded in writing:

        □ Every word I said *went down in* the officer's notebook.

☐ He'll *go down in* history as one of the cleverest men ever to enter Parliament.

2 fail an examination paper:

☐ She passed physics but *went down in* chemistry.

●●(●○)
●●○(●○)
go down (with)   be received or well received by somebody:

☐ Your joke about unemployment didn't *go down with* the Prime Minister, I'm afraid.

☐ I thought that his speech *went down* very well.

☐ The idea of shorter working hours *went down* badly *with* the boss.

●●●○
go down to   **1** be defeated by someone, especially in a sports competition:

☐ I wouldn't mind *going down to* a good team, but losing to that lot is disgraceful!

2 reach as far as a certain date or period in history:

☐ This book only *goes down to* the eighteenth century.

●●●○
go down with   become ill with something:

☐ Their youngest child has *gone down with* German measles.

●●○
go for   **1** go to fetch or get somebody or something:

☐ He's just this minute *gone for* a newspaper.

2 attack somebody either physically or verbally:

☐ The dog *went for* me as I opened the gate.

☐ She'll *go for* you if she thinks you're criticising her.

3 be sold for a certain amount of money:

☐ The flat *went for* over £60,000 eventually, although it took a long time to find a buyer.

4 be attracted by somebody or something:

☐ She tends to *go for* tall men with beards.

5 be applicable to somebody or something:

☐ You'll be in trouble if you don't get to school on time, Jenkins! And that *goes for* the rest of you, too!

6 aim to get, win, or do something:

☐ The team are so confident this year that they are *going for* the championship and have said so.

●●
go in   **1** be hidden by cloud, of the sun, moon, etc:

☐ It's colder now that the sun has *gone in*.

2 be understood or remembered:

☐ I keep telling him what he should do, but none of it seems to *go in*.

●●●○
go in for   **1** enter an examination, competition, etc:

☐ Her teacher recommended her to *go in for* the Lower Cambridge Examination.

2 make something your career, hobby, sport, etc:

☐ I don't know why he chose to *go in for* architecture.

3 do something regularly for enjoyment:

☐ Our neighbours *go in for* large dinner parties, but we don't.

● ● ○   **go into**   **1** examine, consider or investigate something carefully:

☐ The report should be *gone into* very thoroughly before you reach a decision.

☐ We still need to *go into* the question of cost.

2 make a career of something:

☐ They want their son to *go into* medicine.

☐ He decided to *go into* the navy.

3 enter a particular mental or physical condition:

☐ When we saw the egg run down his face, we all *went into* shrieks of laughter.

☐ The doctors are worried that she may *go into* a coma.

4 divide a number mathematically:

☐ How many times does six *go into* seventy-two?

● ●   **go off¹**   **1** explode, be fired or make a loud noise:

☐ Another car bomb *went off* today in London, killing six people.

☐ I nearly fell out of bed when the alarm *went off* this morning.

2 go bad, especially of food and drink:

☐ This milk smells a bit strange. It must have *gone off* in the heat.

3 deteriorate or become worse in quality:

☐ Local craftsmanship has *gone off* a lot since tourists started coming here.

4 cease to operate or be available:

☐ The lights *go off* at midnight and come on again at eight.

☐ What's happened? The water has suddenly *gone off*!

5 become less intense or no longer felt:

☐ Has your headache *gone off* yet?

6 fall asleep:

☐ I can't hear the baby any more. He must have *gone off*.

● ● ○   **go off²**   stop liking somebody or something:

☐ I *went off* motor racing the day I saw a driver get killed.

● ● ○   **go off³**   happen in a particular way:

● ●   ☐ The rehearsal *went off* very well.

● ● ● ○   **go off with**   **1** leave your home, husband, parents, etc, to be with or marry somebody:

☐ She *went off with* her friend's husband.

2 take something without permission and leave with it:
□ Our first gardener *went off with* just about all of
Henry's tools.

go on¹ **1** happen or take place:
□ It sounds as if there was an argument *going on*
upstairs.
□ Did you hear about the strange *goings-on* up at the
farm last night? They think they've got a ghost.
2 be in operation, especially of lights, heating, etc:
□ A lot of drivers would like the lights on the motorway
to *go on* much earlier.
3 pass, especially of time:
□ She became more relaxed as the evening *went on*.
4 behave, especially in an unusual or outrageous way:
□ If they keep *going on* like that, they'll be asked to leave
the restaurant.
5 continue along a route or road, etc, ahead of the other
people you are travelling with:
□ You two *go on*, and we'll catch you up after we've had
a little rest.
6 continue speaking, especially after a pause:
□ If there are no objections, I'll *go on*.
□ 'The next item on the agenda,' he *went on*, 'is housing.'
7 continue, especially for an excessive length of time:
□ How much longer is this ridiculous play going to *go
on*?

go on² **1** continue doing something; usually followed by
-ing:
□ You can't *go on* working all night without a rest.
2 proceed to do, say or become something:
□ Although they only just managed to qualify, they *went
on* to win the competition.
3 be spent on something:
□ Most of his salary *goes on* food for the family.
4 be guided or influenced by something:
□ The jury shouldn't *go on* the evidence of a known
criminal.

go on (about) talk a lot about something, especially in a
boring way:
□ I'm tired of the way she's always *going on about* cat
diseases.
□ That awful woman does *go on*!

go on (at) keep complaining in an angry way about
something:
□ She's always *going on at* me about the money I spend
on cigarettes.

●●(●○) **go on (with)** resume or continue doing something:
    □ If we don't finish the painting today, we can always *go on with* it tomorrow.

●●●○ **go on for** be almost a certain age, time, price, etc:
    □ It's *going on for* ten o'clock. It's time we left.

●●●○ **go on to** change to a new system or scale:
    □ The company has *gone on to* a three-day week.
    □ It's many years since we *went on to* the metric system.

●● **go out** **1** stop burning or giving light:
    □ He put some more wood on the fire to stop it *going out*.
    □ The lights on the island always *go out* at midnight.
2 leave your home and go somewhere, especially for entertainment:
    □ His wife complains that they never *go out*.
3 become obsolete or unfashionable:
    □ That type of design *went out* five or six years ago.
4 be sent, announced or broadcast:
    □ Have all the invitations *gone out*?
    □ The first programme in the new series *goes out* on Thursday.
5 be eliminated from a competition by being beaten:
    □ The London team *went out* in the first round last night, losing 2–0 to Ipswich.
6 reach a lower level, especially of the sea or tide:
    □ Once the tide *goes out*, the children can go and play on the beach.
7 begin a strike:
    □ The men at the car factory are *going out* from tomorrow.

●●(●○) **go out (to)** go overseas or emigrate to another country:
    □ She's *going out to* Australia to see her daughter.

●●(●○) **go out (with)** be regularly in the company of a boyfriend or girlfriend:
    □ Jim *went out with* Rachel for only six weeks.

●●○ **go over** **1** examine or check something:
    □ I *went over* the figures three times, but always reached the same total.
2 repeat something, especially an explanation, details, etc:
    □ Could you *go over* what you have said, for the sake of the people who have just arrived?
3 search somebody or something:
    □ They spent thirty minutes *going over* me at the customs, but forgot to look under my hat.
4 inspect a property when deciding whether to buy it:

□ After *going over* the house very carefully, I realised that it would require a lot of repair work.
5 clean, service or repair something:
□ I need somebody reliable to *go over* the car.
□ She gave the room a good *going-over*.
6 review or rehearse something:
□ The gang *went over* the robbery a dozen times, until each member knew exactly what he had to do.
7 be received by somebody:
□ Considering the bad news it contained, his speech *went over* surprisingly well.

●●●○   **go over to**   change your allegiance or preference to something else:
□ Why don't you *go over to* margarine? It's cheaper than butter and better for you.
□ After all these years, he's suddenly *gone over to* the Worker's Party.

●●   **go round¹**   be sufficient for everybody:
●●○   □ Is the cake big enough to *go round*?
●●   **go round²**   see **go about/around/round**.
●●(●○)   **go round (with)**   see **go about/around/round (with)**.
●●   **go through¹**   **1** be officially approved or accepted:
□ We were rather relieved to hear that the application had *gone through*.
2 be successfully completed:
□ Why didn't the deal *go through*? I thought they were ready to sign?

●●○   **go through²**   **1** use, spend or consume something:
□ You'll soon *go through* your savings if you start gambling.
2 search or examine something, especially to find something that may have been hidden:
□ I must look guilty. They always stop me at the customs and *go through* my bags.
3 suffer or endure something:
□ The poor girl has *gone through* a lot of pain in the last twelve months.
4 review or discuss something:
□ Shall we quickly *go through* the major points again?
5 rehearse something:
□ Let's *go through* that scene again.

●●●○   **go through to**   reach a particular stage in a competition:
□ I'm sure our team will *go through to* the next round.
●●●○   **go through with**   finish doing something you have already started, or do something that you have planned or promised to do:

☐ Once all the arrangements had been made, he felt that he had to *go through with* the marriage.

●●○ **go to** be given or awarded to somebody or something:

☐ The first prize *goes to* Jennifer Smith.

☐ All her money *went to* charity after her death.

●● **go together** **1** be regularly in the company of somebody, especially a boyfriend or girlfriend:

☐ How long have Peter and Mary been *going together*?

2 be a suitable combination:

☐ Do you really think that ice cream and onions *go together*?

3 be commonly found together:

☐ People say that money and happiness don't always *go together*.

●● **go under** **1** sink, dive or be drawn beneath the surface of:

☐ Those who had been rescued watched their ship *go under*.

2 fail or collapse, especially of a business:

☐ We're bound to *go under* unless we can widen our range of products.

●●(●○) **go under (to)** be defeated or overcome by somebody or something:

☐ A lot of small businesses *went under* when supermarkets were introduced.

●● **go up** **1** rise or increase, especially of prices:

☐ I see that the price of petrol has *gone up* again.

2 be built:

☐ Another new factory is *going up* where we live.

3 be destroyed by an explosion or by fire:

☐ If you had lit a match, the whole kitchen could have *gone up*.

●●○ **go with** **1** be included as part of something:

☐ Do the carpets and curtains *go with* the house?

2 match or suit something:

☐ Does this blue hat *go with* my coat?

3 be regularly in the company of somebody, especially a boyfriend or girlfriend:

☐ I didn't know that John was *going with* your sister.

●● **go without** not have or manage without something:

●●○ ☐ He often *goes without* his dinner so that he can get more work done.

☐ If you don't want your fish and chips, you'll just have to *go without*.

●○●○ **goad into** provoke somebody to do something by harassing them:

□ He didn't really want to apply for the job. His mother *goaded* him *into* it.

●○● **goad on** incite or entice somebody, especially to do something mischievous, illegal, etc:
□ He would never have stolen the car if he hadn't been *goaded on*.

●●(●○) **grind away (at)** work laboriously at something:
□ You're not still *grinding away at* that essay, are you?

●○●
●●○ **grind down¹** gradually destroy the vitality or resistance of somebody:
□ All this work is going to *grind* you *down* if you don't get somebody to help you.

●● **grind down²** slow down gradually and come to a halt:
□ Everything *grinds down* towards the end of term.

●● **grind on** move forwards relentlessly:
□ The enemy tanks *ground on* through the night.

●●○ **grow on** become more attractive or appealing to somebody:
□ I didn't like this piece of music at first, but it's slowly *growing on* me.

●●●○ **grow out of** become too old or too big for something; especially of children:
□ She's *grown out of* all the clothes she wore last summer.
□ Most kids are afraid of the dark, but they *grow out of* it sooner or later.

●● **grow up** 1 get older; become an adult:
□ He's beginning to look more like his father as he *grows up*.

N □ Andrew prefers the company of *grown-ups* to children.
2 behave, think or talk sensibly:
□ I wish you would *grow up* and stop acting like a child!
3 arise or originate, of customs, traditions, etc:
□ The custom is believed to have *grown up* in India.

●●○ **guard against** take precautions to avoid something:
□ We must always try to *guard against* bringing innocent people to trial.

●○●
●●○ **gun down** shoot somebody, especially in a cowardly way:
□ The group's latest victim was *gunned down* as he was getting into his car.

●●○ **gun for** seek to attack or take revenge on somebody:
□ He's bound to be *gunning for* you after the awful things you wrote about his last book.

H, h

●●(●○)   **hammer away (at)**   **1** work hard at a task or on a problem:
□ Just keep *hammering away* and you'll soon have the answer.
2 attack somebody with questions, criticisms, arguments, etc:
□ Our lawyer *hammered away at* the witness for at least an hour, but she wouldn't change a single detail.
3 to force a fact, idea, opinion, etc, upon somebody by constantly repeating it:
□ I *hammered away at* the point all night but nobody took any notice.

●○●
 ●●○   **hammer in**   teach somebody something by emphasising it or repeating it many times:
□ The message I'm trying to *hammer in* is that you'll never lose weight if you keep eating so many biscuits.

●○●
 ●●○   **hammer out**   **1** remove or tackle a problem, difficulty, etc, through serious discussion:
□ Sooner or later we shall have to sit down and start *hammering out* the objections that have been raised.
2 produce a solution, policy, agreement, etc, as a result of concentrated effort or serious discussion:
□ The point of the meeting is to *hammer out* ways of saving the college from closure.

●○●(●○)
 ●●○(●○)   **hand back (to)**   **1** return or restore something to somebody, especially to its owner:
□ The islands were *handed back* just two years after the war.
2 return a radio or television audience, etc, to a previous speaker or presenter:
□ Well, that's all we have time for today from the Chelsea Flower Show. I'll now *hand* you *back to* Peter Barker in the studio.

●○●
 ●●○   **hand down/on**   pass something from one person or generation to a younger one:
□ Why throw away the baby's clothes when you can *hand* them *down*?
□ Their religious customs have been *handed down* since time began.

●○●
 ●●○   **hand in**   present or submit something, especially something written, completed or no longer required:

☐ Don't forget to *hand in* your answer sheets before you leave.

☐ Why has he *handed in* his resignation if he doesn't feel responsible?

●○●(●○)
●●○(●○)

hand on (to) **1** pass something, especially something that you have no further use for, to somebody:

☐ Once you've read the book, perhaps you would like to *hand* it *on to* Richard.

2 see **hand down/on.**

●○●
●●○

hand out **1** distribute something, especially printed sheets of paper:

☐ At the beginning he would always *hand out* an outline of the lecture.

N

☐ Some of the *handouts* were unreadable.

2 give food, clothing, money, etc, to people in need:

☐ The government has been *handing out* free milk to families on a low income.

N

☐ He's much too proud to accept *handouts* from the government.

3 offer, give or allocate criticism, work, punishment, etc:

☐ That man is always *handing out* unwanted advice.

●○●
●●○

hand over¹ give or pass something or somebody to another person:

☐ She refused to *hand over* the car keys until he promised to wear his safety belt.

☐ The thief was *handed over* to the police.

●○●
●●○
●●
N

hand over² transfer power, control, responsibility, etc:

☐ He wants to *hand over* all his responsibilities and retire as soon as we can find a replacement.

☐ The outgoing president has suggested July as a suitable month for the *hand-over.*

●●
●●○

hang about/around wait or spend time somewhere, especially doing nothing:

☐ The last guests *hung about* till the early hours of the morning.

☐ Since he lost his job, he just *hangs around* the house all day.

●●(●○)

hang back (from) be slow or reluctant to do something, especially because of shyness, fear, etc:

☐ It's only her modesty that's making her *hang back from* showing you her examination results.

●●

hang on **1** *Informal* remain, stop or wait:

☐ Why don't you *hang on* here while I go and fetch the others.

☐ *Hang on!* Isn't the restaurant closed on a Sunday?

2 continue to do something:

☐ Despite his head injury, the goalkeeper was able to *hang on* until the end of the match.

●●○   **hang on/upon**   depend upon or be conditional upon something:

☐ We want to move as soon as we can, but everything *hangs on* whether we can sell our flat.

●●●○   **hang on to**   keep or retain something, especially instead of selling it or giving it away:

☐ If I were you, I'd *hang on to* that old chair. It might be valuable.

●●   **hang out**   *Informal* live or spend a lot of time in a place:

☐ Until he found a job, he spent most of the day *hanging out* in coffee bars.

N   ☐ If he's not at home, he'll be at his favourite *hang-out*.

●●(●○)   **hang out (for)**   resist, especially by refusing to return to work, in the hope of obtaining something:

☐ The steel workers are still *hanging out for* more money.

●●   **hang together**   **1** remain united or in support of one another:

☐ Unless the party *hangs together*, we're going to lose the next election.

2 be consistent, especially of two or more statements:

☐ Although some of the observations are very interesting, the whole thing doesn't really *hang together* as a book.

●●(●○)   **hang up (on)**   abruptly end a telephone conversation with someone by replacing the receiver:

☐ As soon as I said that I wouldn't be home until late, she *hung up on* me.

●●○   **hang upon**   see **hang on/upon**.

●●○   **hanker after/for**   have a strong wish, urge or yearning for something:

☐ She's been *hankering after* a trip to the States for the last six years.

●●○   **happen on/upon**   find or meet somebody or something by chance:

☐ If you should *happen upon* her address, perhaps you would let me have it.

●●(●○)   **hark back (to)**   recall or refer to something said or done earlier:

☐ His grandfather loved to *hark back to* the good old days, when cigarettes were cheap.

☐ *Harking back* to your first question, it is my firm belief that the safety of the drug has still to be demonstrated.

●●(●○)   **harp on (about)**   mention or criticise something repeatedly, usually with the effect of annoying somebody:
□ My mother is always *harping on about* my hair being untidy.

●○●   **have around/in/over/round**   invite somebody to your home for a drink, meal, social visit, etc:
□ Since it's John's birthday on Friday, we thought we'd *have* a few friends *round* for the evening.

●○●   **have back¹**   have something returned to your possession:
●●○   □ He's had your camera for nearly six weeks now. Don't you think it's about time you *had* it *back*?

●○●   **have back²**   allow a marriage partner, boyfriend, etc, to return to you after a period of desertion:
□ Surely she won't *have* him *back* after all the suffering he has caused her?

●○●   **have in**   **1** have or arrange to have a doctor, builder, etc, at your home:
□ We've *had* the painters *in* all week, but they don't seem to have done very much.
2 see **have around/in/over/round**.

●○●   **have on¹**   **1** have an engagement, appointment, meeting, etc; often used in the negative or as part of a question:
□ How about a drink tonight, or do you *have* something *on*?
2 *Informal* try to make a person believe something untrue or fantastic, usually for fun:
□ He told me that the quickest way to learn a language was to eat the pages of a dictionary. Do you think he was *having* me *on*?

●○●   **have on²**   be wearing something:
●●○   □ Naturally, he *had* his best suit *on* for his daughter's wedding.
□ His wife *had on* one of the most ridiculous hats you've ever seen!

●○●○   **have on³**   **1** have evidence against or information about somebody; usually used in the negative or as part of a question:
□ How can we send them to prison if we don't *have* anything *on* them?
2 be inferior or superior to something:
□ All these modern clothes *have* nothing *on* the old styles, in my opinion.

●○●   **have out**   have something removed or extracted by a surgeon or dentist:
□ Both children have *had* their tonsils *out*.

☐ Poor old Tom is *having* two teeth *out* this afternoon.

●○●(●○)　**have out (with)**　discuss with somebody something which has been causing disagreement or bad feeling, especially in a direct and often angry way:
☐ If you think that he's been paying you too little, why don't you *have* it *out* with him?

●○●　**have over/round**　see **have around/in/over/round**.

●○●(●○)　**have up (for)**　bring somebody to court for an offence:
☐ That's the second time he's been *had up for* drunken driving.

●●○　**head for**　**1** go in the direction of somewhere or something:
☐ The last time we saw them, they were *heading for* the swimming pool.
2 act in a way likely to cause disaster, ruin, defeat, etc; often used as part of a warning:
☐ If you refuse to listen to what the doctor tells you, you're *heading for* trouble.

●○●　**head off**　**1** cause a person or animal to change direction
●●○　by getting in front of them:
☐ We managed to *head off* half the herd, but the rest continued straight into the river and drowned.
2 prevent or avoid something unpleasant:
☐ She was very good at *heading off* embarrassing questions.

●●○　**hear from**　receive a letter, telephone call, etc, from somebody:
☐ I haven't *heard from* Andrew for weeks. I hope he's all right.

●●○　**hear of**　**1** become aware of the existence of somebody or something:
☐ Have you ever *heard of* a little town called Pingy Pongy?
2 receive news or reports of something:
☐ Every day we *heard of* more lives being lost by both sides in the war.
3 allow something to happen or be suggested; usually used in the negative as part of a strong refusal:
☐ 'Won't you let me pay for the meal this time?' 'Certainly not! I wouldn't *hear of* it!'

●○●　**hear out**　listen to the whole of an apology, suggestion, statement, etc:
☐ The judge insisted upon *hearing* the witness *out*.

●○●●○　**help off with**　assist somebody to remove something they are wearing:
☐ I *helped* him *off with* his boots and then made a cup of tea.

● ○ ● ● ○   **help on with**   assist somebody to put on clothes, shoes, etc:
         ☐ Let me *help* you *on with* your jacket.

● ○ ●   **help out**   assist somebody to overcome a problem or
● ● ○   difficult situation:
● ●   ☐ The neighbours were good enough to *help* us *out* by watering the plants while we were away.
         ☐ She's always willing to *help out* in an emergency.

● ○ ● ○   **help to**   serve somebody or yourself with food:
         ☐ Can I *help* anybody *to* more potatoes?

● ○ ●   **hem in**   restrict the movement or freedom of somebody or
● ● ○   something:
         ☐ She felt that marriage was *hemming* her *in*.

● ● ○   **hinge on/upon**   depend or be conditional upon something:
         ☐ The outcome of the debate *hinges upon* which way the chairman decides to vote.

● ● ○   **hit on/upon**   have a new idea or discover something suddenly and unexpectedly:
         ☐ While making a list of his students' mistakes, he *hit upon* the idea of bringing them all together in a book.

● ● (● ○)   **hit out (at/against)**   criticise somebody or something in a wild or violent manner:
         ☐ The speaker *hit out at* the Government for its handling of the crisis.

● ○ ●   **hive off**   *Informal* transfer part of a task, operation, firm,
● ● ○   etc:
         ☐ The government wants to *hive off* parts of the nationalised industries to make different companies.

● ○ ● ○   **hold against**   consider something, especially a past crime, misdeed, etc, as being to somebody's discredit:
         ☐ I know that you spent a year in prison, but I won't *hold* it *against* you as long as you behave yourself while you are working for me.

● ○ ●   **hold back**   **1** refuse or be slow to provide something that is
● ● ○   wanted by somebody:
         ☐ I don't understand why he is *holding back* the examination results, especially since the students keep asking for them.
         2 prevent or hinder the progress of somebody or something:
         ☐ Her lack of qualifications is almost certain to *hold* her *back* sooner or later.

● ● (● ○)   **hold back (from)**   be slow or reluctant to do something, especially because of shyness, fear, etc:
         ☐ Two of the horses immediately came over to us, but the third *held back*, more cautious than his companions.

□ I *held back from* answering the letter for as long as I could.

●○●
●●○   **hold down** **1** prevent a price, figure, level, etc, from rising:

□ I won't be able to *hold down* my expenses once I have to start using the car.

2 force somebody to live with reduced freedom:

□ The faces of the men and women showed that they had been *held down* by a dictatorship for long enough.

●●(●○)   **hold forth (on)** speak on a subject at length or in public; often used in a derogatory way:

□ If that ridiculous woman starts *holding forth on* the dangers of stamp collecting, I'm going home.

●○●
●●○   **hold in** repress the expression of an emotion:

□ She did her best to hide her excitement, but eventually she just couldn't *hold* it *in*.

●●   **hold off¹** **1** not arrive, fall or occur, especially of bad weather:

□ You were lucky that the rain *held off* for your tennis match.

2 refrain from doing something, especially attacking:

□ Our men *held off* for the length of the cease-fire.

●○●
●●○   **hold off²** resist an attack or advance:

□ She always carries a big stick for *holding off* dogs.

●●   **hold on** **1** wait or stop; often used in the imperative:

□ If you *hold on* a minute, I'll come with you.

□ *Hold on*! I'd like some of that apple-pie too, you know!

2 survive, especially in a difficult or dangerous situation:

□ We won't be able to *hold on* for much longer without fresh supplies of food and medicine.

●●●○   **hold on to** keep or retain something, especially instead of selling or returning it:

□ Do you mind if I *hold on to* the book you lent me for another week or so?

●●   **hold out** **1** continue to resist:

□ With just a handful of weapons, we never thought we'd be able to *hold out* for so long.

2 last or be sufficient:

□ I'm worried about the water *holding out* during the trip. Do you think that we have enough?

●●(●○)   **hold out (for)** wait, especially in the hope of a better offer:

□ What will you do if the owners decide to *hold out for* a better price?

●●(●○)   **hold out (on)** refuse to offer or provide something somebody needs, especially information:

☐ I swear I'm not *holding out on* you. If I knew where she was, I'd tell you.

●○● **hold over**   postpone something, especially a discussion:
●●○ ☐ In view of the time, the matter of rent increases was *held over* until the next meeting.

●○●○ **hold to¹**   make somebody keep their promise:
☐ He said he would do anything for her if she married him, and she's certainly *holding* him *to* it.

●●○ **hold to²**   persist in holding an opinion, principle, belief, etc:
☐ I've always *held to* the belief that the more people have, the more they want.

●○● **hold up**   **1** obstruct or stop the progress of somebody or
●●○ something:
☐ Whenever there is an accident on this stretch of the motorway, the traffic is *held up* for hours.

N ☐ Without any *hold-ups*, the whole job shouldn't take more than an hour.
2 seize money or valuables from a bank, post office, security van, etc, by the use of guns:
☐ Four armed men today *held up* a post office in the city centre and escaped with stamps and postal orders to the value of £6000.

N ☐ If there's one more *hold-up* at the bank, I'm going to start keeping my money under the bed.

●●○ **hold with**   approve or be in favour of a principle, fashion, habit, etc; usually used in the negative:
☐ She doesn't *hold with* the present trend in ladies' swimwear. She thinks it vulgar.

●●●○ **home in on**   detect and move towards something, especially a target:
☐ Once one of these new missiles *homes in on* you, you can say goodbye.
☐ I don't know how the sales manager finds all these new markets for us to *home in on*.

●● **horse about/around**   *Informal* play or have fun in a wild or noisy way, especially of young adults:
☐ Will you people stop *horsing around* just for one minute? I'm trying to make a phone call!

●● **hot up**   *Informal* become faster, greater or more intense:
☐ Whenever I hear talk of the nuclear arms race *hotting up*, I simply have to stop listening.

●●○ **hunger after/for**   have a great longing or desire for something:
☐ The child *hungered after* love and affection.

●○●
●●○

hunt out   find something by searching:

 □ I'm not sure where I put my old stamp album, but if I manage to *hunt* it *out*, you can have it.

●○●
●●○

hush up   prevent something from becoming publicly known or discovered:

 □ I don't care who is to blame. Unless we can *hush* the whole shameful business *up*, we're all finished.

I, i

●●
●○●
●●○
ice up   become or cause something to become covered with or full of ice:
   □ During the winter months I often cover the windscreen with a newspaper to stop it *icing up*.

●●
idle about/around   spend time in a lazy way, especially doing no work:
   □ She hates to see people *idling around*, especially when the shop is full of customers.

●○●
●●○
idle away   spend an amount of time in a lazy, relaxed or wasteful way:
   □ He loves to *idle away* an hour or two down by the river, ideally with a fishing rod in his hands.

●○●
●●○
ink in   cover or trace something with ink:
   □ Once the drawing was to his satisfaction, he carefully began to *ink* it *in*.

●●○
inquire after/into   see **enquire/inquire after, enquire/inquire into.**

●○●
invite around/over/round   ask somebody to your home for a drink, meal, social visit, etc:
   □ Why don't we *invite* your sister *over* for dinner tomorrow?

●○●
invite in   ask somebody to enter your house, room, etc, especially for a short social visit and without any previous arrangement:
   □ She was obviously expecting me to *invite* her *in*, but I was too busy.

●○●
invite out   ask somebody to meet or accompany you somewhere, especially for entertainment:
   □ The Bakers have *invited* us *out* for a meal tonight.

●○●
invite over/round   see **invite around/over/round.**

●○●
●●○
iron out   solve a problem or remove a difficulty by means of discussion and action:
   □ It's time we *ironed out* the causes of the disagreement once and for all.

●●○
itch for   feel an urgent need or desire for something to happen:
   □ She talked so much that within five minutes we were both *itching for* her to leave.

J, j

●○● **jack in** *Informal* **1** resign from a job or abandon a
●●○ course, project, etc:
☐ If you think that philosophy would be more
interesting, why don't you *jack in* history and ask for a
transfer?
2 abandon or give up a bad habit:
☐ I didn't know that you had *jacked in* smoking
cigarettes.
3 stop doing something temporarily:
☐ After six hours of trying to mend the radio, they
decided to *jack* it *in* for the night.

●○● **jack up** *Informal* raise or increase a price, figure, salary,
●●○ etc:
☐ In some countries you find that the prices are suddenly
jacked up if the traders realise that you are a stranger.

●○● **jam in**   block the passage of a vehicle:
●●○ ☐ That stupid lorry driver has gone and *jammed* us *in*.

●○● **jam on**   cause something to operate forcibly or suddenly,
●●○ especially the brakes of a moving vehicle:
☐ Although he *jammed on* his brakes, he still couldn't
avoid hitting the dog.

●○● **jazz up** *Informal* **1** rewrite or play a piece of music in a
●●○ style associated with jazz:
☐ I don't care if they want to *jazz up* Bach, but I wish
they would leave Beethoven alone.
2 make somebody or something more lively, colourful,
exciting, etc:
☐ If you're going to be a pop star, we'll have to *jazz* you
up a bit. How about some pink trousers?

●●○ **jockey for** **1** move about in order to gain an advantageous
position, often by pushing or obstructing your
competitors:
☐ One of the Canadian runners fell, as the group
jockeyed for the inside lane.
2 manoeuvre politically in order to win favour,
promotion, etc:
☐ It's amusing to watch members *jockeying for* the Prime
Minister's attention prior to a Cabinet reshuffle.

●●   **jog along/on**   continue in a routine way, with little excitement or progress:
       ☐ He's been *jogging along* in the same job for over twenty years now.

●●   **join up**   become a member of one of the armed forces:
       ☐ She tried to stop him from *joining up*, since one of her sons had already been killed.

●●○   **juggle with**   alter or revise a set of figures, accounts, statistics, etc, especially with the intention of deceiving somebody:
       ☐ He hoped that by *juggling with* the receipts, he would disguise the size of the firm's profits.

●●○   **jump at**   accept an offer, invitation, opportunity, etc, eagerly and without hesitation:
       ☐ If somebody asked me to go to America, I'd *jump at* the chance.

●●○   **jump on**   criticise something or somebody sharply and excitedly:
       ☐ If the boss is in one of his bad moods, he'll *jump on* you for the slightest thing.
       ☐ Her driving instructor *jumped on* every little mistake, which made her very nervous.

K, k

●●   **keel over**   **1** fall to the ground, especially somebody who is ill:

☐ Tourists who are not used to the heat sometimes *keel over* if they stay in the sun too long.

2 overturn or lean to one side, especially of a boat or ship:

☐ The vessel *keeled over* after being hit by enemy fire.

●●○   **keep after**   **1** continue to chase somebody:

☐ We *kept after* the stolen car for twenty minutes.

2 ask or remind somebody repeatedly to do something:

☐ You'll have to *keep after* them if you want the work done. They're so lazy!

●●○   **keep at¹**   continue to make an effort, especially in spite of difficulties or tiredness:

☐ You'll never improve your piano playing unless you *keep at* it.

●○●○   **keep at²**   persuade or force somebody to continue working, etc:

☐ Good teachers know how to *keep* their pupils *at* a task without using threats or punishments.

●○●(●○)   **keep back (from)**   **1** deliberately withhold information:
●●○(●○)

☐ We decided to *keep* the rest of the bad news *back from* her until she was feeling stronger.

2 retain or not return something:

☐ The owner of the boat *kept back* half their deposit to pay for the damage they had done.

●○●   **keep down**   **1** prevent or control the increase or spread of
●●○   something, especially pests, weeds, etc:

☐ Singapore has been very successful in *keeping down* the number of its mosquitoes.

2 restrict the freedom or advancement of a person, group or society:

☐ She thinks that women have been *kept down* by men for long enough.

3 retain or hold food or drink in the stomach:

☐ She'll just get weaker if she can't *keep* her food *down*.

●●○   **keep from¹**   restrain yourself from doing something; usually used in the negative:

☐ I liked his suit so much that I just couldn't *keep from* asking him where he had bought it.

●○●○   **keep from²**   **1** prevent somebody from doing something:

☐ I'm not *keeping* you *from* your work, am I?

☐ The new information *kept* us *from* making a serious mistake.

2 deliberately not give information about something to somebody:

☐ I was so excited that I couldn't *keep* the good news *from* her any longer.

keep in¹ **1** make somebody, especially a child, stay indoors, in school, etc, often as a punishment:

☐ His mother *kept* him *in* until he had finished his homework.

2 keep control of an emotion, especially anger:

☐ As I listened to her, it became harder and harder for me to *keep in* my indignation.

keep in² continue or cause something to continue to burn:

☐ The fire *kept in* all night, so the room was still warm in the morning.

keep in with continue to receive the friendship, favour, sympathy, etc, of somebody:

☐ If you want him to give you a good reference one day, you should try to *keep in with* him.

keep off¹ not arrive, fall or occur, especially of bad weather:

☐ Fortunately, the rain *kept off* for most of our holiday.

keep off² **1** avoid or cause somebody to avoid a subject, topic, issue, etc:

☐ He embarrasses the government by refusing to *keep off* the problem of unemployment.

2 not eat, drink or take something or cause somebody to do this, especially for reasons of health:

☐ The doctor has advised him to *keep off* alcohol.

keep on¹ **1** continue doing something:

☐ Despite the noise of the workmen outside the window, the students *kept on* writing.

2 do something repeatedly or regularly; followed by *-ing*:

☐ She *kept on* writing me letters during the months I was away.

keep on² **1** continue in the same direction, along the same road, etc:

☐ Turn right at the traffic lights and then *keep on* until you come to a large petrol station.

2 persist or continue to try despite difficulties:

☐ Although he failed his driving test five times, he *kept on* and eventually passed.

keep on³ continue to wear something:

☐ Do policemen really *keep* their uniforms *on* in bed?

●○●
●●○

keep on⁴ **1** continue to employ somebody:
    □ The factory can't afford to *keep on* more than a hundred men after July.
2 continue to own or rent a house, flat, etc:
    □ Are you going to *keep* the flat *on* if your company sends you abroad?

●●●○(●○)

keep on at (about) mention or complain about something repeatedly, especially in an irritating way:
    □ His mother *keeps on at* him *about* the length of his hair.

●●●○
●○●●○

keep out of avoid or prevent somebody from becoming involved in something, especially a conflict:
    □ He's a very quiet sort of person and usually tries to *keep out of* arguments.

●●○
●○●○

keep to **1** not wander or not allow somebody to wander from something, especially when travelling or talking:
    □ You'll get to the station more quickly if you *keep to* the main road.
    □ The meeting has to end at four o'clock, so the chairman must *keep* speakers *to* the point,
2 act or cause somebody to act according to a plan, promise, set of rules, etc:
    □ We'll never finish building the boat unless we *keep to* the instructions.
3 stay or cause somebody to stay somewhere, especially in bed or indoors:
    □ Illness has *kept* him *to* his bed since December.

●○●

keep under **1** continue to have control over something, especially a fire, feeling, disease, etc:
    □ They won't be able to *keep* the flames *under* once they reach the paint store.
2 restrict the freedom or advancement of a person, group or society:
    □ The country's prisons are full of men and women who refuse to be *kept under* by a dictator.

●●
●○●
●●○

keep up¹ remain or maintain something at a high or normal level:
    □ Her husband has started working overtime to *keep* his wages *up*.
    □ You must eat properly to *keep up* your strength.

●●

keep up² continue without change, especially of weather:
    □ You won't be playing much tennis today if this rain *keeps up*.

●●
●●○

keep up³ continue or maintain something without stopping or relaxing:

☐ How long can our forces *keep up* the attack?

☐ The stream of questions *kept up* for over an hour.

● ● ○ **keep up⁴** continue or maintain a course, relationship, tradition, etc:

☐ Having arrived in Paris, they wished they had *kept up* their French lessons.

☐ The two girls *kept up* their friendship by writing to each other.

● ○ ● **keep up⁵** maintain a property in good condition:
● ● ○ ☐ It was a lovely house, but they couldn't afford to *keep* it *up*.

N ☐ The *upkeep* of the garden involved a lot of hard work.

● ○ ● **keep up⁶** prevent somebody from going to bed:

☐ She *kept* me *up* half the night, talking about her problems at work.

● ●(● ○) **keep up (with)** maintain the same level, speed, etc, as somebody or something:

☐ Towards the end of the race his legs suddenly tired and he couldn't *keep up*.

☐ Wages haven't *kept up with* price increases over the last twelve months.

● ● ● ○ **keep up with** be informed about recent events, developments, research, etc, by making an effort to obtain news or read reports:

☐ When I'm abroad, I like to *keep up with* what's happening back home.

☐ It's important that a doctor *keeps up with* all the new drugs on the market.

● ○ ● **key up** prepare somebody, usually yourself, physically or mentally for an important event:

☐ The players are already starting to *key* themselves *up* for next month's big match.

● ● **kick about/around** *Informal* **1** lie or remain in a place,
● ● ○ especially of something unwanted or forgotten:

☐ I wonder whose shirt this is? It's been *kicking about* the changing-room for months.

2 travel somewhere in a casual way without a plan or schedule:

☐ He spent a whole month just *kicking around* the countryside, enjoying the peacefulness and the fresh air.

3 be alive and active somewhere:

☐ We never dreamt that old Tom would still be *kicking around* after such a serious operation.

● ○ ●   **kick around**   *Informal*   **1** discuss or consider the possibilities of something in a casual or informal way:
□ We started *kicking* the idea *around* right back in January, but a decision hasn't been made yet.
2 give somebody a lot of orders, especially to display your authority or power:
□ The people who work for him tend to be *kicked around* like slaves.

● ●   **kick off¹**   begin, especially of a football match:
□ The crowd got more and more impatient as they waited for the players to *kick off*.

N   □ The first goal came just two minutes after the *kick-off*.

● ●   **kick off²**   *Informal* begin or cause something to begin:
● ● ○   □ I was surprised when they *kicked off* the interview by asking me about my girlfriend.

N   □ For a *kick-off*, we can't afford a new car, and what's more we don't need one.

● ○ ●(● ○)   **kick out (of)**   *Informal* make somebody leave a room,
● ● ○   school, job, etc, often on account of bad behaviour or work:
□ He was *kicked out of* the club because he was so rude to the manager.

● ● ○   **kick up**   make a lot of noise or fuss:
□ The children *kicked up* a terrible noise as soon as the teacher left the room.

● ●   **kip down**   *Informal* lie down somewhere to sleep:
□ Do you mind if I *kip down* on your floor for the night?

● ○ ●(● ○)   **kit out (with)**   equip somebody or something with clothes,
● ● ○(● ○)   personal items, etc:
□ How much will it cost to *kit* the children *out with* new school uniforms?

● ○ ●   **knock about**   hit, punch or beat somebody:
□ Whenever he gets drunk, he starts *knocking* his wife *about*.

● ●(● ○)   **knock about (with)**   *Informal* have a friendly or sexual relationship with somebody:
□ I wonder why John and Sandra have stopped *knocking about* together?

● ●   **knock about/around**   *Informal*   **1** travel in a casual way
● ● ○   without a plan or schedule:
□ He spent his summer holidays *knocking about* India.
2 be active or seen in a place:
□ You must know Arthur. He's been *knocking around* for years.
3 lie or remain in a place:

□ How much longer are these shoes going to *knock about* the bedroom before you put them away?

●○●
●●○ **knock back**[1] drink something quickly or in great quantities; often used in a humorous way:
□ He certainly knows how to *knock back* the whisky!

●○●
●○●○ **knock back**[2] *Informal* cost somebody an amount of money, especially a large amount:
□ That new dress must have *knocked* her *back* a few pounds!

●○●
●●○ **knock down** 1 make somebody or something fall by hitting them, especially of a driver or moving vehicle:
□ His wife is in hospital after being *knocked down* by a taxi.
2 demolish or remove a building or structure:
□ They're going to *knock* all these old houses *down* to make room for a new block of flats.
3 reduce or make somebody reduce the price of something; often used with an expression of amount:
□ We managed to *knock* the price *down* to five pounds.
□ Can't you *knock* him *down* a pound or two?

●●
●●○ **knock off**[1] *Informal* stop work:
●○● □ What time do you usually *knock off* for lunch?
●●○ **knock off**[2] *Informal* deduct an amount from the price of
●○●○ something:
□ Since we are regular customers, he's agreed to *knock* a few pounds *off* the bill.

●○●
●●○ **knock off**[3] *Informal* 1 steal something:
□ Of course the television is cheap. It was *knocked off*!
2 complete something, especially in a hurried way:
□ Some writers can *knock off* a book in less than three months.
3 kill somebody:
□ People are saying that he *knocked* her *off* for her diamonds.

●○●
●●○ **knock out** 1 cause somebody to become unconscious, especially of a blow, drug, alcoholic drink, etc:
□ All of his last twelve opponents have been *knocked out* within five rounds.
□ If you can't sleep, your doctor can give you something to *knock* you *out*.
N □ People expect that the fight tomorrow night will end in a *knock-out*.
2 *Informal* shock or amaze somebody:
□ We were completely *knocked out* by their generosity.
□ The news of the tragedy really *knocked* us *out*.

●○●(●○)　　　**knock out (of)**　eliminate a person or team from a
●●○　　　　　　competition by defeating them:
　　　　　　　　　□ United's supporters were disappointed when their side
　　　　　　　　　was *knocked out* in the first round.

●○●　　　　　　**knock together/up**　prepare, make or build something,
●●○　　　　　　especially in a hurried or unplanned way:
　　　　　　　　　□ It won't take me more than five minutes to *knock up* a
　　　　　　　　　snack.

●○●　　　　　　**knock up¹**　wake and get somebody out of bed, by ringing
●●○　　　　　　their doorbell, etc:
　　　　　　　　　□ If he's already asleep, we'll just have to *knock* him *up*.

●○●　　　　　　**knock up²**　*Informal* make somebody, especially yourself,
　　　　　　　　　ill or exhausted, usually by working too hard without
　　　　　　　　　enough rest:
　　　　　　　　　□ If you don't take a holiday soon, you're going to
　　　　　　　　　knock yourself *up*.

●●　　　　　　　**knock up³**　practise before the beginning of a tennis match,
　　　　　　　　　squash match, etc:
　　　　　　　　　□ The players were given five minutes to *knock up*.
N　　　　　　　　□ Shall we start straight away, or would you like a
　　　　　　　　　knock-up?

●●(●○)　　　　**knuckle down (to)**　start to concentrate seriously on your
　　　　　　　　　work:
　　　　　　　　　□ Now that the holidays are over, it's time to *knuckle
　　　　　　　　　down* again.

●●(●○)　　　　**knuckle under (to)**　submit or learn to obey somebody or
　　　　　　　　　something:
　　　　　　　　　□ Some of the new boys are not used to obeying rules,
　　　　　　　　　and take a long time to *knuckle under*.

L, l

●●
●●○

lag behind   move or progress more slowly than somebody or something:
□ The youngest child soon got tired and began to *lag behind*.
□ We'll continue to *lag behind* other companies until we invest in new machinery.

●●

land up   finish a journey, career, series of actions, etc, in a particular place or position:
□ Don't forget to leave the motorway at the next junction, or you'll *land up* in Scotland.
□ After trying six different jobs, he *landed up* working for his father.

●○●○

land with   leave somebody with something they don't want:
□ That husband of hers always manages to *land* you *with* the bill!

●○●
●●○

lap up   take in something eagerly, especially praise or entertainment:
□ She sat there *lapping up* the compliments, too stupid to realise that they were mostly insincere.
□ His jokes were really funny: the audience simply *lapped* them *up*.

●●

lark about/around   play or behave in a silly way, especially for fun:
□ If you boys are going to *lark about*, you'd better go outside!

●●(●○)

lash out (at)   attack somebody physically or verbally:
□ The youth *lashed out* with both fists as the police officers tried to arrest him.
□ In his speech this afternoon the President *lashed out at* the press for the way they have reported recent events.

●●(●○)

lash out (on)   spend money freely, especially on luxuries:
□ He's decided to *lash out on* a trip to the States this summer.

●●(●○)

latch on (to)   **1** attach yourself to a person or group, especially in an insistent way:
□ Don't let the vicar's wife *latch on to* you at the meeting, or you won't get the chance to meet anybody else.
2 understand something:
□ These examination papers suggest that very few of the students have *latched on to* the theoretical issues.

● ● ○   **laugh at**   **1** ridicule or make fun of somebody, especially in an unkind way:
□ You shouldn't *laugh at* her just because her English isn't very good.
2 disregard or underestimate the importance, significance, danger, etc, of something:
□ The government's threat to withdraw its support is certainly not to be *laughed at*.

● ○ ●
● ● ○   **laugh off**   dismiss a danger, threat, mistake, etc, by making a joke of it:
□ How do some people manage to *laugh off* their misfortunes?

● ● ○   **launch into**   start a long speech, story, description, etc, especially in an eager way:
□ At the first opportunity he *launched into* one of his long stories about life in the tropics.

● ●(● ○)   **launch out (into/on)**   begin a new business, career, etc, especially in a daring way:
□ What made you decide to *launch out into* journalism?

● ○ ●
● ● ○   **lay aside/by**   save money for a future need:
□ I'm sure that most parents *lay by* a few pounds for their daughter's wedding.

● ○ ●
● ● ○   **lay down**   **1** state or declare a rule, law, condition, etc:
□ These new rules have been *laid down* for the safety of the club's members.
2 put bottles of wine, etc, in a store or cellar to mature:
□ He admitted that, just after the war, he had *laid down* a dozen bottles of port, especially for this celebration.

● ○ ●
● ● ○   **lay in**   provide yourself with a supply of something:
□ We usually *lay in* extra coal in case of emergencies.

● ● ○   **lay into**   *Informal* attack somebody physically or verbally:
□ He's frightened to stay out late in case his mother *lays into* him again.

● ○ ●
● ● ○   **lay off¹**   dismiss somebody from work, especially temporarily:
□ Most of us were *laid off* until the firm received new orders.

N   □ The men have only just returned after a six-week *lay-off*, and now they're being *laid off* again!

● ●
● ● ○   **lay off²**   *Informal*   **1** stop eating, drinking or doing something, especially something that is unpleasant or bad for your health:
□ The doctor advised me to *lay off* the cigarettes.
2 stop worrying, harassing or hurting somebody; often used as an imperative:

□ Just *lay off* and leave me alone!
□ She can't *lay off* the poor child for more than five minutes at a time.

●○●
●●○ **lay on** supply or organise something:
□ As soon as the water and electricity are *laid on*, they'll be able to start using the house.
□ The firm always *lays on* a special meal for the staff round about Christmas.

●○●
●●○ **lay out** **1** arrange things neatly or so that they can be clearly seen:
□ She *laid* all her new clothes *out* on the bed.
2 spend a lot of money on something:
□ Do you realise how much I have to *lay out* on their school fees each year?
N □ After the initial *outlay*, we didn't have anything else to pay.
3 make somebody unconscious by hitting on the head:
□ It was the last punch on the chin that really *laid* him *out*.
4 prepare a body for burial:
□ The bodies of the victims had to be *laid out* before their relatives were asked to identify them.
5 plan or design something, especially a building:
□ The ground floor had been *laid out* very sensibly.
N □ I didn't like the *lay-out* upstairs.

●○●
●●○ **lay up** **1** store or save something:
□ We *laid up* so much fuel for last winter that we haven't had to buy any since.
2 cause somebody to stay in bed or indoors:
□ The flu can *lay* you *up* for more than a week if you're really unlucky.

●●(●○) **lead in (with)** begin or introduce a speech, performance, show, etc:
□ He usually *leads in with* a song and then tells a few jokes.
N □ It was such a long *lead-in* that the speech seemed very short.

●●
●●○ **lead off** begin a speech, performance, meeting, etc:
□ The principal *led off* by welcoming all the new students.

●○● **lead on** encourage somebody to believe or do something, especially in an attempt to fool, deceive, or trick them:
□ If you have no intention of marrying her, you shouldn't keep *leading* her *on*.

●●●○   **lead up to**   **1** happen before something, especially of events:

     ☐ The Prime Minister has demanded an investigation of the incidents that *led up to* the riots.

     2 approach a topic, request, confession, etc, in a gradual or indirect way:

     ☐ I don't know what she's *leading up to*, but I wish that she would hurry up and say it!

●●○   **leaf through**   look at a book, magazine, newspaper, etc, while quickly turning the pages:

     ☐ I *leafed through* a couple of photography magazines while waiting to see the dentist.

●●   **leak out**   become known, especially of a secret:

     ☐ Whatever happens, we must make sure that this information doesn't *leak out*.

●●○   **lean on**   **1** depend upon somebody for support:

     ☐ It was a comfort to know that she could always *lean on* her daughters if the need arose.

     2 *Informal* put pressure on somebody to do something, especially by the use of threats or violence:

     ☐ If you pay the gang the thousand pounds, they'll only *lean on* you for more.

●●○   **leap at**   accept an offer, invitation, opportunity, etc, eagerly and without any hesitation:

     ☐ We *leapt at* the offer of their car for two weeks.

●○●   **leave in**   not remove or delete something:

●●○   ☐ The editor finally agreed to *leave* the paragraph *in*.

●○●   **leave off**[1]   stop wearing something:

●●○   ☐ You'll be able to *leave off* that jacket when the warmer weather arrives.

●●   **leave off**[2]   cease or stop doing something:

●●○   ☐ The rain hasn't *left off* all morning.

     ☐ I *left off* writing to them, because I never got a reply.

     ☐ *Leave off* and go and annoy somebody else!

●○●   **leave on**   let something remain alight, burning or working:

●●○   ☐ It's expensive to *leave* the electric fire *on* all day.

●○●(●○)   **leave out (of)**   fail to include somebody or something:

●●○   ☐ The headmaster won't like it if we *leave* his son *out of* the team.

●○●   **leave over**   delay or postpone something until a later date:

     ☐ In view of the time, perhaps the discussion of these final points could be *left over* until our next meeting.

●○●○   **leave to**   pass a task to somebody:

     ☐ This letter needs answering. Can I *leave* it *to* you?

●○●●○   **leave up to**   give somebody the responsibility for deciding or choosing something:
     □ At some colleges, the amount of work you do is *left* entirely *up to* you.

●○●○   **lend to**   have suitable qualities for a particular treatment or adaptation:
     □ The book really *lends* itself *to* film treatment.

●○●   **let down**   **1** lengthen a piece of clothing:
●●○   □ That coat would still fit you if you got a tailor to *let* it *down*.
     2 disappoint somebody, especially by breaking a promise, or by failing to do what is expected:
     □ You can trust John. He'll never *let* you *down*.

N   □ The 'dream holiday' was a complete *let-down*.
     3 release the air from a tyre, balloon, etc:
     □ I always *let* my tyres *down* a little bit in the warmer weather.

●○●●○   **let in for**   accept or cause somebody to accept responsibility for something, especially for a lot of work, expense, problems, etc:
     □ Do you realise how much work you are *letting* me *in for*?

●○●   **let in/into**   allow somebody or something to enter
●●○/   somewhere:
●○●○   □ These big windows *let in* a lot of light.
     □ They won't *let* you *into* the shop until nine o'clock exactly.

●○●●○   **let in on**   allow somebody to share a secret or take part in something:
     □ The Ministry of Education has agreed to *let* the headmaster and three senior teachers *in on* the discussions.

●○●○   **let into**   **1** put something into a groove, recess, opening, etc, in a surface:
     □ In order to save space, the back of the boiler had been *let into* the wall.
     2 see **let in/into**.

●○●   **let off¹**   **1** cause something to fire or explode:
●●○   □ He shouldn't be allowed to *let off* fireworks at his age. He's only three!
     2 release or excuse somebody without punishment:
     □ It was the first time that he had done anything wrong, so they *let* him *off*.

●○●   **let off²**   **1** allow a passenger to leave a bus, train, ship, etc:
●●○   □ The conductor won't *let* anybody *off* between stops.

● ○ ● ○   **2** excuse from a task, chore, etc:
☐ You're lucky that they *let* you *off* all that washing-up.

● ●(● ○)   **let on (about)**   reveal something that somebody wants to
● ● ○   be kept a secret:
☐ Don't *let on about* the price of the car.
☐ One of the children *let on* that they were trying to sell
the house.

● ● ○   **let out¹**   utter a cry, scream, yell, etc:
☐ She *let out* the most terrible scream I'd ever heard.

● ○ ●   **let out²**   **1** make a piece of clothing wider, especially round
● ● ○   the waist:
☐ I know a tailor who could *let* the trousers *out* for you.
2 cause something, especially a secret, to become known:
☐ Somebody must have *let* the information *out* without
realising the danger involved.
3 release or escape from an unpleasant or tedious activity,
obligation etc:
☐ If neither of us wants to go to the party, we'll have to
find an excuse to *let* us *out*.

● ○ ●(● ○) **let out (of)**   release somebody or something from a prison
● ● ○   or confined space:
☐ After six years they *let* him *out* for good behaviour.
☐ If the tyres are too hard, just *let* some of the air *out*.

● ●   **let up**   relax, diminish or stop:
☐ You'll have a heart attack if you don't *let up* a bit.
N   ☐ It's been pouring all day, without a single *let-up*.

● ○ ● ○   **level against/at**   direct a charge or accusation towards
somebody:
☐ Are you aware of the allegations that have been
levelled against you?

● ○ ● ○   **level at**   aim a gun, etc, at somebody or something:
☐ He *levelled* the rifle *at* the animal and fired.

● ●   **level off/out**   stop climbing and stay at the height that has
been reached:
☐ Five minutes after take-off, the aircraft *levelled out* at
30,000 feet.

● ● ○   **lie behind**   be the reason or explanation for something:
☐ Do you know what *lies behind* her sudden departure
for London?

● ●   **lie in**   stay in bed late:
☐ It's Sunday tomorrow, so you can *lie in*.
N   ☐ You can have a good *lie-in* in the morning.

● ●   **lift off**   leave the ground, especially of a plane or rocket:
☐ The rocket is due to *lift off* at noon on Friday.
N   ☐ We've just witnessed another perfect *lift-off*.

● ● ○   **light on/upon**   discover something, especially by chance:
         ☐ Tell us how you *lit upon* the idea for your invention.

● ●   **light up**   **1** light a cigarette, pipe, etc:
         ☐ He usually *lights up* immediately after supper.
         2 switch on or be switched on, especially of street or car
         lighting:
         ☐ Drivers who forget to *light up* at night often cause
         accidents.
         3 suddenly display emotion, especially happiness or
         excitement:
         ☐ Her eyes *lit up* when I mentioned a holiday.

● ○ ● ○   **liken to**   compare something with something else:
         ☐ His big hands are usually *likened to* bunches of
         bananas.

● ●   **limber up**   do exercises in order to loosen the muscles,
         especially in preparation for more strenuous activity:
         ☐ I like to *limber up* for five minutes before a race.

● ●   **line up¹**   arrange people or things in lines, rows or ranks,
● ○ ●   or cause them to be arranged in this way:
● ● ○   ☐ Every morning the prisoners were *lined up* to be
         counted.
         ☐ He loves to *line* his toy soldiers *up* into rows.

● ●   **line up²**   form a queue:
         ☐ People without tickets had been *lining up* all day
         outside the theatre.

● ○ ●   **line up³**   organize the visit or gathering of a number of
● ● ○   entertainers, sportsmen, etc:
         ☐ The organisers are *lining up* some of the finest
         musicians in the country for next autumn's concerts.
N   ☐ There are two new names in the *line-up* today.

● ●(● ○)   **listen in (on/to)**   deliberately listen to a private
         conversation:
         ☐ It's rude to *listen in on* other people's telephone calls.

● ●(● ○)   **listen in (to)**   listen to a radio broadcast:
         ☐ People used to *listen in* regularly before the days of
         television.
         ☐ I always try to *listen in to* the news.

● ○ ●   **live down**   cause people to forget or ignore your past
● ● ○   behaviour, reputation, etc:
         ☐ Twenty years later, his family are still trying to *live* the
         scandal *down*.

● ● ○   **live for**   have somebody or something as your main or
         only interest in life:
         ☐ He says that he has nothing to *live for* since his wife
         died.
         ☐ Both boys just *live for* football.

●●　　　　　**live in**　have your home where you work, study, etc:
　　　　　　　□ It's cheaper for most nurses to *live in*.

●●○　　　　**live off**　**1** get somebody to provide you with food, shelter, etc:
　　　　　　　□ Since he lost his job, he's been *living off* his parents.
　　　　　　　2 get enough money or what you need to live by doing a particular job or activity:
　　　　　　　□ I don't know how she manages to *live off* her painting.

●●　　　　　**live on¹**　survive or endure:
　　　　　　　□ The composer's work will always *live on*.

●●○　　　　**live on²**　**1** support yourself on a certain income:
　　　　　　　□ How do you manage to *live on* such a small salary?
　　　　　　　2 have something as your only food:
　　　　　　　□ For a whole week we had to *live on* fish and chips.

●●　　　　　**live out**　have your home away from where you work, study, etc:
　　　　　　　□ Most of the students prefer to *live out*.

●●○　　　　**live through**　survive or endure something, especially a bad experience:
　　　　　　　□ We never dreamt we'd have to *live through* another war.

●●　　　　　**live together**　live as husband and wife, but without being legally married:
　　　　　　　□ How long have they been *living together*?

●●●○　　　**live up to**　reach, match or fulfil a particular standard or expectation:
　　　　　　　□ The hotel didn't *live up to* its great reputation.
　　　　　　　□ The child found it hard to *live up to* the school's standards of excellence.

●●○　　　　**live with**　**1** gradually accept or tolerate something unpleasant:
　　　　　　　□ It was very difficult when she first lost her hearing, but she has learnt to *live with* it.
　　　　　　　2 live in the same house, etc, with someone, as husband and wife, but without being legally married:
　　　　　　　□ She lived with him for a couple of years before they got married.

●●　　　　　**liven up**　become or cause somebody or something to become more lively or cheerful:
●○●
●●○　　　　　□ We need some music to *liven* the party *up* a bit.
　　　　　　　□ When I suggested a walk, she *livened up*.

●○●(●○)　**load down (with)**　place a great weight or burden on somebody or something:
●●○　　　　　□ The poor car was completely *loaded down with* all my bags.

□ She's always trying to *load* me *down with* her problems.

●○●   **lock out**   prevent workers from entering their place of
●●○   work, especially of employers:
□ The men were *locked out* in response to their refusal to
operate the new machines.

N   □ The prospect of a *lock-out* may encourage the workers
to agree to our terms.

●○●(●○)   **lock up (in)**   **1** put somebody in prison:
●●○   □ He's been *locked up* for receiving stolen goods.
2 make an investment in something that cannot easily be
changed into cash:
□ All my money has been *locked up in* property for the
last ten years.

●●○   **look after**   **1** take care of somebody or something:
□ I'll give you the piano as long as you promise to *look
after* it.
2 be responsible for something, especially paying a bill:
□ The boys' grandfather has kindly offered to *look after*
their school fees.

●●○   **look at**   **1** examine or inspect something:
□ If your arm isn't better by tomorrow, I'd get the
doctor to *look at* it.
2 consider something:
□ If your offer is too low, the people selling the house
won't even *look at* it.

●●   **look back**   stop making progress; always used in the
negative:
□ Once he had gained a little self-confidence, he never
looked back.

N   □ After his first book was published, there was no
looking back.

●●(●○)   **look back (on)**   think about the past:
□ *Looking back*, it's easy to see where we went wrong.
□ She *looked back on* their relationship with feelings of
deep regret.

●●●○   **look down on**   regard somebody or something as inferior
or unworthy:
□ I'm sure that they *look down on* me because I'm
married to a greengrocer.

●●○   **look for**   try to find somebody or something:
□ He's decided to *look for* a new job.
□ Why are the police *looking for* you?

●●●○   **look forward to**   await something eagerly or excitedly:
□ The children are really *looking forward to* seeing you in
October.

●●(●○)   **look in (on)**   pay somebody a short casual visit, especially when this does not require a long journey:
□ Why don't we *look in on* John and Sally on the way home?

●●●   **look into**   investigate something:
□ The police are *looking into* the disappearance of a five-month-old baby from its home in South London.

●●   **look on**   stand and watch, without taking part:
□ Do you mean to say that the two policemen just *looked on* without doing anything to stop the fight?

N   □ A crowd of *onlookers* gathered to see the film being made.

●(●)●○   **look (out) on/onto**   provide a view of something:
□ Her bedroom window *looks out onto* the back garden.

N   □ The room has a very pleasant *outlook*.

●●○(●○)   **look on/upon (as)**   regard somebody or something in a certain way:
□ I've always *looked upon* Mary *as* somebody I can trust.

●●   **look out¹**   be careful; often used in the imperative:
□ *Look out*! There's a car coming!
□ You're going to cut yourself if you don't *look out*!

●○●   **look out²**   search for or choose something:
●●○   □ I'm sure I have a bicycle pump somewhere at home. I'll see if I can *look* it *out* for you.
□ I've *looked out* a couple of books that I thought might interest you.

●●●○   **look out for**   keep watching attentively for somebody or something:
□ If you're going to be at the party tonight, I'll *look out for* you.
□ He advised us to *look out for* snakes if we were going into the jungle.

N   □ Keep a *look-out* for Robert. We don't want to miss him.

●●○   **look over¹**   do a tour of inspection around an office, factory, house, etc:
□ I always enjoy *looking over* breweries when I'm on holiday in Germany.

●○●   **look over²**   **1** examine or scrutinise somebody or something:
●●○   □ The customs officers *looked* the car *over* very carefully before they let us go through.
2 revise or check something, especially something that you have written:
□ Don't forget to *look over* your work at the end of the exam.

●●○ | **look through¹** **1** read or scan something:
□ I've *looked through* the newspaper twice, but I still can't find the weather forecast.
2 ignore or seem to ignore somebody when you look at them:
□ Ever since we had the argument, she *looks* straight *through* me as if I didn't exist.

●○● | **look through²** examine something carefully, especially a formal written document:
□ We'll have to *look* the last two paragraphs *through* very carefully before we sign the agreement.

●●○(●○) | **look to (for)** approach somebody or something for help, support, comfort, etc:
□ She has always *looked to* her parents *for* advice.

●○●
●●○ | **look up¹** **1** search for something in a dictionary, encyclopedia or other reference book:
□ If you don't know how to spell the word, why don't you *look* it *up*?
2 visit somebody you have not seen for a long time:
□ Now that we're in Cambridge, why don't we *look up* my old tutor?

●● | **look up²** improve, especially of business:
□ Business must be *looking up* if he's got two more men working for him.

●●○(●○) | **look upon (as)** see **look on/upon (as)**.

●●●○ | **look up to** admire or respect somebody:
□ He's a born leader. Even at school the other boys *looked up to* him.

●● | **loosen up** do exercises in order to relax the muscles:
□ I always *loosen up* for five minutes before a match.

●●(●○) | **lose out (on)** suffer a loss or defeat, especially because of unfairness or bad luck:
□ You often *lose out* when you bet on horse races.
□ How much did we *lose out on* the deal?

●●(●○) | **lose out (to)** be defeated, replaced or overtaken by somebody or something:
□ We *lost out* in the election simply because the opposition had more money to run their campaign.
□ Live entertainment is *losing out to* television.

●○●
●●○ | **louse up** *Informal* spoil or disrupt something:
□ The rescue work had been going very well until a sudden downpour *loused* the whole thing *up*.

●○●
●●○ | **lump together** put two or more things together and treat them as a single item:
□ Why don't you just *lump* the two bills *together* and pay with one cheque?

M, m

●●○   **make after**   chase or pursue somebody or something:
                   ☐ She suddenly noticed that he had gone out without leaving her any money, and quickly *made after* him.

●●   **make away/off**   leave or escape in a hurry:
                   ☐ They ran out of the bank and *made away* in a stolen car.

●●(●○)   **make away/off (with)**   hurry away, especially after stealing something:
                   ☐ The bank robbers *made off with* £6,000 in used notes.

●●○   **make for**   **1** move towards something, especially in a determined way:
                   ☐ As soon as they told me how much they would pay me, I got up and *made for* the door.
                   2 rush towards somebody or something, in order to attack:
                   ☐ We didn't want to open the garden gate in case their dog *made for* us.
                   3 help cause something to happen or develop:
                   ☐ Good communications normally *make for* better understanding.
                   ☐ The drop in house prices *made for* an increase in the number of people buying their own homes.

●○●○   **make into**   cause somebody or something to change in some way:
                   ☐ The headmaster is going to *make* me *into* a prefect.
                   ☐ The two houses are being *made into* flats.

●○●○   **make of**   form an impression or understanding of somebody or something; often used with *what* and/or in the negative:
                   ☐ She's a strange girl. I don't quite know what to *make of* her.

●●   **make off**   see **make away/off**.

●●(●○)   **make off (with)**   see **make away/off (with)**.

●○●   **make out**[1]   **1** write or complete something, especially a
●●○   cheque, bill, form, etc:
                   ☐ The cheque was *made out* for sixty pounds.
                   ☐ *Make out* a list and then you won't forget anything.
                   2 manage to see, read, or distinguish something; usually used with *can*:
                   ☐ It got darker and darker until we could no longer *make out* the names on the sides of the ships.

3 understand somebody or something; usually used with *can*:

□ Can you *make out* what he is saying? His voice is very low.

□ Our daughter has changed a lot in the last five years. Nowadays, we just can't *make* her *out*.

●●○   **make out²**   claim or assert something, especially something that is not true:

□ He *made out* that he had never been married before. Then, one day, his first wife appeared on the doorstep.

●●   **make out³**   manage, survive or progress:

□ How's your sister *making out* now that she's living on her own?

●○●(●○)   **make over (to)**   transfer ownership of something to
●●○(●○)   another person, especially by signing a legal document:

□ What will you do with the house that your father *made over to* you?

●○●   **make up¹**   **1** invent a story, excuse, etc:
●●○

□ Is he telling the truth, or *making* it all *up*?

2 compose a tune, rhyme, etc:

□ She's very good at *making up* poems.

3 prepare something, especially medicine, by putting different things together:

□ The chemist only took a minute to *make up* the prescription.

□ If you want to give her something useful, get the shopkeeper to *make up* a basket of groceries.

4 recover, repay or replace something that is owed, missing, or lost:

□ Somehow the company has got to *make up* all the time we've lost through illness.

5 make a number, total, amount, etc, complete:

□ We need just one more player to *make up* a full team.

6 add fuel to a fire, boiler, etc:

□ He always *makes* the boiler *up* before he goes to bed.

7 put sheets, blankets, etc, on a bed:

□ You're welcome to stay the night. I can easily *make* a bed *up*.

8 prepare a page, book, etc, for printing:

□ Bob's report should have gone on the front page but unfortunately the page had already been *made up*.

9 put the surface on a road:

□ When will the road be *made up*?

●●○   **make up²**   form or constitute something:

□ How many countries *make up* the Common Market?

N
□ The arrival of the new manager has changed the whole *make-up* of the team.

● ●
● ○ ●
● ● ○
N
make up³ **1** put powder, lipstick, etc, on your face:
□ You only have five minutes to *make up* before the show begins.
□ She's worried that she won't have enough time to put on her *make-up*.
2 become friendly again with somebody after a quarrel:
□ The two boys soon *made up* once Timothy had been given his ball back.

● ● ● ○
make up for pay or compensate somebody for something:
□ All the sunshine this week *makes up for* the rain we had last week.
□ She's obviously trying to *make up for* all the trouble she has caused.

● ● ● ○
make up to try to gain the sympathy, favour, love, etc, of somebody by being very friendly and pleasant:
□ She started *making up to* him the day she learnt that he was a millionaire.

● ○ ●
● ● ○
mark down reduce the price of something:
□ I wonder why these dresses have been *marked down*.

● ○ ● ● ○
mark out for select somebody for special treatment:
□ Within a week of joining the firm, James had been *marked out for* early promotion.

● ○ ●
● ● ○
N
mark up **1** decide the price at which to sell something:
□ If we *mark* them *up* at that price, we'll never sell them.
□ The *mark-up* is 100 per cent.
2 raise the price of something:
□ Everything in the shop will have to be *marked up* if the tax is increased.
3 prepare a manuscript for printing:
□ The manuscript contained so many mistakes that it took longer to *mark up* than the publisher had expected.

● ● ○
marry above marry somebody higher than yourself in social rank:
□ In spite of our advice, he *married above* himself.

● ● ○
marry beneath marry somebody lower than yourself in social rank:
□ In order to marry the girl he loved, he had to *marry beneath* himself.

● ● ○
marry into become a member of a family, group, class, etc, by marriage:
□ Her dream is to *marry into* the aristocracy.

● ○ ●
● ● ○ **marry off**   find a marriage partner for somebody, especially for your daughter:
☐ After all these years they have finally managed to *marry* her *off*.

● ●(● ○) **measure up (to)**   display qualities, skills, etc, of a required standard:
☐ If she doesn't *measure up to* the job, she'll just have to leave.

● ● ○ **meet with**   encounter or experience problems, resistance, opposition, etc:
☐ The work has taken longer than expected because we *met with* one or two difficulties.

● ● **mess about/around¹**   **1** spend time in a lazy way:
☐ Now and again it's lovely to spend the whole day just *messing around*.
2 behave in a silly, playful or irritating way:
☐ If you'd stop *messing about* for five minutes, I might be able to hear what John is saying!

● ○ ● **mess about/around²**   upset or cause problems for somebody, especially by breaking a promise:
☐ At first they said they definitely wanted to buy our flat, but now they've started *messing* us *about*.

● ●(● ○) **mess about/around (with)**   **1** spend time on a hobby, interest, etc:
☐ Her husband loves *messing around with* car engines.
☐ Susannah would *mess around* in the kitchen all day if you let her.
2 interfere with or use without permission something that does not concern or belong to you; have a casual sexual relationship with somebody:
☐ Who's been *messing about with* my tools? I can't find the hammer.
☐ He's been *messing around with* my wife.
3 handle something in a clumsy or unskilled way:
☐ Why don't you stop *messing about with* the radio and take it to a proper repair shop?

● ○ ●
● ● ○ **mess up**   spoil something or do a job badly:
☐ The weather really *messed up* our holiday.
☐ If she *messes* it *up* again this time, I shan't ask her to type any more letters for me.

N ☐ He's made a complete *mess-up* of the arrangements.

● ○ ●
● ● ○ **miss out**   omit somebody or something, especially by mistake:
☐ Would you like to check the report in case I've *missed out* anything important?

●●(●○) **miss out (on)** fail to experience, profit from or take part in something:

  □ You'll *miss out* unless you get to the shop on the first morning of the sale.

  □ If you don't come to the party, you'll *miss out on* all the fun!

●○●○ **mistake for** confuse the identity of somebody or something with that of somebody or something else:

  □ She looks so young that people often *mistake* her *for* her daughter.

●○● **mix up** make somebody confused about something:

  □ You'll *mix* me *up* if you ask me to do two jobs at once.

●○●(●○) **mix up (with)** **1** confuse the identity of somebody or
●●○(●○) something with that of somebody or something else:

  □ The two colours are so similar that I keep *mixing* them *up*.

  □ I think that you must be *mixing* me *up with* somebody else.

  2 cause something to be in disorder:

  □ Try not to *mix up* these examination papers *with* the ones that have been marked.

N □ I'm afraid there's been a bit of a *mix-up* with the tickets.

●●(●○) **monkey about/around (with)** play or interfere with something in a mischievous way:

  □ One of you is going to get hurt if you don't stop *monkeying around*.

●○● **mop up** complete a task by doing the few minor things that remain; remove the few areas or resistance that remain after a major attack:

  □ All our problems are solved, except for *mopping up* the final details.

  □ The battle isn't over until the last of the enemy guns has been *mopped up*.

●● **move in** transfer your possessions to where you are going
●○● to live, or do this for somebody:
●●○ □ Our new neighbours are *moving in* tomorrow.

●●(●○) **move in (on)** approach, enter or attack an area when trying to get control of it, especially in business or military occupation:

  □ Our sales team have got two whole months before the competition *moves in*.

●●(●○) **move on (to)** **1** change, progress or develop to something else, especially over a long period of time:

  □ Medical science has *moved on* a lot since I was a boy.

2 change the topic of discussion, conversation, etc, to something else:
□ If nobody has any further questions, perhaps we can *move on to* the next item on the agenda.

●●
●○●
●●○
move out remove your possessions from where you have been living, or do this for somebody:
□ They're having to *move out* because they can't afford the rent.

●●
move over/up change your position to make room for another person:
□ Would you mind *moving up* a bit so that I can sit down?

●○●
●●○
mow down murder somebody or kill people in large numbers:
□ Our troops were *mown down* before they had even reached the bottom of the hill.

●○●
●●(●○)
muck about (with) **1** upset somebody, especially by changing a decision:
□ He hates customers who *muck* him *about*.
2 handle something playfully or in a clumsy way:
□ Stop *mucking about with* the bananas if you're not going to eat one.

●●
muck about/around **1** spend time in an aimless or idle way:
□ If I were you, I'd stop *mucking about* and look for a job.
2 behave in a silly, playful or foolish way:
□ I'll send the pair of you to see the headmaster if you don't stop *mucking about*.

●●(●○)
muck in (with) *Informal* share a task or activity with other people:
□ You don't want people to think that you are too proud to *muck in*, do you?

●○●
●●○
muck out clean a place where animals are kept:
□ I'm glad it's not my job to *muck out* the pigsty.

●○●
●●○
muck up spoil something or do a job badly:
□ The hairdresser has really *mucked* my hair *up* this time. He's cut it much too short.
□ Her mother arrived and *mucked up* the whole weekend.

N
□ He made a complete *muck-up* of painting the front door.

●●
muddle through manage to do or complete something, despite lack of knowledge or skill:
□ It always amazes me how Tom manages to *muddle through*.

●○●   **muddle up** cause somebody to become confused about
        something:
        □ Let's concentrate on one job at a time, or you'll
        muddle me *up*.

●○●(●○) **muddle up (with)** **1** cause something to be in disorder:
●●○(●○)   □ The photographs got *muddled up with* the postcards
        and it was difficult to sort them out.
        2 confuse the identity of somebody or something with
        that of somebody or something else:
        □ I've only met her brothers once, and I keep *muddling*
        them *up*.

●○●   **mug up** *Informal* learn something thoroughly, usually for
●●○   an examination or test, by a short period of intensive
        study:
        □ I've forgotten nearly everything that I *mugged up* for
        the last exams.

●●○   **mull over** consider or think about something:
●●○   □ He's asked for a bit more time to *mull over* my
        proposal.

●●(●○) **muscle in (on)** use force, influence, etc, in order to
        become involved in something and benefit from it:
        □ We don't want any of the big companies *muscling in on*
        the project.

N, n

●○●   **nail down**   **1** make somebody express their position,
●●○   opinion, etc:
       ☐ The more we try to *nail* her *down*, the more she refuses
       even to talk about the issue.
       2 make somebody agree to something, especially by
       strong persuasion:
       ☐ See if you can *nail* him *down* to accepting our offer.
       3 establish something firmly or formally, especially a
       written agreement; accurately define something:
       ☐ Our company has just managed to *nail down* a new
       contract worth £60,000.

●○●(●○)   **narrow down (to)**   reduce an issue, number or amount to
●●○(●○)   something; may be reduced to something:
●●(●○)   ☐ The selection committee has *narrowed down* the
       original pile of applications *to* just these five.
       ☐ The whole question *narrows down to* who is going to
       pay for all the damage.

●●   **nod off**   fall asleep unintentionally:
       ☐ Is it really so late? I must have *nodded off*.

●●   **nose about/around**   look inquisitively at other people's
●●○   private possessions; used in a derogatory way:
       ☐ He hates the way her mother goes *nosing around* the
       house each time she visits them.

N   ☐ There's nothing she enjoys more than a good *nose-
       around* when she thinks you're not watching.

●●○   **nose into**   *Informal*   enquire inquisitively into somebody's
       private affairs; used in a derogatory way.
       ☐ She's always *nosing into* other people's business.

●○●   **notch up**   achieve or record a victory, success, gain, etc:
●●○   ☐ The team *notched up* another two points on Saturday
       with their seventh win in a row.

●○●   **note down**   write something down:
●●○   ☐ He *noted down* her address and telephone number in
       the back of his diary.

O, o

●●○ **occur to** enter the mind or thinking of somebody, especially of an idea:
□ It suddenly *occurred to* me that somebody might be able to lend us the money.

●●○ **open onto** be next to or present a view of something:
□ Nobody is going to buy a house whose front door *opens onto* a gas works.

●● **open out** 1 become wider, especially of a road, river, etc:
□ We had to go slowly for a while, and then the motorway suddenly *opened out* and there were three lanes again.
2 become visible over a wider area, especially of natural scenery:
□ Just over the hill the countryside began to *open out*, and we had our first glimpse of the sea.
3 become less shy or nervous in public:
□ He's *opened out* a lot since he went to university.

●● **open up¹** 1 become less shy or more talkative:
□ Once she had got to know us, she began to *open up* and tell us about her problems.
□ China has *opened up* a lot in recent years, and an increasing amount of information about the country is reaching the West.
2 begin to fire, of a gun or gunner:
□ We held our ears as the machine guns *opened up*.
3 develop, arise or emerge, especially of possibilities, prospects, opportunities, etc:
□ Quite unexpectedly a chance has *opened up* for Henry to go and work abroad.
4 open a door; usually used in the imperative:
□ Come on, *open up*! I can't wait here all day!

●○● ●●○ ●● **open up²** become or cause something to become more lively or exciting, especially of a match, contest, etc:
□ It was Kennedy's equaliser, just five minutes into the second half, that really *opened* the game *up*.

●○● ●●○ **open up³** 1 make something, especially land, available for use or development:
□ We are being forced to move because the council wants to *open up* the whole area for redevelopment.
2 cause a gap, division, cut, etc:

□ The champion suddenly *opened up* a two-inch gash over the right eye of his opponent.

●●(●○) **opt out (of)** choose not to do or take part in something:
□ Most of the group were willing to give blood, but Arthur *opted out*.

●○● **order about/around** keep giving somebody orders or instructions, especially in an offensive way:
□ Who does he think he is, *ordering* people *about* like that?

●●(●○) **own up (to)** admit responsibility for a crime, mistake, etc:
□ The headmaster promised not to punish whoever broke the window if he *owned up*.

P, p

●●○
●○●
pack away store something in a box, cupboard, etc:
□ They *packed away* all their toys before they went on holiday.

●●○
●○●
pack in *Informal* **1** stop doing something, especially a job, habit, etc:
□ You're coughing a lot. You should *pack in* smoking.
□ That's a dreadful noise! Please *pack* it *in*!
□ She had only worked in the shop for three months before she *packed* it *in*.
2 end a relationship with a boyfriend or girlfriend:
□ She went out with John for six months, but then she *packed* him *in*.
3 attract large audiences to a theatre, concert, etc:
□ The new pop group is really *packing in* the teenagers.

●○●(●○)
●●○
pack off (to) send somebody away somewhere, especially quickly and without much care:
□ His mother *packed* him *off to* school.
□ She *packed* him *off* with a bottle of lemonade.

●●
pack up **1** stop or abandon an activity:
□ If you haven't learned how to drive after ten years, you may as well *pack up*.
2 stop working or operating, especially of a machine:
□ We had only just got the car out of the garage when the engine *packed up*.

●●○
●○●
pad out make a sentence, story, etc, longer by adding unnecessary detail:
□ Her letter to her aunt was not long enough, so she *padded* it *out* with information about the weather.

●●○
●○●
paint in add something to a picture by painting:
□ He *painted in* a house to add some human interest.

●●○
●○●
paint out cover something by putting paint over it:
□ They *painted out* the old name of the street before they put in the new one.

●●(●○)
●○●(●○)
pair off/up (with) join or cause somebody to join another person to make a pair or couple:
□ The teacher told the children to *pair off*.
□ John *paired up with* Mary to play tennis.
□ Jane's parents want to *pair* her *off*, but she refuses to get married.

●●(●○)
pal up (with) become friends with somebody:
□ John and Bill *palled up* on their first day at school and they have been friends ever since.

●○●(●○)
●●○(●○)   **palm off (on)**   get rid of something you do not want by
          persuading somebody to buy or accept it:
          □ He *palmed* his old washing machine *off on* his aunt,
          even though he knew it was always breaking down.

●○●(●○)
●●○(●○)   **palm off (with)**   persuade somebody to accept something
          worthless or untrue:
          □ He tried to *palm* his boss *off with* the story that he had
          been to the dentist.

●●○   **pander to**   provide something for which there is a strong
          demand or desire, especially for the purpose of gain or
          profit:
          □ Far too many films *pander to* the public's love of
          violence.

●●○   **paper over**   conceal, disguise or repair something,
          especially a fault, mistake, disagreement, etc:
          □ They tried to *paper over* the differences between union
          and management, but the agreement did not last for long.

●●○
●○●   **parcel out**   divide something into parts, shares or
          portions:
          □ After his death, his land was *parcelled out* among his
          family.

●●○
●○●   **pare down**   reduce or minimise something, especially
          costs, expenditure, etc:
          □ If we're going on holiday, we must *pare down* all our
          other expenses.

●●○   **pass as**   see **pass for/as**.

●●   **pass away/on**   die:
          □ Mr Smith *passed away* last night.

●○●   **pass by**   ignore or pay no attention to somebody:
          □ She felt that life was *passing* her *by*.

●●○
●○●   **pass down**   hand or transfer a story, tradition, custom,
          etc, from one generation to another:
          □ The craft of candle-making has been *passed down* for
          many generations.
          □ The secret has been *passed down* from father to son
          over six centuries.

●●○   **pass for/as**   be mistakenly accepted or identified as
          somebody or something:
          □ You could *pass for* a teenager if you cut your beard
          off.
          □ Her dress was so soft it could *pass as* silk.

●●   **pass off**   **1** gradually disappear, especially of an illness or
          emotion:
          □ By the morning her fever had *passed off* and she was
          well enough to get up.
          2 take place:

129

□ The organisers were pleased that the demonstration *passed off* without any police arrests.

●○●(●○)
●●○(●○)
pass off (as)　present somebody or something in a way that is meant to decieve:

□ She tried to *pass* the knives *off as* silver.

□ He tried to *pass* himself *off as* a doctor until he was caught.

●●
pass on　see **pass away/on**.

●●(●○)
pass on (to)¹　proceed to a new point, question, subject, etc, especially during a meeting:

□ I shall now *pass on to* the next item on today's agenda.

●○●(●○)
●●○(●○)
pass on (to)²　transfer a price increase or decrease to customers, shoppers, etc, by making them pay more for something or letting them pay less:

□ They *passed on* the tax increase *to* the customer.

□ The profit can be *passed on to* the traveller who will pay even less next year.

●●
pass out¹　**1** faint or lose consciousness:

□ She thought she would *pass out* in the heat.

2 leave or graduate from a military or police college:

□ Thirty police cadets *pass out* every week.

●●○
●○●
pass out²　distribute something:

□ The salesman *passed out* cigarettes to everybody in the restaurant.

●●○
●○●
pass over¹　**1** not notice or avoid mentioning something:

□ I *passed over* his unpleasantness without commenting on it.

2 not promote or choose somebody who feels he should be promoted:

□ Did you hear that they've *passed over* poor old Henry for a newcomer?

●●○
pass over²　review or summarise something briefly:

□ He quickly *passed over* the decisions which had been taken at the last meeting.

●●○
pass through　**1** finish a course at a college, university, etc:

□ He *passed through* medical school last year and is now a qualified doctor.

2 experience or suffer something, especially a period of difficulty:

□ She *passed through* a difficult time after her son left home.

●●○
●○●
pass up　not accept an invitation, opportunity, etc:

□ He *passed up* the chance of going to New York for a year.

●●○   **paste up**   prepare a page, etc, for printing by sticking text
●○●   and illustrations on to a sheet of paper:
         □ The printer *pasted up* the first chapter to show the
         author what his book would look like.
N   □ The printer did a *paste-up* of the first chapter.
●●○   **patch up**   resolve or settle an argument, disagreement, etc:
●○●   □ They soon *patched up* their disagreement.
●○●(●○)   **pay back (for)**   punish or take revenge on somebody:
●●○(●○)   □ She *paid* him *back for* insulting her by refusing to
         speak to him.
●●○   **pay for**   suffer or be punished for something:
         □ They made him *pay for* his offence by giving him the
         sack.
         □ If you don't work now, you'll *pay for* it later when you
         fail your exams.
●●○   **pay off¹**   **1** pay everything that you owe somebody:
●○●   □ He *paid off* the £500 that he owed his father.
         2 pay somebody their wages and then dismiss them:
         □ The whole ship's crew were *paid off* at the end of the
         voyage.
         3 give somebody money to stop them threatening you:
         □ He agreed to *pay* the gang *off* if they promised not to
         burn down his shop.
N   □ He gave them £50 as a *pay-off*.
●●   **pay off²**   have a favourable or profitable outcome:
         □ His years of hard work *paid off* when they made him a
         director of the firm.
N   □ The *pay-off* made all his work worthwhile.
●●   **pay out¹**   pay a sum of money, especially regularly or in
●●○   small amounts:
●○●   □ I'm sick of having to *pay out* every time you have an
         accident.
         □ Their father must have *paid out* a fortune on school
         fees.
●●○   **pay out²**   cause or allow a rope, cable, etc, to run through
●○●   your hands:
         □ The kite climbed steadily higher until there was no
         more string to *pay out*.
●●   **pay up**   pay all the money you owe, especially unwillingly
●●○   or under pressure:
●○●   □ He eventually *paid up* when the firm threatened to take
         him to court.
●●○   **peel off**   remove some or all of your clothes:
●○●   □ He was so hot that he *peeled off* his jacket.
●●   □ She *peeled off* and dived into the water.

●●(●○)   **peg away (at)**   work hard and steadily at something:
        □ He found maths difficult but he *pegged away at* it every evening and passed the exam.

●●   **peg out**   *Informal* die:
        □ My grandfather finally *pegged out* at the age of ninety.

●○●   **pen in/up**   shut animals or people in a small space:
●●○   □ He *penned* the sheep *in* for the night.

●○●   **pencil in/into**   make preparatory or tentative
●●○/   arrangements for something:
●○●○   □ Let me *pencil in* that date for the meeting and we can confirm it later.
        □ The minister's visit has been *pencilled into* the programme.

●○●   **pension off**   dismiss somebody from a job after many
●●○   years of service, and pay them a pension:
        □ He was *pensioned off* to make way for a younger man.

●○●   **pep up**   become or make somebody or something more
●●○   lively, interesting, etc:
●●   □ A holiday in the sun will *pep* you *up* and you'll soon feel better.
        □ He *pepped up* the fruit juice by adding some gin.
        □ Don't worry! You'll soon *pep up*.

●○●○   **pepper with**   hit somebody or something with a lot of small stones, questions, insults, etc:
        □ The bird had been *peppered with* lead shot.
        □ The journalist *peppered* the Prime Minister *with* questions.

●●   **perk up**   become or make somebody more lively, cheerful,
●○●   etc:
●●○   □ She *perked up* when I suggested that we went to the theatre that evening.
        □ She was feeling depressed but a cup of tea soon *perked* her *up*.

●●○   **permit of**   *Formal* allow something to be possible, especially of a situation, agreement, etc; usually used in the negative:
        □ The travel arrangements do not *permit of* any change whatsoever.

●●○   **pertain to**   *Formal* be connected or associated with something:
        □ The other questions *pertaining to* this matter have yet to be answered.

●●   **peter out**   steadily weaken or decrease, and come to an end:
        □ Her enthusiasm for dancing *petered out* and she stopped going to lessons.

●●○
●○●

phase in   introduce something gradually or in stages:
  □ They *phased in* the new course by accepting just five students in the first year, and ten in the second.

●●○
●○●

phase out   withdraw something gradually or in stages:
  □ British Leyland has announced plans to *phase out* some of its cars next year.

●●○
●○●

phone in   submit a question, complaint, comment, etc, by telephone to a radio or television programme:
  □ Listeners are asked to *phone in* their questions to the Prime Minister who will be in our studio for the next hour.

N

  □ Twenty housewives took part in the *phone-in* this morning.

●●○

pick at   **1** eat very little of something, in an uninterested way:
  □ She *picked at* her dinner for a few minutes and then said she was not hungry.
  2 keep touching or scratching a cut, wound, etc:
  □ If you keep *picking at* that cut, it will never get better.

●●○
●○●

pick off   carefully and deliberately shoot people or animals one after the other:
  □ The gunman *picked off* each policeman as he tried to enter the house.

●●○

pick on   **1** choose somebody, especially to do something unpleasant or boring:
  □ Why do you always *pick on* me to wash the kitchen floor?
  2 speak to somebody angrily and find fault with them:
  □ I wanted the teacher to stop *picking on* my daughter.

●●○
●○●

pick out   **1** choose or select something from a number of similar things:
  □ There were a lot of blue dresses in the shop and I *picked out* one which was very pretty.
  2 recognise or identify somebody or something:
  □ Although he had not seen his sister for twenty years, he *picked* her *out* as soon as she got off the plane.
  3 play a tune on a musical instrument by guessing which notes to play and experimenting:
  □ As soon as she'd sung the first verse, he *picked out* the tune on the piano.

●●○
●○●

pick over   examine something by lifting and inspecting it, especially before making a decision to buy:
  □ She *picked over* the tomatoes, looking for the ripest ones.

● ● ○
● ○ ●

pick up¹ **1** raise somebody or something from the ground or a surface:

☐ Please *pick up* the pieces of paper which you have just thrown on the floor.

2 stop to buy or get something:

☐ I must remember to *pick up* some potatoes for dinner this evening.

3 stop to collect somebody:

☐ The coach will *pick* you *up* at the corner of your road at nine o'clock.

☐ Whilst driving to Edinburgh he *picked up* two students who were hitching a lift.

4 acquire or buy something, especially a bargain:

☐ He *picked up* a beautiful statue when he was in Rome.

5 acquire knowledge of or proficiency in something, especially without lessons or tuition:

☐ She *picked up* French by living in Paris for six months.

6 make the acquaintance of somebody casually or informally, especially for sexual purposes:

☐ I think she *picked* him *up* at a dance.

N

☐ He was surprised that she was such an easy *pick-up*.

7 receive radio signals:

☐ With my new radio I can *pick up* stations all over Europe.

8 rescue somebody from the sea or some other danger:

☐ They *picked up* the survivors in the lifeboat.

☐ The children who were stranded on the cliff were *picked up* by helicopter.

9 earn something, especially an amount of money:

☐ He *picked up* £60 for two days' work.

10 catch or arrest somebody:

☐ The police *picked* the burglar *up* as he was leaving the house.

11 acquire information, especially by chance:

☐ She *picked up* some rumour that the king had died.

12 continue or return to something after a break or interruption:

☐ I found it difficult to *pick up* the discussion again after lunch.

● ●

pick up² **1** improve or recover, especially of trade:

☐ Business has been very poor but we expect it to *pick up* again before Christmas.

2 improve in health:

☐ He has *picked up* slowly since he came out of hospital.

3 start to work properly again, especially of an engine:

☐ The car was very jerky but then the engine *picked up* and we had no more trouble.

●●○
●○●
piece together　**1** join or gather bits, remnants, parts, etc, in order to make something:

☐ She *pieced together* any bits of material she had to make a cover for her bed.

2 gather facts or pieces of information, especially to discover what happened, the whole truth, etc:

☐ After questioning everybody who was there, I eventually managed to *piece* the whole story *together*.

●●/
●●○
pile in/into　push, crowd, be pushed or crowded into a car, room, football ground, etc:

☐ It's not very far. I'm sure we can all *pile into* my car.

●●/
●●○
pile on/onto　push, crowd, be pushed or crowded onto a vehicle, stage, platform, etc:

☐ The children *piled onto* the bus.

●●(●○)
pile out (of)　push, crowd, be pushed or crowded out of a car, room, football ground, etc:

☐ We all *piled out of* the car when we got home.

☐ At the end of the football match, everybody *piled out of* the ground.

●●
pile up　**1** form into a heap or large mass:

☐ I've been on holiday for a month and my work has really *piled up*.

2 crash into each other, especially of vehicles travelling too close together:

☐ Ten cars *piled up* in the fog this morning.

N
☐ There was another bad *pile-up* on the motorway this morning.

●●○
●○●
pin down　**1** accurately define or determine something:

☐ It was impossible to *pin down* exactly what it was that he was trying to say.

2 make somebody commit himself to a firm opinion or promise:

☐ I have been trying to *pin* him *down* to a date for a meeting next week, but with no success.

3 trap somebody, especially of a heavy weight or gunfire:

☐ After *pinning* them *down*, it was only a short time before they surrendered.

●○●○
pin on　place blame or responsibility for something on somebody:

☐ You needn't think you can *pin* the robbery *on* me. I was out of the country at the time.

●●
pipe down　be quiet; often used in the imperative:

☐ Do *pipe down*! I'm trying to work.

●● **pipe up** begin to speak, especially in a high, squeaky voice:
□ Suddenly a little voice *piped up*: 'Could I have a drink, please?'

●○●○ **pit against** put somebody or something in a fight, contest, etc, against somebody or something else:
□ He *pitted* his intelligence *against* my strength.

●●(●○) **pitch in (with)** join an argument, discussion, activity, etc, by saying something or offering help:
□ If you see things going badly in the meeting, just *pitch in with* some good news.

●●/ **pitch in/into** start to do something, especially to eat or
●●○ work with enthusiasm or vigour:
□ I am grateful for the way everybody *pitched in* and got all the work done.
□ After walking on the hills all day, they could hardly wait to *pitch into* their dinner.

●●○ **pitch into** attack somebody, either physically or verbally:
□ The boys had to be separated once they had *pitched into* each other.
□ The teacher *pitched into* her about her careless work.

●○●○ **plague with** annoy or irritate somebody with endless questions, reminders, suggestions, etc:
□ If you mention the exam to the students, you'll be *plagued with* questions all morning.

●●(●○) **play about/around (with)** behave in a silly, irresponsible way:
□ The school told him that if he didn't stop *playing about*, he would fail all his exams.
□ She is *playing around with* a man twenty years younger than she is.

●○● **play along** keep somebody waiting for an answer or a
●●○ decision:
□ The Government have been *playing* the nurses *along* for six months in the pay talks.

●●(●○) **play along (with)** co-operate, conform or pretend to share somebody's ideas, beliefs, etc:
□ He *plays along with* his boss all the time, but I'm sure he does not really agree with him.

●●○ **play at** pretend to do something or do something in a half-hearted way:
□ You must settle down and concentrate. You're only *playing at* doing your homework.

●●○ **play back** play something which has been recorded on a
●○● tape-recorder, video-recorder, etc:

☐ We recorded our English lesson and then *played* it *back*.

N
☐ We studied the *play-back* carefully.

●●○
●○●
play down   try to make something seem less important or serious than it really is:
☐ She *played down* the fact that she had failed to get a degree.

●○●●○
play off against   put somebody in competition with somebody else, so that you benefit from it:
☐ She was always *playing* her two brothers *off against* each other.

●●○
play on/upon   exploit something, especially somebody's feelings, weakness, etc:
☐ He *played on* her good nature and managed to borrow £20.

●●○
●○●
play out   **1** finish something, especially a game, fight or struggle:
☐ In spite of the heavy rain they managed to *play out* the football match.
☐ The long struggle between management and trade unions is not yet *played out*.
2 perform or conduct something:
☐ Their marriage was *played out* in a series of fights and arguments.

●●○
●○●
play up¹   make something seem more important or serious than it really is:
☐ He loves to *play up* her bad qualities.

●○●
●●○
●●
play up²   cause somebody trouble, unhappiness or pain:
☐ My leg always *plays* me *up* in winter.
☐ The new teacher didn't know what to do when the class started *playing up*.

●●●○
play up to   flatter or pretend to admire somebody, especially to gain favour, position, popularity, etc:
☐ She's always *playing up to* the men in the office.

●●○
play with   consider an idea, suggestion, possibility, etc:
☐ He's been *playing with* the idea of leaving his job and buying a farm, but he'll never do it.

●●(●○)
plod away (at)   work slowly and steadily, especially at something that you do not find interesting:
☐ He *plods away at* his studies every night, but he doesn't enjoy the work.

●○●(●○)
●●○(●○)
plough back (into)   reinvest profits in a company:
☐ He *ploughed* as much money *back into* the firm as he could because he wanted to expand.

●●○   **plough through**   read or work your way through something slowly and laboriously:
□ He *ploughed through* the collected works of Charles Dickens.

●●(●○)   **plug away (at)**   keep working hard at something:
□ He's been *plugging away at* his new novel for nearly a year.

●●○
●○●
●●   **plug in**   connect something electrical to an electricity supply, by putting its plug into a socket:
□ *Plug in* the kettle for me, please. I'd like a cup of tea.

●●○   **plump for**   choose something or somebody enthusiastically, especially after a lot of thought:
□ We couldn't decide which car to buy, but we finally *plumped for* a Datsun.
□ The appointments committee *plumped for* the older man with experience rather than the younger one with a degree.

●●○
●○●   **plump up**   make pillows, cushions, etc, soft and round by shaking and patting them:
□ Every evening she *plumps up* the cushions before she goes to bed.

●●/
●●○   **plunge in/into**   begin work or an activity eagerly or abruptly:
□ Instead of just *plunging in*, why don't you seek professional advice?
□ She *plunged into* her new assignment the moment she got it.

●○●○
●●○   **plunge into**   suddenly assume or cause somebody or something to assume a particular mood, condition, state, etc:
□ She switched off the light and *plunged* the room *into* darkness.
□ He was *plunged into* despair by the terrible news.
□ Every month they *plunged* deeper *into* debt.

●○●○   **ply with**   keep supplying somebody with food, drink or questions:
□ She *plied* all her visitors *with* cake until they could eat no more.
□ They *plied* the speaker *with* so many questions that he had no time to answer them all.

●●○
●○●   **point out**   identify, indicate or draw attention to something:
□ I *pointed out* the advantages of the plan.
□ I asked him to *point out* the house where he was born.

●●○   **point to**   suggest or indicate something:
□ All the evidence *points to* his guilt.

●●○   **point up**   emphasise or highlight something:
●○●   □ The special enquiry is expected to *point up* the failure of the police to produce eye-witnesses.

●●   **poke about/around**   move or disturb things while searching for something:
    □ Who's been *poking about* in my desk?

N   □ Somebody's been having a *poke-around* in here by the looks of it.

●●○   **polish off**   *Informal*   **1** finish something, especially work,
●○●   food, etc:
    □ He *polished off* the last of the whisky.
    2 defeat or kill somebody:
    □ The champion soon *polished off* his opponent.

●●○   **polish up**   improve your knowledge of or proficiency in
●○●   something, especially something you have partly forgotten:
    □ If I'm going to live in Paris, I'll have to *polish up* my French.

●●   **ponce about/around**   *Informal* behave in a showy, often effeminate way:
    □ That new young salesman *ponces around* all day, getting in the way and never doing anything useful.

●●   **pop off**   *Informal* die:
    □ I'm not going to *pop off* just yet, so you needn't worry

●●   **pop up**   appear, arise or emerge, especially suddenly or unexpectedly especially something written:
    □ He *pops up* all over the place, so you never know where to look for him.

●●○   **pore over**   study something carefully and with great attention:
    □ He is always *poring over* his books.

●●   **potter about/around**   spend time doing small, unimportant jobs:
    □ He spent all morning *pottering about* in his greenhouse.

●●○   **pounce on/upon**   **1** scold somebody or criticise something sharply:
    □ He *pounced on* my smallest mistake.
    2 grasp an opportunity eagerly:
    □ The children *pounced on* the chance of visiting the television studios.

●●   **pour down**   fall hard and steadily, especially of rain:
    □ The rain *poured down* all day.

N   □ There was a tremendous *downpour*.

●●○
●○●
●●
  pour out say or tell something quickly and without stopping:
   □ Sobbing, she *poured out* the whole story.

●○●○
  preclude from *Formal* prevent somebody from doing something:
   □ Non-residents are *precluded from* private ownership.

●○●○
  predispose to/towards cause somebody to behave in a certain way, especially of a past experience:
   □ His unhappy childhood *predisposed* him *to* spoiling his own children.

●●○
  press for keep demanding or insisting upon something:
   □ The nurses are *pressing for* a bigger increase in salary.

●●
  press on continue to do something, especially without stopping, in spite of problems or difficulties:
   □ I know it's almost midnight, but we'd better *press on* and get the job finished.

●○●○
  press on/upon[1] force somebody to accept something:
   □ He tried to *press* his political beliefs *on* his wife, but she wouldn't listen to him.
   □ The old lady was always *pressing* money *on* him.

●●○
  press on/upon[2] worry or trouble somebody:
   □ He looks as if all the worries in the world are *pressing upon* him.

●●○
  presume upon/on *Formal* take unfair advantage of somebody's good nature, patience, feelings, etc:
   □ He *presumed* too much *upon* her generosity and she was forced to tell him so.

●●○
  prevail upon/on *Formal* persuade somebody to do something:
   □ She *prevailed upon* her daughter to refrain from entering into conversation with complete strangers.

●●○
  prey on/upon **1** exploit somebody or somebody's weakness:
   □ He was a very handsome man and lived by *preying upon* members of the fairer sex.
   2 attack and rob somebody or something:
   □ It was hard to believe that these little boats were being *preyed upon* by pirates.
   3 trouble or worry somebody, especially of sorrow, grief, fear, etc:
   □ His fears and worries *preyed* so much *on* his mind that eventually he comitted suicide.

●●○
●○●
  print out provide a printed record of information, especially of a computer:
   □ I asked the computer to *print out* every word beginning with 'b'.

N
☐ I asked for a *print-out* of phrasal verbs.

●○●(●○)   **prise/prize out (of)**   force information out of somebody:
●●○   ☐ She *prised* the secret *out of* him by threatening to tell his father.

●●○   **proceed against**   take legal action against somebody:
☐ They have decided to *proceed against* the accused, despite the advice of their counsel.

●●○   **proceed from**   be the result of something:
☐ His mistakes *proceed from* carelessness, not ignorance.

●●○   **profit by/from**   learn or benefit from something:
☐ Has he *profited from* his year abroad?

●●○   **prop up**   support somebody or something that would
●○●   otherwise fall or collapse:
☐ The opposition parties decided not to *prop up* the Government any longer.

●●○   **provide against**   do something that lets you avoid foreseeable danger, hardship, distress, etc:
☐ She has *provided against* a bad winter by buying in lots of food.

●●○   **provide for**   1 support somebody or something by earning, producing or saving what is needed:
☐ He has always worked hard to *provide for* his family.
2 make arrangements to overcome all foreseeable problems:
☐ In the space shuttle every possible electrical failure has been *provided for*.

●●○   **puff out**   1 make somebody short of breath:
●○●   ☐ Climbing stairs *puffs* me *out* these days. I must go and see a doctor.
2 put out a flame by blowing on it:
☐ She likes to *puff out* the candles.

●○●   **pull about/around**   handle somebody or something
●●○   roughly or clumsily:
☐ The baby doesn't like it when people start *pulling* him *about*.
☐ Their new puppy has been *pulling* the furniture *about*.

●●(●○)   **pull ahead (of)**   overtake somebody or something:
☐ The winner of the men's 400 metres *pulled ahead* on the last bend.
☐ The Rolls Royce *pulled ahead of* us and disappeared into the distance.

●○●   **pull apart**   criticise somebody or find serious faults in an idea, plan, piece of work, etc:
☐ He *pulled* my argument *apart* and made me feel very stupid.

●●○   **pull at/on**   draw tobacco smoke from a pipe, cigarette, etc, into your mouth:
     □ The old man sat in the corner, *pulling at* his pipe.

●●   **pull away**   start to move, especially of a vehicle:
     □ He leapt onto the train just as it was *pulling away*.

●●●○   **pull away from**   get further ahead of somebody or something:
     □ The car *pulled away from* the lorry as soon as they started going uphill.
     □ She was an extremely intelligent child, and soon *pulled away from* the rest of the class.

●●   **pull back**   withdraw or cause somebody to withdraw from
●●○   a position, especially of a group of soldiers:
●○●   □ The platoon *pulled back* to safety.

●●○   **pull down¹**   destroy or demolish something, especially a
●○●   building:
     □ They *pulled down* my old house and built five new ones.

●○●   **pull down²**   cause somebody to feel weak and depressed, especially of an illness:
     □ A really bad cold *pulls* you *down* and leaves you feeling very miserable.

●●○   **pull in**   **1** *Informal* earn money:
●○●   □ He *pulls in* quite a lot as a milkman.
     2 take somebody to the police station because they are suspected of being a criminal:
     □ The men were *pulled in* on suspicion of having committed a burglary.
     3 attract a lot of people to a theatre, concert, etc:
     □ The Beatles always *pulled in* enormous crowds.

●●/   **pull in/into**   **1** arrive, especially of a train at a station:
●●○   □ The train from Edinburgh *pulled in* five minutes late.
     2 move to or towards one side, especially of a vehicle or driver about to stop:
     □ The lorry driver *pulled into* the side of the road and got out for a cup of tea.

●●○   **pull off**   complete or perform something successfully,
●○●   especially a difficult or daring task:
     □ How did you manage to *pull off* the deal without offering them more money?

●●○   **pull on**   see **pull at/on**.

●●(●○)   **pull out (of)¹**   **1** move out of a line of traffic, especially to overtake another vehicle:
     □ The car in front was travelling very slowly, so I *pulled out* to overtake.

2 leave, especially of a train from a station:
☐ The train *pulled out* exactly on time.
3 recover from an illness, bad mood, etc:
☐ She's been very depressed recently, but I'm sure she'll soon *pull out of* it.

●●(●○)
●○●(●○) **pull out (of)²**   leave or make somebody leave a place or situation where there is trouble:
●●○ ☐ The foreign firm decided to *pull out* because of strikes.
☐ The government *pulled* the army *out of* the trouble-spot.
N ☐ There was a large *pull-out of* troops.

●●
●●○ **pull through**   survive or help somebody survive an illness, accident, crisis, etc:
●○● ☐ He was very ill but he eventually *pulled through*.
●○●○ ☐ It was a miracle that they were able to *pull* her *through* the operation.

●● **pull together**   work as a team:
☐ People always seem to *pull together* in a crisis.

●●
●○● **pull up¹**   stop or cause something to stop, especially of a vehicle or driver:
●●○ ☐ The bus *pulled up* at the stop.
☐ He *pulled up* and we got out.

●●
●○● **pull up²**   improve your position in a race, competition, class, etc:
☐ He's *pulled up* from seventh to second place.
☐ It must have been the history paper that *pulled* him *up*.

●○● **pull up³**   scold or reprimand somebody:
☐ She was *pulled up* by the teacher for running down the corridor.

●○● **push about/around**   order somebody to do something in a rough or bullying way:
☐ I'm not going to be *pushed about* by anybody.
☐ She won't let anybody *push* her *about* these days.

●● **push ahead/forward/on**   advance or continue your journey, especially in a determined way:
☐ The infantry *pushed forward* until they came within range of the enemy guns.
☐ Although we were tired, we *pushed on* through the night.

●●(●○) **push ahead/forward/on (with)**   proceed or continue to do something:
☐ Now that the plans have been accepted, we can *push ahead*.
☐ If you want to *push on with* the decorating, we can leave dinner until later.

●●   **push along**   leave, especially of a guest, visitor, etc:
        □ It's getting late. We'd better be *pushing along*.

●●○
●○●○   **push for**   keep insisting upon something or demanding
        something from someone:
        □ The miners are *pushing for* more money and less work.
        □ They're *pushing* the sales manager *for* better figures.

●●○
●○●   **push forward¹**   **1** try to bring something to somebody's
        attention:
        □ She *pushed forward* her plans for the new theatre.
        2 be assertive or forceful in order to be noticed:
        □ If only he had *pushed* himself *forward* at work, he
        might have been a director now.

●●   **push forward²**   see **push ahead/forward/on**.

●●(●○)   **push forward (with)**   see **push ahead/forward/on**
        (with).

●●   **push off**   **1** *Informal* leave or go away; often used in the
        imperative to express anger:
        □ *Push off!* Can't you see I'm busy!
        □ Tell him to *push off* if he starts annoying you.
        □ I'll be *pushing off* now. It's getting late.

●●   **2** leave in a boat:
        □ We *pushed off* from the shore and were soon out to
        sea.

●●   **push on**   see **push ahead/forward/on**.

●●(●○)   **push on (with)**   see **push ahead/forward/on (with)**.

●○●
●●○
●○●○   **push through**   **1** gain acceptance of a bill, proposal,
        decision, etc, by somebody, using force or persuasion:
        □ Despite a lot of resistance, we managed to *push* the
        proposals *through*.
        2 cause somebody to pass or succeed in doing something:
        □ By giving him extra lessons we managed to *push* him
        through his exams.

●●○
●○●   **push up**   cause something to rise or increase:
        □ Wage increases keep *pushing up* the cost of living.
        □ The hot bath has *pushed* her temperature *up*.

●○●
●●○   **put about**   spread or circulate a rumour, piece of news,
        story, etc:
        □ They've *put* it *about* that the Government's going to
        resign.
        □ Somebody's *putting* vicious rumours *about*.

●○●○   **put across**   deceive or trick somebody into believing or
        accepting something:
        □ You can't *put* anything *across* old Harrison. He's been
        around too long.

●○●   **put across/over**   **1** communicate an idea, message,
●●○   argument, etc, so that it is clear, persuasive or
understood:
☐ He was too full of emotion to *put across* his ideas
properly.
2 project your personality or a song, story, etc, in a way
that is liked or admired:
☐ He just doesn't know how to *put* himself *across* at an
interview.

●●○   **put aside**   **1** save or reserve money, goods, time, etc:
●○●   ☐ Every month he *puts aside* £20.
☐ Can't you manage to *put aside* five minutes to talk to
your children?
2 ignore or pay no attention to something:
☐ During the war everybody *put* their political
differences *aside* and worked together.

●○●○   **put at**   guess or estimate the weight, height, size, etc, of
somebody or something:
☐ I don't really know how old she is, but I would *put* her
at about forty.

●●○   **put away**   **1** *Informal* eat or drink, especially a lot:
●○●   ☐ He *put away* nearly half a bottle of whisky last night.
2 confine somebody in prison or a mental hospital:
☐ He became unstable and thought that he was a giant
banana, so we had to have him *put away*.
☐ They've *put* him *away* for thirty years.

●●○   **put away/by**   save something, especially money, for use in
●○●   the future:
☐ How much have you *put away* for your holiday?

●●○   **put away/down**   kill an animal, especially one that is old,
ill or injured:
☐ If the horse's leg is broken, it'll have to be *put down*.

●○●   **put back**   **1** move the hands of a clock or watch backwards
●●○   so that it shows an earlier time:
☐ Don't forget to *put* the clock *back* an hour tonight.
2 move an event, appointment, etc, to a later time or date:
☐ We had intended to get married in April but we had to
put the wedding *back* to September.
3 cause something to be delayed:
☐ Heavy rains *put back* the harvesting of the corn this
year.

●○●   **put down**[1]   **1** record something in writing:
●●○   ☐ He *put* the meeting *down* in his diary.
2 stop and let a passenger get out, of a driver or vehicle:
☐ Where would you like me to *put* you *down*?

3 pay a deposit or make a down payment:
- □ She *put down* £100 on some furniture.

4 see **put away/down**.

●●
●○●

put down² land or cause something to land, especially an aircraft:
- □ The plane *put down* in a field.
- □ The pilot *put* the plane *down* safely, despite the storm.

●○●

put down³ humiliate somebody:
- □ He seems to enjoy *putting* his wife *down* in public.

●●○

put down⁴ subdue a riot, rebellion, revolt, etc:
- □ The army will soon *put down* the revolt.

●○●●○

put down as form a particular opinion of somebody or reach a certain explanation for something:
- □ We *put* him *down as* a dreadful fool.

●○●●○

put down for **1** write down somebody's name on a list because they are willing to give, buy or do something:
- □ How many raffle tickets can I *put* you *down for*?

2 put somebody's name on the waiting-list for a school, club, team, etc:
- □ We *put* our son *down for* his father's old school when he was two years old.

●○●●○

put down to **1** attribute something to a particular cause:
- □ She *put* his rudeness *down to* tiredness.

2 charge something to a particular account:
- □ She *put* the dress *down to* her mother's account.

●●○
●○●

put forward **1** offer an idea, proposal, plan, etc, for consideration:
- □ We *put forward* our ideas on how the club should be run.

2 recommend somebody or advance yourself for a job or position:
- □ He *put* himself *forward* for secretary.
- □ We *put forward* four names for the committee to consider.

3 move the hands of a clock or watch forwards so that it shows a later time:
- □ We *put* the clocks *forward* in March.

4 move an event, appointment, etc, to an earlier time or date:
- □ We had to *put* our holiday *forward* one month.

●●○
●○●

put in¹ **1** submit a request or application:
- □ If any of the goods arrive in a damaged condition, you must *put in* a claim within three days.

2 spend a particular amount of time doing something:
□ Altogether, he must have *put in* about four years' work on his thesis.
3 elect a government:
□ Voters *put* a Conservative government *in* at the last election.
4 install, fit or supply something:
□ We *put* central heating *in* when we moved into our new house.

●● **put in²** interrupt or interject:
□ 'Don't forget the work involved,' I *put in*.

●●(●○) **put in (for)** submit a request or application for
●●○(●○) something, especially for a job, promotion, rise, etc:
●○●(●○) □ The miners have *put in* a claim *for* a thirty per cent wage increase.
□ You won't get the money if you don't *put in for* it.

●○●●○ **put in for** **1** enter somebody or something in a competition:
□ He *put* his beans *in for* the 'Best Vegetable' prize.
□ She *put* herself *in for* the marathon.
2 recommend somebody for a job, award, prize, etc:
□ They *put* his name *in for* the Distinguished Service Medal.

●●/ **put in/into** enter a port, used of a ship:
●●○ □ The liner *puts in* at Bombay, Singapore and Hong Kong.
□ We *put into* Amsterdam to unload.

●○● **put inside** *Informal* put somebody in prison:
□ He was *put inside* for murder:

●●○ **put off¹** **1** postpone something:
●○● □ He had to *put off* his trip to Japan for two weeks.
2 distract, prevent or hinder somebody or something:
□ The slightest noise *puts* me *off* when I'm concentrating.
3 avoid seeing, meeting, talking, etc, to somebody:
□ He *put* her *off* with the excuse that he had too much work to do.
4 discourage somebody or cause them to lose interest in something:
□ I tried to learn French but my teacher was so unpleasant that she *put* me *off*.

●○● **put off²** **1** cause somebody to lose their liking, desire or
●○●○ appetite for something:
□ Don't let the price of the carpet *put* you *off*.
□ The awful smell coming from the kitchen *put* me *off* my dinner.

2 let or make somebody get out of a vehicle, especially a bus:

☐ The stupid conductor *put* me *off* at the wrong stop.

● ● ○
● ○ ●

put on¹ 1 cause electricity, gas or water to start flowing, by moving a switch or turning a tap:

☐ He opened the door and *put on* the light.

2 gain weight:

☐ She *put on* a lot of weight last winter.

3 provide extra trains, buses, etc:

☐ British Airways are *putting on* an extra flight to Rome every day.

4 present or produce a play, exhibition, etc:

☐ They are *putting on* a new production of 'Romeo and Juliet'.

5 move the hands of a clock or watch forwards so that it shows a later time:

☐ He forgot to *put* the clock *on* last night.

6 assume or adopt a particular manner, tone, attitude, etc, especially to impress or deceive somebody:

☐ She always *puts on* a posh voice to talk to the vicar.

☐ He's not really angry. He's just *putting* it *on*.

● ○ ● ○
● ● ○
● ○ ●

put on² 1 add to the cost of something:

☐ The rise in taxation will *put* pounds *on* the cost of living.

2 bet or risk money on something, especially on a horse:

☐ I *put* £5 *on* Black Beauty in the two o'clock at Newmarket.

● ● ○

put on/upon be a trouble or nuisance to somebody:

☐ I don't want to *put upon* you, but could you possibly mind the baby for me for just ten minutes?

● ○ ● ● ○

put on to 1 give somebody information about somebody or something which will be interesting or useful to them:

☐ My friend *put* me *on to* a very good restaurant.

2 bring the attention of an authority to something or somebody, especially a criminal or suspect:

☐ We *put* the police *on to* them as soon as we discovered the gun in their room.

● ○ ●
● ● ○

put out¹ 1 cause a light or fire to stop burning, by moving a switch, etc:

☐ She *put out* the light and closed the door.

2 extinguish a fire or flame, especially by using water:

☐ The firemen took an hour to *put* the fire *out*.

3 publish, broadcast or circulate something:

☐ The government is about to *put out* a statement on its wages policy.

4 dislocate a part of the body:
□ You can imagine how painful it was when he *put* his shoulder *out*.
5 cause figures, results, calculations, etc, to be wrong or inaccurate:
□ The rise in transportation costs has really *put* our estimate *out*!
6 cause somebody to become unconscious, especially with a drug or blow:
□ His last words before they *put* him *out* for the operation were: 'If only I'd listened to that life-insurance salesman!'
□ He *put out* his opponent in the seventh round.

●●○   **put out²**   **1** produce or manufacture something, especially of a factory:
□ The company *puts out* 900 cars a week.

N   □ Our *output* is twice that of our nearest competitor.
2 generate a particular amount of power:
□ The engine *puts out* thirty horsepower.

N   □ What's the *output* of this engine?
3 sprout new shoots, leaves, etc, especially of a tree or plant:
□ She loves it when the trees start *putting out* their fresh green shoots in the spring.

●○●   **put out³**   **1** inconvenience somebody:
□ You're not *putting* us *out* at all! On the contrary, we're glad to see you.
2 annoy or anger somebody:
□ You could tell that his rudeness had *put* her *out* by the way she slammed the door.
3 remove somebody from a room by force:
□ If you keep talking in class, I'll have to *put* you *out*.

●●   **put out⁴**   set sail or move away from the shore:
□ We *put out* at the crack of dawn.

●○●(●○)   **put out (to)**   **1** transfer or subcontract a job to somebody:
●●○(●○)   □ He *puts* a lot of his work *out to* other people, including carpenters and electricians.
2 lend money to somebody in order to get interest on it:
□ The banks have started *putting out* money *to* people wanting to buy their own homes.

●○●   **put over**   see **put across/over**.
●●○   **put through¹**   successfully complete a plan, scheme,
●○●   programme, etc:
□ He *put through* an important business deal yesterday.

● ○ ● ○   **put through²**   cause somebody or something to undergo or experience a test, upheaval, misery, etc:
      ☐ All the students are *put through* an English test before starting their course.
      ☐ Engineers are *putting* the new train *through* rigorous safety checks.

● ○ ● ○   **put to**   **1** submit a question, belief, proposal, etc, to somebody for consideration:
      ☐ I would like to *put* a question *to* the speaker, if I may.
      ☐ I *put* it *to* you, Minister, that unemployment will continue to rise.
      ☐ The plans for the new building were *put to* the committee last week.
      2 ask somebody to decide something; resolve something by voting or discussing it:
      ☐ May we *put* the proposal *to* the meeting?
      3 subject somebody to a lot of worry, trouble, distress, etc:
      ☐ We've been *put to* a great deal of inconvenience by your irresponsible behaviour.

● ● ○
● ○ ●   **put together**   construct or mend something by joining its parts together:
      ☐ If you have some glue, I'll try and *put* the vase *together* again.
      ☐ He *put* the story *together* by asking lots of people what had happened.

● ● ○
● ○ ●   **put up¹**   increase the price of something:
      ☐ Universities have just *put up* their fees.

● ● ○   **put up²**   **1** give or lend somebody a sum of money needed for a project:
      ☐ He hopes that one of the major banks will agree to *put up* the bulk of the capital.
      2 offer a struggle, resistance, defence, etc:
      ☐ The losers certainly didn't *put up* much of a fight, did they?
      3 offer or submit something for consideration:
      ☐ Don't tell me they're going to *put up* yet another proposal: They've had four rejected already!

● ○ ●
● ● ○
● ●   **put up³**   provide food and a bed for somebody; stay somewhere overnight:
      ☐ I'm afraid we can't *put* you *up* tonight. We're full.
      ☐ Perhaps we could *put up* at this hotel.

● ○ ●(● ○)   **put up (for)¹**   suggest or propose somebody for a job, official position, etc:
      ☐ We *put* him *up for* chairman, but he refused.

●●(●○) **put up (for)**[2] offer yourself as a candidate for an election:
●○●(●○) □ He is *putting up for* Parliament next year.
●●○ **put upon** see **put on/upon**.
●○●●○ **put up to** encourage or entice somebody to do something wrong or mischievous:
□ He's not usually naughty. Somebody must have *put him up to* it.
●●●.○ **put up with** suffer or tolerate somebody or something patiently and without complaining:
□ I'm not going to *put up with* their shouting and banging any longer!
●●○ **puzzle out** find an answer or solution to something by
●○● thinking hard and carefully:
□ He finally *puzzled out* how to use the dishwasher.
●●○ **puzzle over** try to understand something difficult or confusing:
□ He spent all day *puzzling over* his income tax form.

Q, q

●●○   **quarrel with**   dispute or disagree with something; often
used in the negative:
□ We're not *quarrelling with* the decision itself, just the
timing of it.

●○●
 ●●   **quieten down**   become or cause somebody or something
to become calm, especially after being anxious, busy, etc:
□ There was nothing we could say or do to *quieten* her
down while her husband was in hospital.
□ The baby was very restless during the night, but
quietened down after a feed.

R, r

●●○   **rake through**   search somewhere carefully:
He *raked through* the attic trying to find the trunk.

●●○
●○●   **rake up**   **1** mention or introduce a past event, especially an unhappy or unpleasant one, which was forgotten or hidden:
☐ Please don't *rake up* that awful quarrel.
2 produce or find money, people, enthusiasm, etc, with a lot of effort:
☐ I'm busy *raking up* support for the cricket match.

●●
●●○   **rally round**   come together, especially of a group, to help and support somebody or something:
☐ When she was ill, all her family *rallied round*.
☐ The nation will *rally round* the flag in a time of crisis.

●●○
●○●   **rattle off**   say or repeat something quickly and easily from memory or by reading:
☐ The boy *rattled off* all the names of the England football team.

●●○   **rave about/over**   praise somebody or something in an excited and enthusiastic way:
☐ The girls *raved about* the rock concert.

●●(●○)   **reach out (to)**   extend a message, appeal, offer of help, etc, to somebody, especially to a particular group:
☐ Local church leaders are making a new attempt to *reach out to* the younger generation.

●●○   **read for**   study for a qualification, especially a university degree:
☐ When the children are older, she intends to *read for* a BSc at London University.

●○●○   **read into**   find more meaning in something than was expressed or intended:
☐ My book is widely misunderstood: people *read* things *into* it which aren't there.

●○●
●●○   **read off**   read, often aloud, words or figures on an instrument, gauge, dial, etc:
☐ I peered at the dial and *read off* the numbers.

●○●
●●○   **read out**   read something aloud, usually to a group:
☐ First the secretary *read out* the minutes of the last meeting.

●●○
●○●   **read over/through**   read a letter, document, etc, usually in order to check or judge it:
☐ The BBC *read* the script *over* before allowing the programme to be made.

● ● ○   **read up**   find out facts, details, information, etc, by reading:
     □ Out of curiosity, I *read up* all the details on the murder case.

● ● ● ○   **read up on**   study something in detail, by reading:
     □ I had *read up on* the Renaissance before my trip to Italy.

● ● ○   **reason with**   try to persuade or convince somebody with logical arguments:
     □ I tried to *reason with* him, but it was no use.

● ● ○   **reckon on**   expect or depend on something happening:
     □ We are *reckoning on* increasing profits by 20 per cent next year.

● ● ○   **reckon with**   take something into account or consider something or somebody to be a serious obstacle or opponent:
     □ The hikers didn't *reckon with* the possibility of snow and fog when they set off.
     □ When he is angry he is a force to be *reckoned with*.

● ● ○   **reckon without**   fail to take something into account:
     □ The organisers had *reckoned without* a train strike on the day of the show.

● ● ○
● ○ ●   **reel off**   say, repeat, or write something from memory, especially a list of things:
     □ When I asked him to recommend a good restaurant, he *reeled off* a long list of places.

● ● ○   **relate to**   form an understanding and establish a relationship with somebody or something:
     □ I don't get on with other people at work, but I can *relate to* David.

● ●
● ● ○
● ○ ●   **rev up**   push the accelerator of a motor vehicle, causing the engine to run fast while the vehicle is not moving:
     □ The youths *revved up* their motorbikes as they waited at the traffic lights.

● ● ○
● ○ ●   **ride out**   come through a difficult situation, crisis, etc:
     □ The company faces severe financial problems, but we hope to *ride* them *out*.

● ●   **ride up**   move upwards out of its proper position, especially of clothing:
     □ This shirt keeps *riding up* and won't stay tucked in.

● ● ○(● ○)
● ○ ●(● ○)   **rig out (in/with)**   provide or equip somebody with something, especially clothes:
     □ He had *rigged* himself *out in* a dinner jacket and bow tie.
     □ They *rigged* him *out with* everything he needed for the journey.

●●○ **rig up** arrange, assemble or construct something, usually
●○● temporarily:
    □ We *rigged up* the record-player in the dining-room for
the party.
    □ The girls had *rigged up* a kind of bunk-bed using some
planks and a few wooden boxes.

●● **ring around/round** make several telephone calls for a
●●○ particular purpose:
    □ If you need to hire a car, *ring round* first and get the
best price.
    □ Let's *ring round* a few friends and have a party.

●● **ring off** finish a telephone conversation:
    □ I must *ring off* now. I'm in rather a hurry.

●● **ring out** make a loud and clear sound, especially of a bell,
voice, gunshot, etc:
    □ Their shouts *rang out* in the clear night air.

●○● **ring up** record the amount of money paid for a purchase
●●○ on a cash register:
    □ The shop assistant made a mistake and *rang up* £15
instead of £1.50.

●●○ **rip off** *Informal* **1** steal something:
●○●   □ Those kids *ripped off* two boxes of sweets while the
shopkeeper wasn't looking.
    2 charge somebody a very high price:
    □ Don't buy a car from that garage! They'll *rip* you *off*.
N   □ Sixty pounds for a pair of shoes! That's a real *rip-off*.

●● **roll about/around** laugh, especially wildly or loudly:
    □ It was a really funny show. Everyone was *rolling about*
with tears of laughter streaming down their faces.

●● **roll in¹** **1** arrive or come home:
    □ What time did you *roll in* last night?
    2 arrive in large quantity at a steady rate, especially of
money or people:
    □ When the hospital asked for donations, the cash *rolled
in* from all over the country.

●●○ **roll in²** have plenty or more than you need of something,
especially money:
    □ The Smith family are simply *rolling in* money.

●●○ **roll on** hurry, of time, a date, etc; used to express a wish:
    □ *Roll on*, summer!
    □ *Roll on* five o'clock when I can go home!

●● **roll up** arrive, especially late or in a particular manner:
    □ We waited for three hours for John to *roll up*.
    □ The Lord Mayor *rolled up* in a chauffeur-driven car.

● ● ○   **root for**   cheer or support somebody, especially in a
           contest:
           □ Dave was *rooting for* the Scottish football team in the
           World Cup.

● ● ○   **root out**   **1** produce or find something after careful
● ○ ●   searching:
           □ When I get home, I'll see if I can *root out* a few of my
           old essays for you.
           2 destroy, remove or get rid of somebody or something:
           □ The Government is determined to *root out* MPs who
           criticise its policies.

● ○ ●   **rope in/into**   persuade somebody to take part in
● ● ○/   something, especially to join a group or give help:
● ○ ● ○   □ If they think you're interested in the club, they'll soon
           rope you *in*.
           □ Every year I was *roped into* helping with the school
           sports.

● ● ○   **rough out**   outline a plan, idea, scheme, etc:
● ○ ●   □ Let me *rough out* for you the design for the new wing.

● ● ○   **rough up**   use physical violence, especially to frighten
● ○ ●   somebody:
           □ The gang *roughed up* the doorman and then forced
           their way in.

● ● ○(● ○)   **round off (with)**   complete or conclude something in a
● ○ ●(● ○)   suitable way:
           □ The orchestra *rounded off* the concert with Brahms'
           Third Symphony.

● ● ○   **round on/upon**   **1** turn and attack somebody or something
           unexpectedly:
           □ The dog suddenly *rounded on* the little boy who was
           playing nearby.
           2 turn against somebody unexpectedly in anger or
           annoyance:
           □ The old lady *rounded on* the ticket collector because
           the train was five minutes late.
           □ The Prime Minister *rounded on* his critics.

● ○ ●   **round out**   give something more content, body, details,
● ● ○   etc:
           □ If you *rounded out* the story a bit, you could get it
           published as a novel.
           □ The board won't accept the scheme until we *round* it
           out with some figures.

● ● ○   **round up**   **1** collect people or things together in one place,
● ○ ●   especially sheep or cattle:
           □ The farmer *rounded up* the cows for milking.

2 bring a fraction to the nearest or most convenient higher whole number:
  □ The bill should have been £29.54 so I *rounded* it *up* to £30.

●● **rub along** have a satisfactory relationship with somebody; live together in a friendly way:
  □ My wife and I have *rubbed along* all right for twenty-five years.

●○●
●●○ **rub in** talk repeatedly about something which somebody wants to forget or is embarrassed or angry about:
  □ 'I'm really surprised you failed your exams.'
  'OK. Don't *rub* it *in*.'
  □ She kept *rubbing in* the fact that she was prettier than me.

●●(●○) **rub off (on/onto)** pass from one person to another as a result of close contact, especially of habits, qualities, attitudes, etc:
  □ Now that Sue and John are married, perhaps some of her intelligence will *rub off on* him.

●●○ **rule out** **1** prevent something from happening; make something impossible:
  □ It's pouring with rain, so that *rules out* tea in the garden.
  2 exclude, dismiss or decide not to consider a possibility, idea, suggestion, etc:
  □ We can't *rule out* the possibility of a nuclear war within the next decade.

●●○ **run across/into** meet somebody or find something by chance or unexpectedly:
  □ I *ran across* an old school friend at the party on Thursday.

●●○ **run after** pursue somebody, especially of the opposite sex, to gain their attention and affection:
  □ She loves money and is always *running after* rich bachelors.

●●(●○) **run around (with)** **1** be very often in the company of somebody:
  □ I wish my son wouldn't *run around with* those hooligans.
  2 be unfaithful to your marriage partner, lover, boyfriend, etc:
  □ She's threatened to leave him if he doesn't stop *running around*.

●●(●○) **run away (from)** escape from somewhere or from the control of somebody, especially of a child:

□ He hated his stepmother and eventually *ran away from* home.

●●●○ **run away with** **1** leave or escape from your home, husband, parents, etc, with somebody of the opposite sex:
□ Did you know that her daughter has *run away with* the greengrocer?
2 consume a great deal of something, especially fuel:
□ His new car just *runs away with* the petrol.
3 win a sports match or competition very easily:
□ Argentina *ran away with* the World Cup a few years ago.
4 become too strong and take control of somebody, especially of feelings, emotions, imagination, etc:
□ When he saw his dead son, his grief *ran away with* him and he shot himself.
5 steal something and escape with it:
□ He *ran away with* the firm's money.

●●●○ **run back over** review, repeat or discuss something again:
□ Let's *run back over* the events that led up to the outbreak of the Second World War.

●●(●○) **run behind (with)** fail to progress at the speed required
●●○ by a schedule, programme, timetable, etc:
□ The doctor missed lunch because he was *running behind with* his appointments.
□ Hurry up! We're *running behind* schedule.

●○● **run down¹** **1** knock something or somebody to the
●●○ ground, especially of a car, bus, driver, etc:
□ The train *ran down* several sheep on the track.
□ Mr Smith *ran* an old lady *down* in the High Street.
2 criticise or disparage somebody or something:
□ You shouldn't *run down* members of your own family.
□ She's always *running down* my work to the manager.
3 catch or find somebody or something after a chase or search:
□ The police eventually *ran down* the criminal on the moors.

●● **run down²** **1** lose or cause to lose power, strength, etc,
●●○ especially because of age, use, or neglect:
●○● □ The clock has *run down* again. Did you forget to wind it up?
□ If you leave the car lights on, they will quickly *run* the battery *down*.
2 decline; cause something to decline or become less active, especially of a factory, school, organisation, etc:
□ The local council is *running down* the Arts Centre over the next two years.

☐ The steelworks is slowly being *run down*.

●○●   **run in**   **1** prepare a new car engine for normal daily use by
●●○   driving carefully and slowly:
     ☐ Don't drive at more than 50 m.p.h. when you are
     running in a new car.
     2 *Informal* arrest somebody, especially of the police:
     ☐ That's the second time he's been *run in* for speeding.

●○●○   **run into¹**   crash a vehicle into something:
     ☐ Some crazy driver *ran* his car *into* the back of our taxi
     this morning.

●●○   **run into²**   **1** meet somebody unexpectedly or by chance:
     ☐ I *ran into* Mary in town this afternoon.
     2 crash into something, especially in the case of a car,
     bus, driver, etc:
     ☐ The taxi *ran into* the back of my new car.

●○●   **run off**   **1** print or make copies of a document, letter,
●●○   article, etc, on a photo-copier, duplicator or printing
     machine:
     ☐ When you've finished typing this letter, could you *run
     off* four copies for me, please?
     2 cause a liquid to flow or drain from a container:
     ☐ Before the beer is served, a few pints should be *run off*
     from the barrel.

●●(●○)   **run off (with)**   leave or escape from your home, husband,
     etc, with somebody of the opposite sex:
     ☐ His wife has *run off with* another man.

●●●○   **run off with**   steal something and escape with it; take
     something that isn't yours by mistake and leave with it:
     ☐ That silly girl has *run off with* my scissors.

●●   **run on**   **1** continue:
     ☐ The war could *run on* for another year yet.
     2 talk without pause:
     ☐ The old man *ran on* for hours about his childhood.

●●   **run out**   **1** be used, spent or consumed, especially of food,
     supplies, fuel, time, etc:
     ☐ Their food was *running out* fast so the climbers had to
     return.
     ☐ Hurry up! Time is *running out*.
     2 end, expire or cease to be valid, especially of a contract,
     lease, licence, etc:
     ☐ My employment contract *runs out* at the end of this
     month.

●●(●○)   **run out (of)**   have no more of something:
     ☐ The car *ran out of* petrol after ten miles.
     ☐ 'Have you got any eggs?'
     'Sorry. We've *run out*.'

●●   **run over¹**   overflow, especially of a container or its contents:

□ Turn off the tap! The bath is *running over*.

●●○
●○●   **run over²**   accidentally crash into and knock down a person or animal, especially of a vehicle or driver:

□ The car *ran over* a duck crossing the road.

□ Her little boy was *run over* on his way to school.

●●○   **run over/through**   say or read something again, especially notes, a speech, lines of a play, etc, for practice or as a check:

□ I must *run over* this speech before the meeting tonight.

●○●   **run through¹**   **1** review or give a summary of something:

□ I'll *run through* the main points of the news again.

2 rehearse:

□ OK. Let's *run through* the whole thing again.

N   □ This will be the final *run-through* before the performance.

3 spend money quickly and extravagantly:

□ She could *run through* a year's salary in a week if you let her.

●●○   **run through²**   stab or wound somebody with a sword, knife, bayonet, etc:

□ St George *ran* the dragon *through* with a golden spear.

●●○   **run to**   **1** afford something; usually used in the negative:

□ On my salary I can't *run to* a colour television.

2 extend to or reach a certain amount:

□ The book *runs to* 300 pages.

●●○   **run up¹**   **1** raise something, especially a flag or banner, by pulling on a rope:

□ They *ran up* a flag in honour of the president's visit.

2 incur a bill or debt, especially a big one:

□ He *ran up* a huge overdraft at the bank.

●○●
●●○   **run up²**   make something quickly, especially a piece of clothing:

□ Give me the material and I'll *run up* a dress in no time.

●●●○   **run up against**   encounter, meet or discover something, especially a difficulty, problem, obstacle, etc:

□ Everything was going well until we *ran up against* opposition from the Government.

●●○
●○●   **rush out**   produce, make or publish a large number of things in a very short time:

□ They *rushed out* half a million souvenir programmes for the Pope's visit to Britain.

●●○
●○●
●○●○   **rush through**   cause a proposal, order, document, etc, to be officially accepted, processed or dealt with as quickly as possible by a committee, parliament, etc:

☐ The Socialists want to *rush* this legislation *through* Parliament.

☐ The office *rushed through* his order and the goods were quickly delivered.

● ○ ●
● ● ○
rustle up   **1** make or produce something quickly when required, especially a meal:

☐ Can you *rustle up* something for dinner in half an hour?

2 search for and find somebody or something for a particular purpose or occasion:

☐ I'll *rustle up* a few more guests for the party tonight.

S, s

● ○ ● ○   **saddle with**   give somebody something they do not want, especially an extra responsibility:
□ He has *saddled* his wife *with* a house and five children to look after.

● ○ ●
● ● ○   **scale down**   decrease or reduce something in size, amount or scope, especially in proportion:
□ He thinks that the project is much too ambitious, and that the whole thing should be *scaled down*.

● ○ ●
● ● ○   **scale up**   increase or expand something, especially in proportion:
□ Taxes have been *scaled up* this year to keep pace with inflation.

● ● ○   **score off**   make yourself appear clever by making somebody else appear stupid:
□ She enjoys trying to *score off* other people.

● ○ ●
● ● ○   **score out**   draw a line through something, especially a mistake:
□ He *scored out* both calculations and did them again.

● ●(● ○)   **scout about/around (for)**   go and try to find something:
□ He *scouted around for* a shop that sold milk.

N   □ I've lost my glasses. Have a *scout-around* for them, will you?

● ●(● ○)   **scrabble about (for)**   try to find or recover something in a hurried or clumsy way:
□ She dropped the tickets on the floor and *scrabbled about for* them.

● ●(● ○)   **scrape along (on)**   manage to live on a small amount of money:
□ When he was a student, he *scraped along on* what he earned as a waiter in the holidays.

● ●(● ○)   **scrape by (on)**   manage to live through a difficult time with very little money; have just enough of something for your needs:
□ It won't be easy if you lose your job, but we'll *scrape by* somehow.

● ●/
● ● ○   **scrape in/into**   just manage to get into a school, college or profession, especially with the minimum entrance qualifications:
□ He just *scraped into* university, to the surprise of all his teachers.

162

●●   **scrape through**   pass a test or examination with the
●●○   lowest marks possible:
     □ She *scraped through* her English exam with fifty per
     cent.

●○●   **scrape together/up**   collect or save an amount with great
●●○   difficulty:
     □ Can we *scrape up* enough to buy a new car?

●○●○   **screw out of**   *Informal* obtain something, especially
     money, from somebody by using a lot of persuasion or
     pressure:
     □ He *screwed* ten pounds *out of* his grandmother, even
     though she could not really afford it.

●●○   **screw up**   *Informal* do something badly; make a mess of
●○●   something; used in a derogatory way:
     □ We couldn't go on holiday because he *screwed up* all
     the arrangements.

●●○   **see about**   give your time and attention to something that
     needs to be done:
     □ I've got to *see about* the car. It's been making a funny
     noise recently.

●○●   **see off**   **1** cause somebody or something to stop troubling
●●○   or attacking you and chase them away:
     □ Some boys were stealing my apples, but my dog soon
     saw them *off*.
     2 go to an airport, station, etc, to say goodbye to
     somebody:
     □ We *saw* them *off* at the airport.

●●○   **see out**   last until the end of something:
●○●   □ We have enough food to *see out* the winter.

●○●   **see through¹**   help somebody survive a difficult time or
●○●○   crisis:
     □ She was very upset when her husband died but her
     friends *saw* her *through*.

●○●   **see through²**   get to the end of something, especially a
     task of some kind:
     □ Before I leave, I would like to *see* the project *through*.

●●○   **see through³**   not be fooled by somebody or something:
     □ We easily *saw through* the man and his lies.

●●○   **see to**   give your time and attention to somebody or
     something:
     □ There is a lot to *see to* before you go on holiday.
     □ I'll cook the dinner if you *see to* Grandma.

●●○   **seize on/upon**   accept an idea or suggestion with
     eagerness:
     □ She *seized on* the chance of going to New York to
     work.

●●   **seize up** become stuck and stop working, especially of
       machinery:
       □ The car *seized up* on the motorway.

●●(●○) **sell out (to)** betray your principles or your friends,
       especially for money:
       □ He used to write serious novels but now he has *sold
       out* and writes thrillers.
       □ The workers' leaders *sold out to* their employers.

N   □ They were accused of a *sell-out* by their members.

●○●   **send down** expel a student from a university:
●●○   □ He was *sent down* for gross indecency.

●●○   **send out** emit something, especially a light or sound:
●○●   □ The lighthouse *sent out* a very bright light.

●●○   **send up** ridicule somebody or something, especially by
●○●   imitating them:
       □ At the end of the session, the students wrote a play in
       which they *sent up* their teachers.

N   □ They did a good *send-up* of their teachers.

●●○   **set about** **1** begin to do something:
       □ He *set about* his work as soon as he had finished his
       meal.
       2 attack somebody verbally or physically:
       □ If those boys steal any more of my fruit, I'll *set about*
       them with my spade.

●○●○   **set against** make somebody dislike a person:
       □ He *set* the children *against* their mother.

●○(●)●○ **set (off) against** balance one thing against another:
●(●)○●○ □ You can *set* the cost of a new car *against* the cost of
       repairing your old one.

●○●(●○) **set apart (from)** make somebody or something be or
       seem to be special or different from others:
       □ His intelligence *set* him *apart from* the other boys in
       his class.

●●○   **set aside** **1** dismiss or pay no attention to something:
●○●   □ My objections to the plan were *set aside* by the other
       members of the committee.
       2 cancel or reject something:
       □ The Appeal Court *set aside* the prisoner's sentence.
       3 keep something for a special purpose:
       □ She *set aside* five hours a week to learn French.

●●○   **set back**[1] delay or hinder the progress of something,
●○●   especially by a certain amount:
       □ The snow this winter *set back* the building of our new
       house by two months.

N
□ Our plans for moving received a *setback* when our buyer said he could not get a mortgage.

●○●
●○●○ **set back²** cost somebody an amount of money, especially a large amount:
□ Her new boots *set* her *back* seventy pounds.

●○●
●●○ **set down¹** let somebody out of a bus or other vehicle:
□ The driver will *set* you *down* just outside our house.

●○●
●●○ **set down²** write something down:
□ He was good at *setting* his thoughts *down* on paper.

●● **set forth/off/out** begin a journey:
□ We *set off* at nine o'clock and finally arrived at five.

●● **set in** begin and last for a long time, especially of an illness, bad weather, etc:
□ The snow *set in* in November and did not go until March.

●●○
●○● **set off** **1** cause somebody to start laughing, crying, talking, etc:
□ She had stopped crying but his shouting *set* her *off* again.
2 cause something explosive to explode:
□ Be careful that you don't *set* the fireworks *off* by mistake.
3 make something look very good, especially by providing a contrast to it:
□ That dress *sets off* her jewellery to perfection.

●● **set off** see **set forth/off/out.**
●○●○ **set off on** cause somebody to start telling stories, talking about favourite subjects, etc:
□ Don't mention Italy; you'll *set* him *off on* his holiday adventures again.

●○●○
●●○ **set on** attack or cause a person or animal to attack somebody or something:
□ He *set* his dog *on* the burglar.

●● **set out¹** **1** decide upon and work towards an objective or ambition; followed by *to* and an infinitive:
□ He *set out* to make a lot of money.
2 see **set forth/off/out.**

●●○
●○● **set out²** arrange or organise something clearly:
□ He *set out* all the pieces on the floor.
□ My plans for the firm have been *set out* in this document.

●● **set to** **1** begin something eagerly and with determination:
□ They *set to* and cleaned the whole house in two hours.
2 begin arguing or fighting:
□ The boys *set to* and the teacher could hardly separate them.

N
    □ We started talking quietly about the problem, but the discussion soon developed into a terrible *set-to*.

●○●
●●○
    set up¹   **1** establish a business, organisation, committee, etc:
    □ The Prime Minister *set up* an investigation into corruption in the police force.
    2 get something assembled or ready to use, especially a piece of apparatus:
    □ It took him three hours to *set* his new stereo *up*.
    3 help somebody to open a shop, start a business, etc, especially by providing the money required:
    □ His father *set* him *up* in a restaurant.

N
    □ He's got an excellent *set-up* there.

●○●
    set up²   **1** make somebody feel healthier, happier, etc:
    □ My holiday really *set* me *up* for the winter.
    2 claim that you or somebody is special in some way; followed by *as* or *to be*:
    □ He *sets* himself *up* as an expert in this field.

●●○
    set up³   **1** cause or produce something:
    □ The heavy rain *set up* dangerous conditions on the motorway.
    2 achieve or establish something:
    □ The French team *set up* a new record at tonight's meeting.

●●
    settle down   **1** get married and establish a home:
    □ You're thirty-five now; it's time you *settled down* like other people.
    2 give your whole attention to something:
    □ I really must *settle down* to my work this morning.

●●○
    settle for   accept something which is not as good as you hoped for:
    □ She wanted to be a lawyer but she had to *settle for* being a secretary.
    □ He is so keen to sell his houses that he is willing to *settle for* less than the asking price.

●○●○
    settle on   give money or property to somebody by signing a legal document:
    □ He *settled* £200 *on* each of his grandchildren.

●●○
    settle on/upon   agree or decide about something, often after a lot of argument or discussion:
    □ We finally *settled on* Greece for our holiday.

●●(●○)
    settle up (with)   pay a bill or debt:
    □ I asked for the bill and *settled up*.

☐ You paid for the theatre tickets and the meal. I'd better *settle up with* you now.

●●○ **settle with** take revenge on somebody:
☐ I'll *settle with* him one day for telling people I am a thief.

●●○ **sew up** complete, settle or finalise something:
●○● ☐ He was determined to *sew up* the deal before the meeting ended.

●●(●○) **shack up (with)** *Informal* live with somebody you are not married to:
☐ They *shacked up* just after leaving university.

●● **shake down** become used to a new place of work, way of living, etc:
☐ It took the team a few weeks to *shake down*.

●●○ **shake off** get rid of an unwanted companion, illness, bad
●○● habit, etc:
☐ Although he tried very hard, he could not *shake off* his assailants.
☐ It took him three months to *shake off* his illness.

●○●●○ **shake out of** make somebody change their behaviour or attitude by giving them a shock or surprise:
☐ He is so lazy. We must do something to *shake* him *out of* it.

●●○ **shake up** **1** make something, especially an institution or
●○● business, more efficient:
☐ I've a feeling that the new headmaster will soon *shake* the school *up*.
N ☐ There is to be a *shake-up* in the Government soon.
2 cause somebody to be more lively, alert, disciplined, etc, especially by scolding or threatening them:
☐ The warning at the bottom of her school report really *shook* her *up*.

●●○(●○) **shell out (for/on)** *Informal* spend money reluctantly,
●○●(●○) especially because you have to do it regularly:
●●(●○) ☐ I'm always being asked to *shell out for* my child's dancing lessons.
☐ It's not worth *shelling out* any more money *on* my car.

●●○ **shin up** climb up something, especially a wall, tree or rope:
☐ The boy *shinned up* the tree to rescue a cat.

●●○ **shoot down** criticise and dismiss an idea, suggestion,
●○● proposal, etc:
☐ The headmistress *shot down* my plan for making money for the school.

●●(●○) **shoot out (of)**   emerge or cause something to emerge
●○●(●○) quickly and suddenly from somewhere:
●●○ ☐ The snake *shot out* its tongue.
☐ The dog *shot out of* the house and ran away.

●● **shoot up 1** grow quickly, especially of children and plants:
☐ Mary *shot up* eight centimetres in one year.
2 increase rapidly or by a large amount:
☐ Prices have *shot up* in the last year.
☐ When he was ill, his temperature *shot up* to nearly
39°C.

●● **shop around**   compare the prices and quality of goods in
different shops before buying something:
☐ I need a new washing machine, but I'm going to *shop
around* first.

●●○ **shore up 1** support something, especially a house or wall,
●○● with lengths of wood or metal:
☐ They had to *shore up* the back of the church after it
had been damaged by fire.
2 strengthen or support something which is weak or in
danger of collapse, especially by means of economic
measures:
☐ The government took action to *shore up* the coal
industry.

●●○ **shout down**   make it difficult to hear somebody by
●○● shouting loudly:
☐ The crowd *shouted down* the speaker who approved of
nuclear weapons.

●● **shove off**   *Informal* go away: often used in the imperative:
☐ I'm busy, so *shove off* and leave me alone!

●● **show off¹**   try to impress people with your possessions or
abilities:
☐ Nobody's watching you, so there is no point in
showing off.
N ☐ She's an awful *show-off*. She loves it when people
admire her clothes.

●●○ **show off² 1** display somebody or something that you are
●○● proud of:
☐ He enjoys *showing off* his new car to people.
2 display something in a suitable or attractive way:
☐ The room is too small to *show off* the piano properly.

●● **show up¹**   become or cause something to become clearly
●○● visible:
●●○ ☐ The sun *shows up* the dirt on the windows.
☐ The scratches don't *show up* unless you look very
closely.

●●   **show up²** arrive, especially when you are late:
                ☐ We thought that you were never going to *show up*.

●○●   **show up³** embarrass somebody by behaving badly when
           they are present:
                ☐ My friend always *shows* me *up* by laughing too loudly
           in the theatre.

●○●(●○) **show up (as/for)** reveal the nature or character of
           somebody, especially as being unpleasant, dishonest, etc:
                ☐ His behaviour *showed* him *up for* a cheat.

●●○   **shrug off** dismiss something as not worth worrying
●○●   about:
                ☐ He finds it easy to *shrug off* criticism.
                ☐ You can't *shrug off* all your responsibilities onto other
           people.

●●○(●○) **shuffle off (onto)** try to rid yourself of responsibility for
●○●(●○) something by passing it onto somebody else:
                ☐ Although he had made the mistake himself, he tried to
           shuffle the blame *off onto* his son.

●●   **shut down** stop operating or cause something to stop
●●○   operating, either temporarily or permanently:
●○●   ☐ The factory *shuts down* for three weeks every summer.
                ☐ The business was losing so much money that the
           owner had to *shut* it *down*.
N   ☐ The *shut-down* in the steel industry lasted for two
           months.

●●○   **shut off** stop or cease to operate, especially of a gas
●○●   supply, electricity supply, etc, or an electrical or
           mechanical device; cause something to do this, especially
           by means of a switch:
                ☐ He always *shut off* his electricity and gas when he went
           on holiday.
                ☐ I've turned the key but the engine won't *shut off*.

●○●(●○) **shut off (from)** isolate yourself or cease to communicate
           with other people:
                ☐ She has threatened to *shut* herself *off from* the family.

●●   **shut up** *Informal* stop or cause somebody to stop talking
●○●   or making a noise; often used in the imperative to express
●●○   anger or irritation:
                ☐ Oh, *shut up*! I'm trying to work.
                ☐ He *shut up* when he realised nobody was listening to
           him.
                ☐ Can't you *shut* those noisy children *up*?

●○●(●○) **shut up (in)** keep somebody or something locked in a
●●○(●○) room, box, safe place, etc:

□ He *shut* the girl *up in* the house and refused to allow her to leave.

□ She kept her jewellery *shut up in* a safe.

●●●○ **shy away from** avoid something which you find unpleasant, difficult, etc:

□ She *shies away from* anybody touching her.

□ They *shied away from* buying a horse when they realised how much it would cost to keep it.

●●○ **sicken of** become tired of somebody or something:

□ She finally *sickened of* his behaviour and left him.

●●○ **side with** give support to somebody, especially in an argument or quarrel:

□ She always *sides with* her mother.

□ He was careful to *side with* the winning team.

●●(●○) **sidle up (to)** approach somebody in a way which is not intended to attract attention:

□ A man *sidled up to* me in the street and tried to sell me a watch.

●●○
●○● **sign away/over** formally give up rights, property, money, etc, by signing a document:

□ He *signed away* his share of the house to his daughter.

●● **sign in** record your arrival by writing your name and the time or date, especially at work or at a club:

□ He *signed in* at 8 am.

●○●
●●○/
●○●○ **sign in/into** put your signature against someone's name in order that they may enter a club, etc, with you, especially of a member:

□ If you'd like to come to Raffles with me one day, I'll *sign* you *in*.

●● **sign off¹** **1** mark the end of a radio programme or of broadcasting for the day, especially by playing a piece of music:

□ The announcer *signed off* by playing his signature tune.

2 end a letter:

□ I must *sign off* now. Love, Mary.

3 stop work for the day:

□ Because of the snow, we *signed off* at three o'clock.

●○●
●●○ **sign off²** sign a piece of paper to say that somebody is too ill to work, especially of a doctor:

□ The doctor *signed* me *off* for two weeks when I had influenza.

●●
●○●
●●○ **sign on¹** sign or cause somebody to sign an agreement to work for a company, join a team, etc:

□ He *signed on* for five years.

□ We've *signed on* a hundred machine operators.

●●   **sign on²** **1** register as unemployed at an office of the Department of Health and Social Security (in Britain):
□ When the steel works closed, a thousand men had to *sign on*.
2 begin a radio programme or broadcasting for the day, especially by playing a piece of music:
□ The BBC *signs on* at six o'clock every morning.

●●(●○)   **sign out (of)** record your departure, especially from work
●○●(●○) or a club, etc, by writing your name:
●●○   □ We *signed out of* college on Friday evening and returned on Monday morning.

●●○   **sign over** see **sign away/over**.
●○●

●●   **sign up** join or cause somebody to join a club, group,
●○●   class, etc:
●●○   □ The football team *signed up* three new players during the summer.
□ He *signed up* for a course in French at the local college.

●●   **silt up** become or cause something to become blocked or filled with mud, sand, soil, etc:
□ The mouth of the river has gradually *silted up* over the years.

●●   **simmer down** become calmer after being angry, excited, etc: often used in the imperative:
□ *Simmer down*, John! I can't talk to you when you are so angry.
□ I told him to *simmer down* or go away.

●●   **sing out** *Informal* call out loudly.
□ If you need anything, just *sing out* and I'll come.

●○●   **single out** select one person or thing from among many
●●○   for special treatment:
□ Why the critics *singled* me *out*, I'll never know. The whole cast was magnificent.

●●   **sink in** be absorbed, understood or acknowledged:
□ It took a long time for the bad news to *sink in*.
□ I think it has finally *sunk in* that she must be more careful: she won't forget her passport again!

●○●○   **sink in/into** put a lot of money into a business, property, deal, etc:
□ He *sank* all his savings *into* the firm.

●●○   **siphon off** take something, especially money, gradually
●○●   and illegally:
□ He *siphoned off* a lot of the club's savings for his own use.

●●   **sit about/around**   sit and do nothing, especially while other people are working:
         □ She *sat around* all day and watched me clean the house.

●●   **sit back**   relax and do nothing, especially when your help is needed or when you have been working hard:
         □ He's happy just to *sit back* and let others take the decisions.
         □ It's marvellous to be able to *sit back* after a hard day's work.

●●   **sit by**   observe but fail to act as needed:
         □ Even when his daughter was in trouble, he just *sat by* and did not help.

●●○   **sit for**   **1** take an examination:
         □ His teachers said he should *sit for* university.
         □ He *sat for* a scholarship and got one.
         2 be a member of parliament for a certain place:
         □ He has *sat for* Worcester for twenty years now.

●●   **sit in**   occupy a building or part of a building as a protest:
         □ The students have been *sitting in* for the last two weeks.

N   □ They organised a very successful *sit-in* at the factory and prevented it from being closed.

●●(●○)   **sit in (for)**   take somebody's place at a meeting or on a committee, etc:
         □ The chairman is ill, so I am *sitting in for* him this evening.

●●●○   **sit it on**   attend a meeting or a course without taking active part in it:
         □ The professor said I could *sit in on* his linguistics lectures.

●●○   **sit on**   **1** delay taking action on something:
         □ They have been *sitting on* my job application for weeks.
         2 serve as an official member of a committee, jury, etc:
         □ He has been *sitting on* the English committee ever since he came to university.
         3 quickly subdue somebody who behaves rudely or impertinently:
         □ Her brothers *sat on* her firmly whenever she was too noisy or silly.

●○●   **sit out**   **1** remain seated during a piece of dance music:
●●○   □ I'm too hot to dance. Let's *sit* this one *out*.
         2 stay until the end of a meeting, film, performance, etc, especially when you are not enjoying yourself:

□ I hated the play, but I *sat* it *out* to the very end.

●●○ **sit through**   stay in your seat while you attend, watch or listen to something, especially when you are not enjoying yourself:
□ We had to *sit through* the first half of the film without any sound.

●● **sit up**   **1** not go to bed:
□ I *sat up* until four o'clock waiting for you last night.
□ I'll be late tonight. Don't *sit up* for me.
2 become alert and pay attention to somebody or something:
□ You should have seen them all *sit up* as soon as I mentioned money.
□ Coming bottom of the class certainly made Jill *sit up* and think about her work.

●●○ **sit with**   nurse or attend somebody who is ill:
□ You go to bed for an hour. I'll *sit with* your mother while you are asleep.

●●○
●○● **size up**   form an opinion or judgement of somebody or something:
□ He *sized up* the situation and phoned the police immediately.
□ I have difficulty in *sizing* people *up*.

●●○ **skate over**   treat a problem or serious matter lightly:
□ He simply *skated over* the difficulties there would be if we moved to Singapore.

●● **skip off/out**   leave hurriedly and without attracting attention, especially to avoid something:
□ He *skipped off* quickly when the waiter brought us the bill.
□ She is always *skipping out* when there is washing-up to be done.

●○●
●●○ **slap down**   firmly prevent somebody from doing something:
□ He soon *slapped* her *down* when she wanted to speak.

●○●
●●○
●○●○ **slap on/onto**   add an amount to the price of something, especially in a way that seems unfair:
□ The builder *slapped* another £1000 *onto* the price of the house we had hoped to buy.

●● **sleep around**   *Informal* have sexual relations with a lot of different people:
□ She *slept around* a lot before she got married.

●● **sleep in**   **1** sleep in the place where you work:
□ They have two maids who *sleep in*.
2 sleep until later than usual:
□ I *slept in* and missed my bus.

●○●   **sleep off**   get rid of a bad feeling or emotion by sleeping:
●●○   □ He *slept off* the effects of all the drink he had at the
         party the previous night.

●●○   **sleep on**   have a night's sleep before making a decision
         about something:
         □ I can't decide what to do. I'll *sleep on* it and let you
         know tomorrow.

●●   **sleep out**   sleep away from the place where you work:
         □ They have a gardener who *sleeps out*.

●●   **sleep together**   have sexual relations:
         □ They've been *sleeping together* for a long time, but I
         don't think they're going to get married.

●●○   **sleep with**   have sexual relations with somebody:
         □ He has been *sleeping with* his girlfriend for two
         months.

●○●   **slick down**   make hair smooth and shiny by using oil,
●●○   water, etc:
         □ He *slicked down* his hair with haircream before he went
         to meet his girlfriend.

●○●   **slip in/into**   mention something in a conversation or
●●○/   discussion in a casual way:
●○●○   □ She *slipped* the news of her wedding *into* the
         conversation.

●○●   **slip on/into**   put on an item of clothing easily and quickly:
●●○/   □ She *slipped* her shoes *on*.
●●○   □ She *slipped into* her dress.

●●●○   **slip out of**   take off an item of clothing easily and quickly:
         □ She *slipped out of* her skirt.

●●(●○)   **slip up (over)**   make a mistake in something:
         □ They *slipped up* badly *over* the appointments for the
         new project.
N   □ There was a *slip-up* in the university administration.

●●○   **slobber over**   show too much love or affection for
         somebody; used in a derogatory way:
         □ I hate the way she *slobbers over* her children.

●●   **slop about/around**   move about lazily, doing nothing:
●●○   □ When my son is home from college, he just *slops about*
         the house and never does any work.

●●   **slope off**   go away secretly or unobtrusively, especially to
         avoid something:
         □ He's always *sloping off* when I want him to help clean
         the house.

●●○   **smack of**   have a slight trace or suggestion of something,
         especially something unpleasant:
         □ His opinions *smack of* disloyalty to his firm.

●●○   **smell of**   strongly suggest something rather unpleasant:
         □ Don't listen to him. His ideas *smell of* dishonesty.

●●○   **smell out**   discover something by noticing certain signs:
●○●   □ The teacher *smelt out* the culprit by the ink on his
         fingers.

●○●(●○)   **smoke out (of)**   force somebody out of hiding by using
●●○   smoke or clever tactics:
         □ The police *smoked* the gunman *out of* the house.

●●○   **smooth away**   get rid of difficulties or problems:
●○●   □ With a bit of effort, we will *smooth away* any problems
         we encounter.

●●○   **smooth over**   make problems, difficulties, etc, seem less
●○●   important; resolve an argument or conflict:
         □ He tried hard to *smooth over* the quarrel.

●●○   **snap at**   accept something eagerly:
         □ She *snapped at* the chance of going to America.

●●●○   **snap out of**   *Informal* make yourself stop feeling
     miserable, depressed, bad-tempered, etc; often used in the
     imperative:
         □ You're so miserable today! *Snap out of* it before I lose
         my temper with you.

●●○   **snap up**   take or buy something quickly and eagerly:
●○●   □ She *snapped up* a lot of bargains in the sales.
         □ If you don't marry me soon, I'll be *snapped up* by
         somebody else!

●●○   **snatch at**   try quickly and eagerly to seize or take
     advantage of something:
         □ She *snatched at* the chance of happiness she was being
         offered.

●●○   **sneeze at**   refuse to consider something seriously; usually
     used in the negative:
         □ Such a chance is not to be *sneezed at*.
         □ I wouldn't *sneeze at* the opportunity of working for
         such an interesting person.

●●○   **sniff at**   show contempt for something or consider
     something unworthy of attention; often used in the
     negative:
         □ His offer is certainly not to be *sniffed at*.
         □ You're silly to *sniff at* such a good opportunity.

●●○   **sniff out**   discover or detect something, especially a secret,
     criminal activity, etc:
         □ He tried to *sniff out* the reason for the unpleasant
         feelings between them.

●○●(●○)   **snow under (with)**   overwhelm somebody with a large amount of work or too many things to do; often used in the passive:

☐ I'm *snowed under with* work at the moment. I'm afraid I can't accept any more jobs.

☐ When we moved, we were *snowed under with* invitations to visit people.

● ● ○   **snuff out**   put an end to something:

☐ The Government quickly *snuffed out* the rebellion in the army.

● ○ ● ○   **soak in**   absorb as much of something as possible, especially by study; usually reflexive:

☐ For a whole year he *soaked* himself *in* the history of the Roman Empire.

● ● ○   **soak up**   absorb, learn or remember something:
● ○ ●

☐ I've never known a child who *soaked up* so much information.

● ●   **sober down**   become or cause somebody to become calm
● ○ ●   or quiet, especially after being excited or jolly:
● ● ○

☐ Come on, children! *Sober down* or you will never get to sleep!

● ●   **sober up**   **1** recover or cause somebody to recover from
● ○ ●   being drunk:
● ● ○

☐ He drank a lot of water to *sober* him *up* after the party.

2 become or cause somebody to become serious:

☐ He soon *sobered up* when he heard the awful news.

● ● ○   **soften up**   **1** weaken an enemy before a major attack:
● ○ ●

☐ Our aeroplanes bombed the enemy and *softened up* their defences before the army landed and attacked.

2 make it difficult for somebody to resist something, especially by using persuasion, seduction, etc:

☐ He sent her a huge box of chocolates to *soften* her *up* before he asked her to marry him.

● ●   **soldier on**   continue or persevere, in spite of difficulties:

☐ In spite of feeling ill, he *soldiered on* and finished the job.

● ○ ●   **sop up**   remove liquid by putting something absorbent in
● ● ○   it, especially a cloth:

☐ He has spilt his orange juice. *Sop* it *up* quickly with a towel.

● ● ○   **sort out**   **1** arrange things neatly or into groups:
● ○ ●

☐ The child was *sorting out* the bricks into different colours.

N   ☐ Your bedroom is very untidy. It could do with a good *sort-out*.

2 resolve an argument:

□ You will have to *sort out* your differences yourselves.

3 organise somebody or something:

□ He took just one month to *sort out* his new office and the secretarial staff.

□ She told him to *sort* himself *out* or she would leave him.

4 *Informal* attack somebody either verbally or physically:

□ If you don't stop fighting, I shall come and *sort* you *out*.

●●(●○)   **sound off (about)**   *Informal* talk loudly and pompously, especially when expressing opinions; used in a derogatory way:

□ He is always *sounding off about* how awful the Government is.

□ Do we have to listen to her *sounding off* again *about* her holiday?

●●○
●○●   **sound out**   try to discover somebody's opinions, feelings, or plans in a cautious and tactful way:

□ I'm not sure what he intends to do. Will you try to *sound* him *out*?

●●○
●○●   **soup up**   improve the performance of an engine, especially a car or motorcycle engine:

□ He asked the garage to *soup up* his bike.

●●○
●○●   **space out**   place things apart from one another:

□ Her family was well *spaced out*; she had three children in nine years.

□ He carefully *spaced out* his rows of peas in the garden.

●●○
●○●   **spark off**   **1** cause something to erupt or explode:

□ Just one match *sparked off* a terrible forest fire.

2 be the immediate cause of something violent or frightening:

□ The whole war was *sparked off* by a minor disagreement.

□ I have no idea what *sparked* their quarrel *off* this time.

●●○   **speak for**   **1** express thoughts and opinions on behalf of somebody:

□ I know I am *speaking for* everyone when I thank our hostess for a wonderful party.

□ Just be quiet a minute and let John *speak for* himself.

2 make a speech in support of something:

□ He was asked to *speak for* the motion that nuclear weapons should be abolished.

3 need no defence or justification; followed by *itself* or *themselves*:

☐ Our record on unemployment is so good that it *speaks for* itself.

4 book or reserve something; usually passive:

☐ All the rooms in the hotel have been *spoken for* by the organisers of the conference.

●●(●○)   **speak out against**   give your opinions about something bravely and freely:

☐ She *spoke out* strongly *against* cruelty to animals.

●●   **speak up**   **1** speak more loudly:

☐ Please *speak up* so that the people at the back of the room can hear you.

2 speak boldly about a subject:

☐ She *spoke up* in defence of her views on capital punishment.

●●   **speed up**   go faster or cause something to go faster:

●●○
●○●   ☐ You're driving very slowly. Do *speed up* a bit or we'll never get to Edinburgh.

☐ The new government has *speeded up* the building of new houses.

N   ☐ There has been a *speed-up* in the road building programme.

●●○
●○●   **spell out**   **1** read something very slowly and with difficulty:

☐ He is eight now, but he still has to *spell out* nearly everything he reads.

2 explain something in a very clear, simple way:

☐ He is so stupid. You have to *spell out* the most basic things to him.

☐ His speech *spelt out* the Government's plans for the army.

●●   **spew up**   *Informal* vomit:

●●○
●○●   ☐ The dog *spewed up* all over the kitchen floor.

●●   **spill over**   flow or spread beyond certain limits; used especially of people in urban areas:

☐ The housing estate *spilled over* into the very centre of the town.

N   ☐ They built a new town to house Birmingham's *overspill*.

●○●   **spin out**   make something last as long as possible:

●●○   ☐ That's all the money there is, so you'll just have to *spin* it *out* for the rest of the week.

☐ He *spun out* his story for twenty minutes.

●○●   **spirit away/off**   make somebody or something disappear

●●○   quickly or in a mysterious way; often used in the passive:

☐ The pop star was *spirited off* through the back door.

●●○
●○● **spit out**   say something angrily or sharply:
    □ He *spat out* an obscenity at the old man blocking his way.
    □ I'll never forget the way he *spat out* our names.

●○● **splash about/around**   spend money in an extravagant way; often used ironically:
    □ You won't have a penny left if you keep *splashing* your money *about* like that.

●● **splash down**   land in the sea, especially of a space vehicle which has returned to earth:
    □ The astronauts *splashed down* exactly on time.

N   □ It was a perfect *splash-down*.

●●(●○)
●●○(●○) **splash out (on)**   spend a lot of money on something that you want but do not need:
    □ She *splashed out* all her month's salary *on* a beautiful fur coat.
    □ Let's *splash out* this evening. How about going to that new French restaurant?

●●(●○) **split away/off (from)**   leave a group or organisation, especially in order to form a new one:
    □ Some of the members *split away from* the sports society and formed their own tennis club.

●●○ **split on**   *Informal* give information to somebody in authority which will get somebody else into trouble; usually used by children:
    □ Don't *split on* me if I don't go to school tomorrow. It's swimming and I hate it!

●● **split up**   cease to live or work together, especially of a married couple, family, group, etc:
    □ Did you know that John and Mary have *split up*?

●●○ **spring from**   1 appear suddenly from somewhere:
    □ He wasn't here a minute ago. Where on earth did he *spring from*?
    2 be the result or outcome of something:
    □ Her happiness *springs from* her love of her family.

●○●○ **spring on**   tell something to somebody so that they are surprised by it:
    □ She *sprang* the news *on* us without a warning.

●● **spring up**   suddenly appear, arise, or develop:
    □ New buildings are *springing up* all over the city.

●○●
●●○ **spruce up**   make yourself, somebody else or something clean and tidy:
    □ Go and *spruce* yourself *up*, Mary, before we go to the party.

□ She *spruced up* the children because their grandfather was coming.

●○●   **spur on**   encourage somebody to try harder:
●●○   □ Father *spurred* us *on* to do even better at school.
     □ The thought of winning the race *spurred* her *on*.

●●○   **spy on**   watch secretly what somebody else is doing:
     □ Our neighbours are always looking out of their windows, *spying on* us.

●●○   **spy out**   investigate an area, situation, etc, in a secret way, in order to get information about it:
     □ Go and see if you can *spy out* what the opposition is up to.

●●(●○)   **square up (with)**   pay somebody money that you owe them:
     □ Will you *square up with* the waiter while I go and get the car?
     □ If you tell me how much the meal was, we can *square up* later.

●●●○   **square up to**   **1** stand as if ready to fight somebody:
     □ The boys *squared up to* each other, but the teacher stopped them.
     2 acknowledge or accept misfortune in a courageous way:
     □ He *squared up to* the possibility of losing his job.

●●○   **squeal on**   inform the police or somebody in authority about something illegal, especially of a criminal:
     □ One member of the gang *squealed on* the others and they were arrested while robbing the bank.

●●○   **squeeze in**   find time to do something, see somebody, etc:
●○●   □ If I have a quick lunch, I might just manage to *squeeze in* a visit to the library.
     □ I know the professor is very busy, but could he possibly *squeeze* me *in*?

●○●(●○)   **squeeze out (of)**   obtain something from somebody by
●●○   applying pressure:
     □ The government hopes to *squeeze* even more money *out of* the public by raising taxes.

●●○   **stake off/out**   mark an area of land with tall pieces of
●○●   wood:
     □ He *staked off* the land where he was going to build his hut.

●○●○   **stake on**   bet or risk your money, reputation, life, etc, on something:
     □ He *staked* five pounds *on* the winning horse.
     □ I'll *stake* my life *on* his honesty.

●●○
●○●   **stake out**   see **stake off/out**   watch a place secretly, especially of the police:

☐ The police *staked out* the house where they thought the gunman was hiding.

●●○   **stamp on**   suppress something by acting decisively:

☐ We must *stamp on* any act of vandalism in the school.

●●○
●○●   **stamp out**   put an end to something by acting decisively:

☐ The Government quickly *stamped out* the rebellion.

☐ Many infectious diseases have been *stamped out* by the use of new drugs.

●●   **stand about/around**   stand doing nothing, especially because of laziness:

☐ Don't just *stand around*. Help me cut the grass.

●●   **stand aside**   move out of the way, especially to let somebody go past:

☐ The crowd were asked to *stand aside* to let the players go in.

●●(●○)   **stand back (from)**   **1** be situated some distance from something:

☐ The house *stands back from* the main road.

2 distance or detach yourself from something, especially to understand or appreciate it better:

☐ When he managed to *stand back from* his subject, the author realised he had misunderstood her motives.

●●○   **stand between**   be a barrier or difficulty between somebody and the thing that they want:

☐ Only one candidate *stood between* him and the job.

●●   **stand by¹**   **1** watch something and do nothing:

☐ He could not *stand by* and watch the child being beaten.

2 be ready for action, especially of the armed forces:

☐ The regiment is *standing by* to go to Northern Ireland.

N   ☐ The army is on permanent *stand-by*.

3 wait and be ready to act quickly:

☐ *Stand by* to receive a telephone call from India.

●●○   **stand by²**   **1** defend or loyally support somebody:

☐ He is the sort of person who will always *stand by* a friend.

☐ The football supporters *stood by* their team, even when they were losing.

2 be faithful to a promise, undertaking, agreement, etc:

☐ Even if I lose my job by complaining, I must *stand by* my principles.

☐ I *stand by* every word I said.

●●   **stand down**   **1** leave the witness box in a court of law:
    □ If there are no more questions, the witness may now
    stand down.
    2 withdraw from something, especially in favour of
    somebody else:
    □ He *stood down* as a candidate because he felt a younger
    man would be more suitable.

●●○   **stand for**   **1** tolerate or accept something; usually used in
    the negative:
    □ I will not *stand for* behaviour of that kind in my house.
    2 represent, mean or be a symbol or abbreviation for
    something:
    □ I hate the woman and everything she *stands for.*
    □ What does 'BBC' *stand for?*
    3 be a candidate for something:
    □ She is *standing for* Parliament in the next election.

●●(●○)   **stand in (for)**   take somebody's place or job for a short
    time, especially of an actor or actress:
    □ Paul's understudy is *standing in for* him just for
    tonight's performance.
    □ I'm *standing in for* the secretary while she is sick.

N   □ Her *stand-in* looks just like her.

●●○
●○●   **stand off**   dismiss workers, especially for a short time
    when there is no work to do:
    □ The management had to *stand off* a hundred men this
    week.

●●   **stand out**   be noticeable or special in some way:
    □ Two of the girls *stood out* as being exceptionally good
    dancers.
    □ She *stands out* from other detective-story writers.

●●●○   **stand out against**   be firm in your opposition to
    something:
    □ The soldiers *stood out against* the enemy for as long as
    they could.
    □ We must *stand out against* any evidence of racism in
    our country.

●●●○   **stand out for**   wait stubbornly for something that you
    have demanded to be given or allowed:
    □ The union *stood out for* another twenty pounds a week
    for each member.

●●○   **stand over**   watch somebody very carefully:
    □ He never does his homework unless I *stand over* him.

●○●   **stand up**   fail to keep an appointment with somebody:
●●○   □ She *stood* him *up* because she was too tired to go out.

●●(●○) **stand up (to)** **1** be accepted as true or be able to withstand an investigation:
    □ The charges against him will not *stand up* in court.
    □ His alibi *stood up to* all our questions.
    2 endure or withstand something:
    □ I could never *stand up to* another week like last week.
    □ Will the chair *stand up to* your weight?

●●○ **stand up for** defend somebody or something against attack:
    □ He has got to learn to *stand up for* himself when he goes to school.
    □ It is important to *stand up for* your rights as a mother.

●○●
●●○ **stare out** look fixedly at somebody until they look away, blink, become silent, etc:
    □ The two boys decided to see which one could *stare* the other *out*.

●● **start back** begin a return journey:
    □ What time do we have to *start back*?

●● **start off/out** begin a journey:
    □ We *started out* at 8 am and arrived at 6 pm.

●●(●○)
●○●(●○) **start off (on)** begin or cause somebody to begin doing something, especially talking in a way which other people find boring:
    □ Don't let him *start off on* his holiday stories again or we'll be here all night.

●●●○ **start out of** wake quickly and suddenly from sleep, a daydream, etc:
    □ He *started out of* his dream when he heard the telephone ring.

●● **start up** begin a career, business, working life, etc:
    □ He's thinking of *starting up* as a private consultant.
    □ She *started up* in dressmaking and then changed to typing.

●●○
●○● **starve out** force somebody to surrender or leave a hiding place by preventing food from reaching them, especially of an army or the police:
    □ It took just a week to *starve* the prisoners *out*.

●○●
●●○ **stash away** *Informal* hide or put something in a safe place:
    □ The old man *stashed* his money *away* in a box in his cellar.

●●○ **stave off** delay or prevent something from happening:
    □ He borrowed money from the bank to *stave off* bankruptcy.
    □ He ate a crust of bread to *stave off* his hunger.

●●   **stay behind**   remain after other people have left, especially for a particular purpose:
         □ He *stayed behind* when the shop shut to tidy the shelves.
         □ Would somebody *stay behind* after the meeting and put the chairs away?

●●   **stay down**   remain in the stomach, especially of food and drink:
         □ She kept being sick and nothing she ate would *stay down*.

●●   **stay in**   **1** remain at home:
         □ If you *stay in* for a few days, you'll soon feel better.
         2 remain in school after the other children have left, especially as a punishment:
         □ If you don't stop talking, you'll *stay in* for an hour after school.
         3 not be dismissed or defeated, especially of a batsman:
         □ He *stayed in* for two hours and scored seventy runs.

●●   **stay off**[1]   not go to work, school, etc:
●●○   □ I don't feel very well. I think I'll *stay off* tomorrow and have a day in bed.

●●○   **stay off**[2]   not eat, drink, smoke, etc, things which may be bad for you:
         □ You'll have to *stay off* beer if you really want to lose weight.

●●(●○)   **stay on (at)**   remain at school, college, work, etc, after other people have left:
         □ I'll *stay on* this evening and help you if you like.
         □ He is *staying on at* school for another year.

●●   **stay out**   **1** remain out of doors or away from home:
         □ She lets her children *stay out* until ten o'clock in the summer.
         2 remain on strike:
         □ The miners threatened to *stay out* all winter if their pay claim was not accepted.

●●   **stay up**   not go to bed:
         □ They *stayed up* until midnight watching television.

●●   **steal away**   leave quietly and often secretly:
         □ He *stole away* while everyone else was watching the film.

●●○   **steal over**   slowly and quietly take hold of somebody, especially of feelings, emotions, etc:
         □ A feeling of happiness *stole over* the girl when she thought about the days ahead.

●●●○ **steal up on** approach somebody slowly and quietly, especially in order to surprise them:
□ Her friend *stole up on* her and made her jump.

●● **steam up** cover or become covered with steam:
●●○ □ The car windows *steamed up* in the rain.
●○● □ The rain *steamed up* his glasses and he could hardly see.

●○●○ **steep in** make yourself thoroughly familiar with something:
□ He *steeped* himself *in* the traditions of the English countryside.

●●○ **stem from** be traceable to or caused by somebody or something:
□ Her interest in Italy *stems from* her uncle.
□ Their hatred of him *stemmed from* fear.

●● **step down** resign, especially from an important position:
□ The chairman announced that he would *step down* at the next meeting.

●● **step in** enter a discussion or argument:
□ I *stepped in* to prevent John from saying something stupid.
□ If the government does not *step in*, there will be no trains on Monday.

●● **step out** **1** start walking faster, especially by taking longer strides:
□ When he realised how late it was, he *stepped out* to get home before dark.
2 enjoy yourself socially:
□ She's really *stepping out* these days: the theatre last night, dinner tonight and dancing tomorrow.

●●○ **step up** increase something in size, number or speed:
●○● □ If we are to make all the cars we can sell, we must *step up* production this year by fifteen per cent.

●● **stick about/around** *Informal* remain, especially waiting for something to happen:
□ If you *stick around* long enough, he'll be sure to notice you.

●●○ **stick at** continue to work hard and steadily at something:
□ If you really *stick at* that essay, I'm sure you can finish it by Monday morning.

●●○ **stick by** continue to help and support somebody:
□ His wife *sticks by* him whatever he does.

●○● **stick down** *Informal* put something down on the floor, etc:

☐ Just *stick* those books *down* over there. I'll put them away later.

●● ●○● ●●○

stick out[1] protrude or make something protrude or project:

☐ Her teeth *stick out*.

☐ Don't *stick* your tongue *out* at me.

●●○ ●○●

stick out[2] *Informal* endure or tolerate something:

☐ Try to *stick out* the party for another hour and then we can go home.

●●●○

stick out for wait stubbornly for something that you have demanded to be allowed or given:

☐ The students *stuck out for* three seats on the University Senate.

☐ The union are *sticking out for* a twenty per cent increase.

●●○

stick to 1 keep a promise, not change a plan, decision, etc:

☐ I'll *stick to* my promise whatever happens.

☐ Now we've made a decision, let's *stick to* it.

2 concentrate on a particular point, subject, etc:

☐ I hate listening to him; he never *sticks to* the point.

☐ Why doesn't he *stick to* the subject of the lecture?

●●

stick together remain united, especially when threatened:

☐ If we all *stick together*, there won't be any trouble.

●●○ ●○●

stick up *Informal* rob somebody, a bank, etc, with the aid of a gun:

☐ If you are so desperate for money, you could always *stick up* the post office.

N

☐ 'This is a *stick-up*! You've got two minutes to empty the safe!'

●●●○

stick up for speak or act in defence of somebody or something:

☐ You have got to *stick up for* your rights.

☐ My mother always *sticks up for* me against my brother.

●●○

stick with stay close or loyal to somebody or something:

☐ If you *stick with us*, you will come to no harm.

☐ He *stuck with* the Labour party all his life.

●●○ ●○●

stir up cause or encourage trouble, hatred, bad feelings, etc; make somebody angry or agitated:

☐ Please don't *stir up* trouble between them.

☐ I think she enjoys *stirring* him *up* now and then.

●●(●○)

stock up (with) store a large amount of supplies, especially for a particular purpose or occasion:

☐ She *stocked up with* food and drink for the Christmas party.

●●(●○)   **stoke up (with)**   **1** put fuel on a fire:
●○●(●○)   □ Don't forget to *stoke up* before you go to bed.
●●○   **2** *Informal* fill yourself with a great deal of food:
          □ She *stoked up with* chocolates as if she would never eat
          again.

●●○   **stoop to**   lower your standard of behaviour; often
          followed by *-ing*:
          □ He even *stooped to* stealing money from his own
          children.
          □ He would *stoop to* anything to get what he wanted.

●●○   **stop at**   stay in a hotel, etc:
          □ For two days we *stopped at* a lovely little inn in the
          mountains.

●●(●○)   **stop away (from)**   be absent from something:
          □ Why did you *stop away from* the meeting? We expected
          to see you there.

●●   **stop behind**   remain after other people have left, especially
          for a particular purpose:
          □ He *stopped behind* to ask the speaker some questions.

●●(●○)   **stop by (at)**   visit or stop somewhere for a short time,
●●○   especially on your way to somewhere else:
          □ We were passing your house, so we thought we would
          stop by for a few minutes.

●●○   **stop for/to**   stay somewhere to share a meal, etc:
          □ You will *stop to* dinner, won't you?

●●   **stop in**   **1** stay at home:
          □ I'm *stopping in* tonight to wash my hair.
          2 remain at school late as a punishment:
          □ If there is any more trouble, you will all *stop in* for two
          hours.

●●   **stop off**   interrupt a journey, especially to visit friends,
          shop, rest, etc:
          □ They *stopped off* for a meal.
          □ We'll *stop off* at Oxford and see them on our way to
          London.

●●(●○)   **stop on (at)**   remain at school, college, etc, especially after
          other people have left:
          □ She *stopped on at* school until she was nineteen.

●●   **stop out**   **1** remain out of doors or away from home:
          □ She *stopped out* until one o'clock and her father was
          furious.
          2 remain on strike:
          □ The workers decided to *stop out* until their conditions
          of work were improved.

●●	**stop over** interrupt a journey by air for a short time and then continue it:
	□ He *stopped over* in Paris for a day.
N	□ They decided on Brussels for their *stop-over*.
●●○	**stop to** see **stop for/to**.
●●	**stop up** not go to bed:
	□ We shall be home late, so please do not *stop up* for us.
●●/	**storm in/into** enter a room or building noisily and often
●●○	angrily:
	□ He *stormed into* the manager's office, shouting and swearing.
●●	**stow away** hide secretly on a ship or plane in order to travel on it free:
	□ He *stowed away* on a ship going to New York.
N	□ There was a *stowaway* on the ship.
●○●	**straighten out** **1** resolve a problem or difficulty:
●●○	□ My daughter was having problems at school but we soon managed to *straighten* them *out*.
	2 cause somebody to stop being confused, anxious, critical, etc:
	□ He doesn't seem to understand what I'm trying to do. Perhaps if you talked to him you could *straighten* him *out*.
●●○	**strain at** pull hard on something, especially a rope:
	□ The sailors *strained at* the rope, but couldn't lift the anchor.
●○●	**strain off** remove liquid from something by using a sieve,
●○●○	etc:
●●○	□ She *strained* the water *off* the beans and put them on the table.
●○●	**strap in** fasten a seat-belt, especially in a car or plane:
●●○	□ Don't forget to *strap* yourself *in*.
	□ The plane will not take off until everybody is *strapped in*.
●○●	**strap up** fasten something with straps, bandages, etc:
●●○	□ Your ankle is swollen. You'd better *strap* it *up*.
	□ They *strapped up* their luggage and took it downstairs.
●●	**stretch out** **1** extend your body or part of it, especially to
●●○	relax, take something, or greet somebody:
●○●	□ He *stretched out* on the grass in the sunshine.
	□ She *stretched out* her hand and took the ice cream.
	2 be enough or cause something to be enough:
	□ You should have phoned me. I don't think I can *stretch out* the food to feed three more people.

●●○   **strike at**   try to hit somebody or something:
        □ She *struck at* him with a hammer.
        □ This *strikes at* the very heart of democracy.

●○●   **strike down**   make somebody unable to lead a full, active
●●○   life:
        □ He was *struck down* by a heart attack at the age of
        forty.

●○●○   **strike into**   penetrate or cause something to penetrate,
●●○   especially of fear, cold, etc:
        □ The headmaster *struck* terror *into* the new teacher by
        telling her about his pupils.
        □ Her cold words *struck into* his heart.

●○●   **strike off¹**   remove something, especially a name from a
●○●○   list; end somebody's membership of a professional group:
●●○   □ The doctor was *struck off* for prescribing illegal drugs.
        □ He was *struck off* the register.

●●○   **strike off²**   print copies of something:
        □ They *struck off* 5000 copies of the election leaflet.

●●○   **strike on/upon**   discover something suddenly and
        unexpectedly:
        □ He *struck on* a way of making diamonds.

●●   **strike out**   start to do something new and different,
        especially on your own:
        □ He decided to leave his father's firm and *strike out* on
        his own.

●●   **strike out/through**   remove or draw a line through a piece
        of writing:
        □ She *struck out* the sentence she had just written and
        added a new one.

●●(●○)   **strike out (at)**   try to hit somebody in a wild or
        uncontrolled way:
        □ The little boy was frightened and *struck out* madly.

●●(●○)   **strike out (for/towards)**   move quickly in a certain
        direction, especially by swimming:
        □ He dived off the boat and *struck out for* the island.

●●   **strike up**   begin playing a piece of music or singing a song:
●●○   □ The orchestra *struck up* the National Anthem.
        □ People won't get up to dance until the band *strikes up*.

●●○(●○)   **strike up (with)**   begin a friendship with somebody,
        especially in a casual, unplanned way:
        □ They *struck up* an acquaintance *with* each other on the
        beach and soon became very friendly.

●●○   **strike upon**   see **strike on/upon**.

●○●   **string along**   deceive somebody, especially by giving them
        false hopes:

☐ She's been engaged to Jim for five years, but she'll never marry him. She's just *stringing* him *along*.

●●(●○) **string along (with)** *Informal* accompany or be friendly with somebody, especially for as long as it suits you:
☐ We're going to John's party too. You can *string along with* us if you like.

●●
●●○
●○● **string out** be spread or spread something at intervals in a line:
☐ The police *strung out* across the field looking for clues.
☐ She was *stringing out* the clothes on the washing line when it started to rain.

●○●
●●○ **string together** combine words, sentences, etc, in a meaningful way:
☐ He says he can speak fluent German but I have never heard him *string* more than three words *together*.

●●○
●○● **string up** **1** hang something high, especially as a decoration:
☐ They *strung up* pretty lights all over the room.
2 *Informal* kill somebody by hanging:
☐ They *strung up* the captured terrorist for everybody to see.

●●○
●○● **strip down** take something to pieces, especially an engine, machine, etc:
☐ He is never happier than when he is *stripping down* the car.

●● **strip down/off** take your clothes off:
☐ She *stripped off* and went for a swim.

●○●○ **strip of** take something valuable from somebody:
☐ The convicted spy was *stripped of* all his public honours.

●●○
●○● **stub out** stop a cigarette burning by pressing it against something hard:
☐ He *stubbed out* his cigarette in the ash-tray.

●●○ **stumble across/on/upon** discover or meet somebody or something unexpectedly:
☐ They *stumbled across* the entrance to an old tunnel.
☐ Coming out of the airport, he *stumbled on* an old friend.

●●○ **stumble over** hesitate and make mistakes when you are speaking or reading:
☐ The little girl *stumbled over* nearly every word until the teacher told her to stop reading.

●○●○ **subject to** **1** bring a country or person under your control, especially by the use of force:
☐ The Romans never succeeded in *subjecting* the Scots *to* their rule.

2 make something have to undergo a test, treatment, etc:
- ☐ All cars are *subjected to* various tests before they leave the factory.

3 expose somebody to something, especially to something unpleasant:
- ☐ The audience *subjected* the speaker *to* a lot of difficult questions.

●●○ **subscribe to** **1** agree with something that is said or done:
- ☐ I could never *subscribe to* torture, no matter what the reason.

2 pay regularly in order to receive a newspaper, magazine, etc:
- ☐ Many teachers *subscribe to* that periodical.

●○●○ **subsume under** *Formal* place something in a particular group or class; usually used in the passive:
- ☐ Sugar, tea and coffee can be *subsumed under* the heading 'groceries'.

●○● **suck down/under** pull somebody or something below the surface of a liquid or something similar to liquid:
- ☐ He was *sucked under* by the river's strong current.

●●(●○) **suck up (to)** try to make somebody like you, especially by using flattery:
- ☐ She is always *sucking up to* her teachers but they do not like her for it.

●○●○ **suit to** choose or adjust something so that it is appropriate for a particular situation or purpose:
- ☐ It is important to *suit* the punishment *to* the crime.

●●
●●○
●○● **sum up¹** **1** summarise or give the main points of an argument, lecture, etc:
- ☐ The chairman *summed up* the speaker's talk and asked for questions.
- ☐ To *sum up*, for the reasons I have just given, I think my plan is better.

N
- ☐ He was congratulated on his excellent *summing-up*.

2 summarise and comment on the main points of a legal case:
- ☐ The judge *summed up* for twenty minutes.

N
- ☐ His *summing-up* lasted twenty minutes.

●○●
●●○ **sum up²** form a judgement or opinion of somebody or something:
- ☐ She *summed* the man *up* as incompetent.
- ☐ He could *sum up* situations at a glance.

●●○ **summon up** gather the necessary courage, strength, patience, etc, to do something:
- ☐ He had to *summon up* all his courage before he dared enter the room.

☐ He found it impossible to *summon up* enough strength to finish the marathon.

● ● ○
● ○ ●
suss out *Informal* discover or find out something, often in a secret way:
☐ I'm not sure how she will vote. See if you can *suss* her *out.*

● ● ○
● ○ ●
swallow up consume or absorb something quickly, especially money or natural resources:
☐ New clothes for the children seem to *swallow up* all her money.
☐ My new car *swallows up* petrol.

● ○ ● ○
swamp with overwhelm somebody with a great amount or excess of something:
☐ They were *swamped with* replies to their advertisement.

● ● ○
swarm with be full of or crowded with people, animals, etc:
☐ The whole town is *swarming with* tourists during July.

● ○ ● ○
swathe in wrap something or somebody tightly in a cloth, bandage, etc:
☐ He came out of hospital *swathed in* bandages from head to foot.

● ● ○
swear by praise or recommend something, especially as an aid to health:
☐ She *swears by* aspirin as the best remedy for a headache.

● ○ ●
● ● ○
swear in make somebody take an oath to be truthful, loyal, obedient, etc:
☐ They will *swear* the jury *in* for the murder trial this morning.
☐ The new president was *sworn in* last week.

N
☐ The whole senate was present for the *swearing-in* of the president.

● ● ○
swear to say that you are certain of something; often used with *can/could, will/would* and a negative:
☐ I can't *swear to* it, but I don't think he would lie to me.
☐ I am prepared to *swear to* his honesty.

● ● ○
● ○ ●
sweat out get rid of an illness by sweating:
☐ He went to bed with a hot-water bottle and *sweated out* his cold.

● ● ○
● ○ ●
sweep aside dismiss comments or objections:
☐ He *swept aside* all criticism and continued to explain his plan.

● ● ○
● ○ ●
sweep away abolish or get rid of something:
☐ The government promised to *sweep away* all tax privileges.

●●○ **swill down** drink something rapidly in large quantities:
●○● □ He *swilled down* six whiskies in half an hour.
●○● **swill out** wash or rinse something with a lot of water:
●●○ □ She *swilled* the saucepan *out* with plenty of clean
water.
●○●●○ **swindle out of** get money from somebody by cheating
them:
□ He *swindled* the old lady *out of* fifty pounds.
□ He *swindled* fifty pounds *out of* the old lady.
●● **swing round** turn round quickly:
□ He *swung round* to see who had pushed him.
●● **swing to** close or almost close, especially of a door, gate,
etc:
□ The gate *swung to* with a bang.
●●○ **switch off¹** stop the flow of light, water, gas, electricity,
●○● etc, by moving a switch:
□ Don't forget to *switch off* the electricity before you go
away.
●● **switch off²** stop listening, responding or being attentive:
□ Whenever Bill starts talking, Jim simply *switches off*.
●●○ **switch on** 1 start the flow of water, light, gas, electricity,
●○● etc, by moving a switch:
□ She *switched on* all the lights to make the house seem
welcoming.
2 *Informal* make somebody become lively, excited or
responsive:
□ Parties really *switch* her *on*: she becomes a completely
different person.
●● **swot up** learn something thoroughly, usually for a test or
●●○ examination, by a short period of intensive study:
●○● □ He *swotted up* his history the night before the exam.

T, t

●○●   **tack on/onto**   add or join something to the end of
●●○/   something else:
●○●○   □ He *tacked on* another paragraph at the end of the
letter.
□ The publisher *tacked* some notes *onto* the book before
it was printed.

●●(●○)   **tag along (with)**   accompany somebody somewhere,
especially because you have no other plans:
□ We're going to the pub. Do you want to *tag along*?
□ I had nothing better to do, so I *tagged along with* the
others.

●●   **tail away/off**   fade or become gradually quieter until the
sound stops, especially of a voice, music, sound, etc:
□ Their voices *tailed away* down the corridor.

●●   **tail off**   gradually decrease in quantity, especially of trade
or business:
□ Demand for new cars has *tailed off* since the fuel crisis.

●○●   **take aback**   surprise, astonish or shock somebody; usually
preceded by *completely*, *somewhat*, *rather*, etc:
□ I was rather *taken aback* by her rudeness.
□ The violent reaction of the crowd quite *took* him
aback.

●●○   **take after**   be similar to a parent or other relation in
character, appearance or behaviour:
□ He's a very solemn boy. He *takes after* his mother in
that respect.

●○●   **take apart**   **1** criticise somebody or something severely:
□ When the play was first shown the critics *took* it *apart*.
2 defeat somebody easily, especially a team, army,
opposition, etc:
□ United defended well for the first twenty minutes, but
after the first goal City began to *take* them *apart*.

●●○(●○)   **take away (from)**   subtract one number from another:
●○●(●○)   □ Five *take away* three equals two.
□ If you *take* £5 *away from* the total, you're left with
£10.

●●○   **take back**   admit that something you said was wrong or
●○●   that you should not have said it:
□ I was very unfair to you just now. I'm sorry. I *take* it
all *back*.

●○●(●○)　**take back (to)**　cause somebody to remember something
which happened much earlier in their life:
□ Hearing that song *takes* me *back* a few years.
□ The old photograph *took* him *back to* his days at
school.

●○●　　　**take down**　**1** write down or make notes on what
●●○　　　somebody is saying, especially of a secretary, student, etc:
□ The clerk will *take down* the details of the accident.
□ The students were *taking down* notes on the lecture.
2 dismantle or remove something:
□ At the end of the week we have to *take* the fireplace
down.

●○●○　　　**take for**　**1** judge somebody's character in a particular way,
usually incorrectly:
□ I *took* him *for* a fool, but I was wrong.
□ I won't hurt you. What do you *take* me *for* ?
2 assume or believe wrongly that somebody or something
is somebody or something else:
□ I'm sorry. I *took* you *for* the secretary.

●○●　　　**take in¹**　**1** alter an item of clothing to make it smaller:
●●○　　　□ The trousers are slightly too big but I can *take* them *in*.
2 understand and absorb something:
□ She warned him about the danger but he didn't *take* it
in.
3 fool, deceive or cheat somebody:
□ I hope you weren't *taken in* by the advertisement.

●●○　　　**take in²**　**1** include something:
□ The UK *takes in* Scotland, Wales and Northern
Ireland.
2 undertake work, especially washing, laundry, sewing,
etc:
□ She *takes in* laundry to earn a bit of extra money.
3 provide accommodation or food for somebody:
□ He *took in* one or two down-and-outs as a sign of his
generosity.

●○●　　　**take off¹**　**1** imitate or copy the speech or appearance of
●●○　　　somebody, especially in order to make people laugh:
□ It's very funny when Giles *takes off* the headmaster.
2 remove something from service, especially a bus or
train:
□ The London–Edinburgh express service has been *taken
off*.

●○●　　　**take off²**　**1** remove somebody from a job or task:
●○●○　　　□ Because he is so inefficient, we have *taken* Mr Jones *off*
the job.

2 remove a particular item from a menu in a restaurant:
☐ 'Duck à l'orange' has been *taken off* tonight.
3 have a holiday or period of time away from work, school or college:
☐ When I broke my leg I had to *take* three weeks *off*
☐ When I was ill I had to *take* time *off*.

●● **take off³ 1** rise up from the ground into the air, especially of an aeroplane or space-rocket:
☐ The plane is scheduled to *take off* at 17.30.

N ☐ The astronauts were getting ready for *take-off*.
2 become very successful or popular:
☐ Despite a few early difficulties, the idea really *took off*.
3 increase very quickly, especially of sales, profits, etc:
☐ In the last few years, sales of microcomputers have really *taken off* in a big way.

●●○ **take on¹ 1** employ or give a job to somebody:
●○● ☐ The steelworks *took on* 300 extra workers last month.
2 have a fight or quarrel with somebody; accept somebody as an opponent:
☐ He said he would *take on* anybody who stood in his way.
3 accept a job or responsibility:
☐ Her health has begun to suffer since she *took on* the extra work.

●●○ **take on²** acquire or be seen to have a new or different quality, meaning, appearance, etc:
☐ The novel *takes on* a new meaning when you know more about the author.

●●○ **take out¹** obtain or pay a fee for an official document or a
●○● service, especially an insurance policy, subscription, legal summons, etc:
☐ I'd like to *take out* a subscription to 'The Times'.

●○● **take out²** take somebody somewhere for recreation, pleasure or exercise:
☐ Let me *take* you *out* to a night club on Saturday. You'll enjoy it.

●○●●○ **take out on** get rid of an unpleasant feeling such as anger or frustration by making somebody else suffer:
☐ You may have had a difficult day at the office, but there's no need to *take* your anger *out on* me now you're home!

●●○ **take over** get control of something, especially of one
●○● company getting financial control of another:
☐ The state airline has *taken over* two small airline companies this year.

N

●●(●○)
●○●(●○)
●●○(●○)

□ The *take-over* is worth many millions of pounds.

take over (from)   take responsibility for or control of something from somebody else:

□ Dave *took over* the driving while his mate slept for a few hours.

□ I'm retiring at the end of this year. Mr Clark will *take over from* me.

●●○

take to   **1** quickly develop a liking for somebody or something:

□ He *took to* Sally from the moment he met her.

2 begin to do something regularly or as a habit:

□ I've *taken to* playing tennis once a week.

3 go away somewhere, especially to escape or hide from somebody or something:

□ The criminal *took to* the hills when she heard that a police hunt had begun.

●●○

take up¹   start doing some activity regularly, especially a job, sport, hobby, etc:

□ I *took up* squash only a few months ago.

●○●
●●○

take up²   **1** occupy or fill time, space, room, etc:

□ Move over! You're *taking up* far too much room. John can't sit down.

2 shorten a dress, skirt, curtains, etc:

□ Anyone who can sew can *take up* a skirt.

3 become soaked with a liquid:

□ A paper tissue will soon *take up* that spilt coffee.

4 accept or agree to do something, especially an invitation, offer, challenge, etc:

□ I had an invitation to the dinner, but I didn't *take* it *up*.

5 resume or return to something:

□ I *took up* the story where Helen had left off.

●○●(●○)

take up (on)   argue with somebody about something they have said:

□ The lecturer was talking excitedly until someone *took* him *up on* one of his wilder observations.

●●○(●○)
●○●(●○)

take up (with)   raise an issue, matter, complaint, etc, for discussion with somebody:

□ If you have any complaints, *take* them *up with* the manager.

●○●●○

take up on   accept somebody's offer, challenge, invitation, etc:

□ If he has said that he will pay for you, why not *take* him *up on* his offer?

●●●○   **take up with**   become friendly with somebody and be frequently in their company:
□ She has *taken up with* an unpleasant fellow she met in London.

●○●   **talk down**   **1** make it difficult to hear somebody by talking loudly:
□ The objectors *talked* the speaker *down*.
2 give instructions to a pilot to guide the landing of an aircraft:
□ The control tower *talked* the plane *down*.

●●(●○)   **talk down (to)**   speak to somebody in a way that makes them feel less intelligent or of a lower social position than yourself:
□ He's so arrogant: he is always *talking down to* people.

●○●○   **talk into**   persuade somebody to do something:
□ The salesman *talked* the customer *into* buying a new suit.

●○●●○   **talk out of**   persuade somebody not to do something:
□ Her friends *talked* her *out of* getting married.

●○●
 ●●○   **talk over**   discuss something, especially a problem, in a relaxed and informal way:
□ When we've got time, we must *talk* the whole thing *over*.

●○●   **talk round**   persuade somebody to agree to something, especially despite their reluctance:
□ He said he wasn't interested in helping out, but I'll try to *talk* him *round*.

●●
 ●○●
 ●●○   **taper off**   gradually decrease or cause something to decrease in size, number or intensity:
□ The stick *tapered off* to a point.
□ Sales of new cars have been *tapering off* since October.

●●○
 ●○●   **tart up**   *Informal* try to make somebody or something look attractive or smart; used in a derogatory way:
□ She always *tarts* herself *up* before she goes out in the evening.
□ The house had obviously been *tarted up* before it was offered for sale.

●●(●○)   **team up (with)**   start working with somebody as a team:
□ John and Susan *teamed up* to produce a book.

●●○   **tear into**   attack somebody or something violently, either physically or verbally:
□ The teacher *tore into* the poor girl for being late for class.

●○●
 ●●○   **tell off**   scold or reprimand somebody:
□ The little boy's mother *told* him *off* for being naughty.

●●○   **tell on**   **1** have a bad effect on somebody's health or appearance:
□ These late nights are beginning to *tell on* me.
2 reveal a secret about somebody to somebody else:
□ Don't *tell on* me when Dad comes in!

●●   **thaw out**   become or cause something to become
●○●   unfrozen:
●●○   □ You must leave the chicken to *thaw out* completely before cooking it.

●●   **thin out**   become or cause something to become less dense,
●●○   packed or crowded:
●○●   □ The crowds in town *thin out* when the shops close.
□ A good gardener will *thin out* the plants regularly.

●○●   **think out/through**   consider or think carefully about
●●○   something:
□ I can't make a decision until I've *thought* the matter *out*.

●○●   **think over**   take time to consider something carefully:
●●○   □ You've got a few weeks to *think* the matter *over*.

●●○   **think up**   invent or produce a new idea, plan, scheme, etc:
●○●   □ The manager *thought up* a scheme to increase sales while reducing the number of staff.

●○●   **thrash out**   **1** solve a problem by intense discussion and
●●○   argument:
□ The management and union leaders *thrashed out* their disagreement.
2 produce a plan, agreement, document, etc, by intense discussion:
□ The committee *thrashed out* a proposal for a new children's hospital.

●○●   **throw about/around**   be very generous or wasteful with something, especially money:
□ Since John was promoted, he's been *throwing* his money *about*.

●○●   **throw away**   **1** discard, reject or waste something, often
●●○   foolishly or thoughtlessly:
□ You had a marvellous opportunity and you *threw* it *away*.
2 speak words casually or carelessly:
□ You *threw away* the last line and nobody could hear what you said.

●○●   **throw back**   delay the progress of something:
●●○   □ The fire has *thrown* production *back* badly.
●○●○   **throw back at**   remind somebody of something they have done wrong in the past:

199

☐ Whenever he tried to get a job, his time in prison was *thrown back at* him.

● ○ ● ● ○   **throw back on** force somebody to depend more on something:

☐ The failure of all her plans *threw* her *back on* her own resources.

● ○ ●
● ● ○   **throw in** **1** include something extra, usually unexpectedly, in the price of something else:

☐ The car is only £10,000 and I'll *throw in* delivery and a year's road tax.

☐ It was £10 for the coach trip, with a free meal *thrown in*.

2 add a comment, suggestion, remark, etc, to a conversation or discussion:

☐ Can I just *throw in* a few ideas on what's been said so far?

3 resign from a job or abandon a course, project, etc:

☐ He *threw in* the job after only two weeks.

● ○ ● ○   **throw into** involve yourself enthusiastically in a job or task:

☐ The team really *threw* themselves *into* the project, and it was soon finished.

● ● ○
● ○ ●   **throw off¹** **1** escape from somebody who is following you:

☐ The two men *threw off* their pursuers after a dangerous car chase.

2 reject or get rid of something, especially something unpleasant:

☐ He's had a heavy cold for weeks but at last he's beginning to *throw* it *off*.

● ● ○
● ○ ●
● ○ ● ○   **throw off²** upset or disconcert somebody; disturb somebody's work or routine:

☐ The loud noise *threw off* my concentration.

☐ The sudden disturbance *threw* me *off* just as I saw the answer.

● ○ ●
● ● ○   **throw out¹** **1** reject or discard something:

☐ I *threw out* a lot of old junk from the garage.

☐ The committee *threw out* the Finance Officer's proposals.

2 cause figures, results, calculations, etc, to be inaccurate or wrong:

☐ Errors in the computer have *thrown out* the inflation figures for this month.

3 spoil or disrupt something:

☐ The arrangements were *thrown out* by the bad weather.

4 be a source of light, heat, etc:
   ☐ This radiator *throws out* a good heat.

●○●   **throw out²**   upset or disturb somebody or their work or routine:
   ☐ I'd like to bring the family to see you on Sunday, as long as it doesn't *throw* you *out* too much.

●●○   **throw out³**   say or write something, especially a suggestion, idea, plan, etc, in a casual way:
   ☐ Tom wasn't serious. He was just *throwing out* a few suggestions for discussion.

●○●(●○) ●●○   **throw out (of)**   **1** dismiss or expel somebody from a company, school, club, etc, especially because of bad work or behaviour:
   ☐ He was *thrown out of* the school for bullying.
   ☐ The team lost every match until they *threw* Jim *out*.
2 make somebody leave a room, bar, restaurant, etc, especially by using physical force:
   ☐ His teacher *threw* him *out* for talking.

●○● ●●○   **throw together¹**   produce or construct something in a rush or without care:
   ☐ I *threw together* a quick meal for a few unexpected guests.

●○●   **throw together²**   cause two people to meet:
   ☐ Fate *threw* them *together* during the war and they got married soon after.

●● ●○● ●●○   **throw up¹**   *Informal* vomit something:
   ☐ He got terribly drunk and was *throwing up* for most of the evening.
   ☐ The dog *threw up* its dinner.

●●○   **throw up²**   produce or give rise to somebody or something, especially a famous person or an interesting idea, etc:
   ☐ This decade has *thrown up* very few notable architects.
   ☐ The conference has *thrown up* a number of interesting problems.

●○● ●●○   **throw up³**   **1** build something quickly:
   ☐ They *threw up* a new cabin in a couple of hours.
2 abandon, reject or resign from a career, opportunity etc:
   ☐ John *threw up* his job to go to Africa as a missionary.

●●○ ●○●   **tick off¹**   scold or reprimand somebody:
   ☐ The headmaster *ticked* the boy *off* for disobedience.

●●○ ●○● ●○●○   **tick off²**   place a mark alongside somebody's name or an item on a list, usually to indicate that the person or item has been treated, included, checked etc:
   ☐ When you have paid me, I'll *tick* you *off* the list.

☐ As the goods were unloaded, the foreman *ticked* them *off*.

●● **tick over** 1 operate or run slowly and smoothly, especially of the engine of a vehicle:

☐ I've left the car *ticking over* outside, so we can go straightaway.

☐ Is everything at work *ticking over* OK?

2 live or work at a steady rate without achieving much:

☐ He's just *ticking over* in the job until he finds something more interesting.

●○● **tide over** be sufficient for somebody for a period of time, especially of money:

☐ Can you lend me £20 to *tide* me *over* until I'm paid?

●○● **tie down** restrict or limit somebody's freedom with responsibilities or duties:

☐ She wouldn't marry him because she didn't want to *tie* him *down*.

☐ We were both *tied down* with a family and a full-time job.

●●(●○) **tie in (with)** be or cause something to be compatible with
●○●(●○) something else:

☐ The book is designed to *tie in with* the series of television programmes.

☐ Tim is very depressed. I hear his wife is very ill, so that *ties in*.

●● **tie up¹** fit together or be logically compatible, especially of two or more testimonies, reports, accounts, etc:

☐ The police got two eye-witness accounts but they didn't *tie up* at all.

●○● **tie up²** 1 keep somebody busy:
●●○
☐ This report will probably *tie* me *up* for about a week.

☐ I'm *tied up* at the moment. Can I see you later?

2 complete or finish making arrangements for something:

☐ Have you *tied up* the arrangements for the trip to London yet?

●○●(●○) **tie up (in)** invest money, capital, savings, etc, so that the
●●○(●○) money cannot be used for anything else:

☐ Jane would have bought the car if she hadn't *tied up* all her money in the house.

☐ The Government has a lot of money *tied up in* European development.

●○● **tighten up** make rules, regulations, laws, etc, more strict
●●○ or harsh:

☐ The company has *tightened up* the rules governing overtime.

●●(●○)	**tighten up (on)** become more severe and firm about something, especially of a group or person in authority: □ The police are really *tightening up on* drunken driving this Christmas.
●○● ●●○	**tip off** warn somebody that something is going to happen; inform the police of a crime which is going to be committed: □ Scotland Yard had been *tipped off* about the bank robbery.
N	□ I got a *tip-off* that the company was in trouble, so I sold my shares.
●○● ●●○	**tire out** make somebody very tired or exhausted: □ Looking after the children *tires* me *out*. □ After a day at the office she comes home *tired out*.
●●(●○) ●○●(●○)	**tog up (in)** *Informal* dress yourself or somebody else in formal or unusual clothes: □ The people entering the theatre had really *togged* themselves *up*. □ The army *togged* us *up in* full battle-gear and sent us off to the desert.
●●○ ●○●	**tone down** make something less strong, loud or shocking: □ If he *toned down* his arguments, people would be more sympathetic.
●●(●○) ●○●(●○)	**tone in (with)** be or cause something to be compatible or in harmony with something, especially in terms of appearance: □ The new buildings in the village *tone in* nicely *with* the older ones. □ It would be nice to *tone* the curtains *in with* the green carpet in the lounge.
●○● ●●○	**tone up** make something, especially your body, skin, muscles, etc, more vigorous, strong or healthy-looking: □ This exercise will *tone up* flabby tummy muscles. □ Daily jogging will *tone* you *up* and help you to lose weight.
●○● ●●○	**top up** **1** fill to the top a container which is partially empty: □ The car radiator should be *topped up* with water each week. **2** fill somebody's glass with more drink: □ More sherry, John? Let me *top* you *up*.
N	□ Would you like a *top-up*, Mary?
●○● ●●○	**toss off** produce or create something, often something artistic, quickly, and with little effort:

        □ The composer was able to *toss off* a complete sonata in two days.

●●   **toss up**   spin a coin to decide a matter, especially which team will bat, kick off, etc, in games like cricket and football:

        □ The referee *tossed up* to decide which team was to play against the wind.

        □ We can't both go out tonight. We'll *toss up* to see who goes.

●●○   **tot up**   calculate the total of something:
●○●   □ When we've *totted up* the votes, we'll announce the result of the election.

        □ I'll just *tot up* the cost of my holiday in France this summer.

●●   **touch down**   land on the ground, especially of an aircraft:

        □ TWA flight 402 is scheduled to *touch down* at 17.25.

●●○   **touch off**   **1** cause some violent action or reaction to take place:

        □ Police harrassment *touched off* a wave of inner-city riots.

    2 cause gunpowder, a bomb, a firework, etc, to explode:

        □ The slightest spark will *touch off* the whole ammunition dump.

●●○   **touch on/upon**   mention or talk briefly about something:

        □ Later in the lecture, I will *touch on* the issues of free will and determinism.

●○●   **touch up**   **1** improve the appearance of something by
●●○   adding small areas of paint, etc:

        □ You'd better *touch up* those rust spots before you sell the car.

    2 *Informal* make sexual advances by touching somebody:

        □ Mr Smithers is vile! He *touches* me *up* whenever I go near him.

●○●   **tout about/around**   offer something for sale somewhere,
●●○   especially something which has been dishonestly
●○●○ obtained:

        □ There are always people *touting* tickets *around* during the Wimbledon tennis championship.

●○●(●○) **trace back (to)**   find evidence of the origin of something
●●○(●○) in the past:

        □ He *traced* his ancestors *back to* the mid-sixteenth century.

        □ We must find out when the fault occurred. Can you *trace* it *back*?

●○● **track down**   find somebody or something by collecting
●●○ evidence and clues:
  □ The police *tracked* the murderer *down* after a three-
  week hunt.
  □ I've *tracked down* that book I was looking for.
●○● **trade in**   give something second-hand and used in partial
●●○ payment for something newer:
  □ He *traded* his old car *in* for a new hatch-back.
●●○ **trade on/upon**   use somebody's good nature, kindness,
  etc, for unfair advantage or benefit:
  □ He's *trading on* his wife's generosity by selling the
  house.
●● **trail away/off**   gradually become quieter, especially of a
  voice:
  □ As the figure in black moved past the window, Jim's
  voice *trailed off* into silence.
●●○ **trigger off**   cause some event, action or series of events to
●○● take place:
  □ The minister's remarks *triggered off* a fierce debate in
  the daily papers.
●● **trip up¹**   **1** stumble and possibly fall because your feet or
  legs hit some obstacle:
  □ I didn't see the step and I *tripped up*.
  2 make a mistake or be inefficient:
  □ I *tripped up* with the arrangements for the party, and
  forgot to buy any wine.
●○● **trip up²**   **1** cause somebody to stumble and possibly fall by
●●○ putting some obstacle in their way:
  □ The boys think it's funny to *trip up* the girls in the
  playground.
  2 deliberately cause somebody to make a mistake:
  □ The interviewer tried to *trip* me *up* with his questions.
●●○ **trot out**   produce or say something in a casual way,
  without careful thought:
  □ Frank *trotted out* the same feeble excuse for not
  attending the meeting.
●●○ **trump up**   invent a charge, accusation, story, etc,
  especially in order to send somebody to prison:
  □ The police *trumped up* false evidence in order to get the
  man convicted.
●○● **truss up**   tie or bind something firmly with rope, string,
●●○ etc:
  □ The prisoners had been *trussed up* and left to die.
●○● **try on**   put on an item of clothing to see whether it fits and
●●○ looks nice:
  □ Would you like to *try on* a larger size, sir?

●○●(●○)   **try on (with)**   do something deceitful, unlawful, improper, etc, to see if it will be allowed or tolerated:
☐ If you *try* your old tricks *on with* the new headmaster, you'll soon be in trouble.

●○●   **try out**   test a new invention, scheme, product, etc:
●●○   ☐ The design of the new car seems excellent, but we haven't *tried* it *out* on the road.
N   ☐ We could always give the idea a *try-out* to see if it works.

●○●●○   **try out on**   test the effect of something, especially a new
●●○●○   drug, on somebody or something:
☐ The manufacturers *tried out* the drugs *on* rats and mice.

●○●   **tuck away**   **1** put something in a drawer, cupboard or safe
●●○   place, especially in order to hide or store it:
☐ When she heard his voice, she *tucked* the money *away* under her pillow.
2 eat something quickly or eat a lot:
☐ You should see him *tuck away* a steak! Like lightning!

●●/   **tuck in/into**   start to eat something, especially a meal, in a
●●○   hungry way:
☐ Dinner's ready at last. Do *tuck in*, everybody!
☐ They *tucked into* the cake as if they were starving.

●○●   **tuck up**   wrap sheets and blankets around somebody,
●●○   especially a child, to make them comfortable and warm:
☐ Mummy will read you a story and *tuck* you *up* in a minute.

●●(●○)   **tune in (to)**   adjust a radio so that it receives the broadcast from a particular radio station:
☐ *Tune in* at the same time next week for another edition of your favourite programme!

●●   **tune up**   adjust a musical instrument so that the notes
●○●   produced are correct or in tune with other instruments:
●●○   ☐ The musicians need a few minutes to *tune up* before the concert can start.

●○●(●○)   **turf out (of)**   *Informal* ask or force somebody to leave or resign from somewhere:
☐ The landlord will *turf* you *out* if you get too drunk.
☐ Poor Andy was *turfed out of* the cricket club for trying to bribe the umpires.

●●○   **turn against**   become or cause somebody to become
●○●○   hostile or opposed to another person or thing:
☐ Why on earth should I want to *turn* your son *against* you?
☐ After ten years of friendship, Susan suddenly *turned against* Alice for no apparent reason.

206

●●○
●○●

turn away   refuse to admit or give help to somebody:
□ The show was sold out. Hundreds of people were *turned away* at the door.
□ A doctor can't simply *turn away* a dying man.

●○●
●●○

turn down   **1** adjust the volume control of a radio, record-player, tape-recorder, etc, to reduce the noise:
□ *Turn* that radio *down*! I'm trying to go to sleep!
2 adjust the controls of a cooker, heater, oven, etc, to reduce the heat:
□ If you're too hot, I'll *turn* the fire *down* a bit.
3 refuse an offer, request, invitation, etc:
□ This opportunity is too good to *turn down*.
□ Chris offered to lend me his car but I had to *turn* it *down*.

●●

turn in¹   go to bed:
□ It's late. I think I'll *turn in*.

●○●
●●○

turn in²   **1** deliver somebody to or put somebody under the control of the police, authorities, etc:
□ I promise never to do it again! Please don't *turn* me *in*.
2 produce and submit an essay, report, etc:
□ The teacher says that Paul is *turning in* some excellent pieces of homework.

●●○
●○●○

turn into   change or cause somebody or something to change into somebody or something different:
□ He used to be a nasty little boy but now he's *turned into* a charming young man.
□ I've discovered how to *turn* iron *into* gold.

●○●
●●○

turn off¹   **1** stop the supply of gas, water or electricity, by turning a tap or moving a switch:
□ *Turn* the tap *off*! The basin is overflowing!
2 stop a machine or appliance, especially a radio, record-player, television, etc, by moving a switch or button:
□ If you don't like the programmes, you can simply *turn* the television *off*.

●○●○
●○●

turn off²   *Informal* cause somebody to dislike or lose interest in somebody or something:
□ Television debates are guaranteed to *turn* anybody *off* politics.
□ That man is so arrogant! He really *turns* me *off*.

●●○
●○●

turn on¹   **1** start the supply of water, gas or electricity, by turning a tap or moving a switch:
□ He *turned* the water *on*.
2 start a machine or appliance, especially a radio, television, engine, etc, by moving a switch or button:
□ He *turned* the radio *on* to listen to the midday news.

●●○   **turn on²**   attack somebody suddenly and unexpectedly, either physically or verbally:
□ What made the dog suddenly *turn on* him after all these years?

●○●   **turn on³** *Informal* excite somebody, especially sexually:
□ The silk dress she was wearing really *turned* him *on*.

●○●   **turn out¹** **1** make something, especially a light or fire, stop
●●○   burning by moving a switch:
□ Will the last person to leave please *turn out* the lights?
2 produce, manufacture or construct something, especially of a factory, company, machine, etc:
□ This factory *turns out* thirty cars a day.
3 empty or remove the whole contents of something:
□ He *turned out* all his pockets trying to find the ring.

●●○   **turn out²**   prove or eventually be seen, felt, or judged to be
●●   something:
□ After a bad start, the party *turned out* to be a great success.
□ It *turned out* that she had known their intentions right from the start.
□ Let me know how things *turn out*, won't you?

●●   **turn out³**   leave your home and go outside:
□ I'm not *turning out* in this rain!
□ People *turned out* in their thousands to see the new president.

N   □ For such an important election, the *turn-out* was very low.

●○●(●○)   **turn out (of)**   ask or force somebody to leave or resign
●●○   from somewhere or something:
□ The manager *turned* the youth *out of* the cinema for being noisy.

●●○   **turn over**   sell goods or do business worth a particular amount:
□ This company has the potential to *turn over* a million pounds per year.

N   □ Our London branch has a much larger *turn-over*.

●○●(●○)   **turn over (to)**   deliver somebody or give control of
●●○   somebody to the police, authorities, etc:
□ The customs officials *turned* the man *over to* the French police.
□ At the request of Scotland Yard, the French police *turned over* their prisoner.

●○●○   **turn over to**   transfer control of something to somebody else:
□ When I retire I'll *turn* the family business *over to* my son.

●●   **turn up¹** **1** arrive, appear or be found:
□ He's always late. Yesterday he didn't *turn up* until six.
□ I lost my wallet in town last week and today it *turned up* at the bus station.
2 arise or become available unexpectedly, especially of an opportunity, chance, job, etc:
□ I'm still unemployed but I'm hoping something will *turn up* next week.

●●○   **turn up²** **1** discover, reveal or expose something:
●○●   □ While I was digging the garden I *turned up* a lovely Victorian brooch.
□ I went to the library and *turned up* a few more facts about the private life of Louis XIV.
2 adjust the controls of a radio, television, fire, etc, to increase the sound, brightness or heat:
□ *Turn* the record-player *up*. I can't hear it properly.
□ She felt cold and *turned* the heating *up* a little.

U, u

●○●   **urge on**   **1** force or encourage a person or animal to move or continue to move forward:
□ If the group leader hadn't *urged* them *on*, they would have been stuck in the forest for the night.
2 encourage or try to persuade somebody to do or to continue to do something:
□ The book would never have been written if the editor hadn't *urged* the writer *on*.

●○●   **use up**   finish a supply or remainder of something:
●●○
□ Why don't you *use up* the rest of the chicken in a soup? It's a shame to waste it.
□ If I'd known that you'd *used up* all the milk, I'd have bought some more.

●○●   **usher in**   introduce or mark the beginning of a new period,
●●○
fashion, generation, etc:
□ The invention of the telescope *ushered in* a new way of thinking about the universe.

V, v

●●○   **verge on/upon**   come very near to being in a certain condition, especially one which is undesirable:
- Several of his paintings *verge on* the obscene.
- His poor wife seems to be *verging on* senility.

●●○   **vie with**   compete with somebody, especially in order to win something or show yourself to be superior:
- The two children *vied with* each other for their father's attention.

●●○   **vouch for**   **1** guarantee the truth, reliability, etc, of something:
- I certainly wouldn't like to *vouch for* the accuracy of these figures, unless I had checked them myself.
- We can't *vouch for* the chair remaining at this price for much longer, you know.

2 declare your support for or confidence in somebody:
- How can I *vouch for* you when I hardly know you?

W, w

●●○ **wade into** attack somebody, either physically or verbally:
□ The boys *waded into* each other, kicking and punching.
□ The teacher *waded into* the girl for not doing her homework.

●●○ **wade through** read or work through a large amount of material slowly and laboriously:
□ If you expect me to *wade through* 200 pages of this nonsense, you're mistaken.

●● **wait about/around** remain somewhere, usually doing nothing, especially because the person that you are meeting is late:
□ Where have you been? I've been *waiting around* here for two hours.

●● **wait behind** remain somewhere after other people have left:
□ I'd like to ask you something in private. Could you *wait behind* for a couple of minutes, please?

●●○ **wait on/upon** 1 serve somebody with food and drink in a restaurant, etc:
□ We were *waited on* by a pretty girl in a pink pinafore.
2 take care of somebody's needs and wants:
□ The old man expected his entire family to *wait on* him.

●●(●○) **wait up (for)** not go to bed until somebody comes home:
□ I'll be very late tonight, so don't *wait up for* me.

●●(●○)
●○○●○ **wake up (to)** become or cause somebody to become aware of a problem, situation, etc:
□ She *woke up to* the problems of growing old.
□ If only we could *wake* them *up to* the dangers of the situation.

●●●○ **walk away/off with** win a prize, race, contest, etc, very easily:
□ He is so clever he *walked off with* all the prizes at school.

●●○ **walk into** 1 get a job, position, place on a course, etc, very easily:
□ He did so well at university that he *walked into* the first job he applied for.
2 enter a trap or difficult situation, especially because you have not been warned:
□ He *walked* straight *into* the same mistake that we all made.

●●○
●○●
      walk off   get rid of weight, a headache, a bad mood, etc.
by walking:
☐ He is determined to *walk off* some of his fat this week.

●●●○
      walk off with   **1** take something which belongs to
somebody else, either by mistake or on purpose:
☐ The burglars *walked off with* all my jewellery.
2 see **walk away/off with.**

●●
      walk out   leave a factory or place of work and go on
strike:
☐ The men *walked out* when they were asked to work for
lower wages.

N
      ☐ They staged a *walk-out* over their working conditions.

●●/
●●●○
      walk out/out of   leave a meeting, conference, etc, as a
protest:
☐ When the new member began to speak, everybody got
up and *walked out.*

N
      ☐ The talks ended abruptly with an angry *walk-out* by
union leaders.

●●●○
      walk out on   leave, abandon or desert somebody or
something, especially when you are needed or expected to
stay:
☐ He *walked out on* his wife and children and went to
live in Australia.

●●○
      walk over   **1** defeat somebody very easily in a race,
contest, etc:
☐ Our candidate will *walk over* the opposition. You'll
see.

N
      ☐ His election was a complete *walk-over.*
2 treat somebody with contempt:
☐ I can't understand why she allows her children to *walk
over* her as they do.

●○●
●●○
      wall in   enclose somebody or something with a wall or
some barrier:
☐ He was *walled in* by the crowd.

●●○
      wallow in   enjoy or indulge in something more than you
should:
☐ She *wallowed in* the praise she received.

●●●○
      waltz off with   win something, especially a prize, by
defeating other people easily:
☐ He *waltzed off with* six gold medals.

●●○
      want for   lack or be in need of something; always used in
the negative:
☐ Her little girl never *wants for* anything: she has
everything she could possibly need.

● ● ○   **ward off**   prevent something, especially a blow, illness, emotion, etc, from hitting or overwhelming you:
        □ She moved out of the way to *ward off* his blow.
        □ What can you recommend for *warding off* a cold?

● ● ○   **warm to**   gradually become more interested in or enthusiastic about something:
        □ She began to *warm to* her subject after a few minutes and spoke with real enthusiasm.

● ● ○   **warm to/towards**   gradually begin to like somebody and to feel interested in them:
        □ I *warmed to* the girl as soon as she came into the room.
        □ She *warmed towards* him when she realised he was lonely too.

● ●   **warm up**[1]   prepare for a contest or strenuous physical activity by doing exercises:
        □ The footballers *warmed up* for half an hour before the match.

N   □ They had an hour's *warm-up* before the match.

● ●   **warm up**[2]   become or cause somebody or something to
● ● ○   become more interested or lively:
● ○ ●   □ The magician *warmed up* his audience with a few quick tricks.
        □ The game suddenly *warmed up* when the other side scored a goal.

● ○ ●   **warn off**   try to prevent somebody from going somewhere
● ○ ● ○   or doing something, especially by threatening them:
        □ We wanted to have a picnic in the woods, but a large notice *warned* us *off*.

● ○ ● (● ○)   **wash down (with)**   help something be swallowed by
● ● ○ (● ○)   having a drink:
        □ This bread's rather dry. *Wash* it *down with* a cup of tea.

● ○ ●   **wash out**   cause an outdoor game, contest or event to be
● ● ○   cancelled, postponed or abandoned, especially of bad weather:
        □ The match was *washed out* by the heavy rain.

N   □ The match was a complete *wash-out*.
N   □ His idea turned out to be a total *wash-out*.

● ● ○   **wash over**   have no effect on somebody's attitude, understanding or behaviour:
        □ He is so used to receiving complaints that they just *wash over* him nowadays.

● ●   **wash up**[1]   wash the dishes, glasses, cutlery, etc, after a meal:

☐ Her husband *washed up* while she put the children to bed.

N

☐ Whose turn is it to do the *washing-up*?

●●○
●○●
wash up²   bring something onto the shore, especially of the sea:

☐ The waves *washed* the oil *up* onto the sand.

☐ A lot of rubbish was *washed up* by the high tide.

●●
waste away   lose weight and strength, especially of a part of the body or somebody who is ill:

☐ We could see him *wasting away* because of his illness.

●●
watch out   be careful, especially to avoid a dangerous situation or upsetting other people; often used in the imperative:

☐ *Watch out!* This is a very busy road.

☐ If you do that again you'll be in trouble, so you had better *watch out*.

●●(●○)
watch out (for)   remain alert, attentive or observant, so that you notice somebody or something:

☐ He asked me to *watch out for* his uncle who would be wearing a green suit.

☐ The doctor told me to *watch out for* any sickness or high temperature.

●●○
watch over   protect and be responsible for somebody or something:

☐ She asked me to *watch over* her daughter on the journey.

☐ He has been appointed to *watch over* the interests of the disabled.

●●○
●○●
water down   **1** dilute a liquid by adding water to it:

☐ I'm sure this whisky has been *watered down*.

2 make something weaker, less intense, less severe, etc:

☐ He agreed to *water down* his criticisms of the Government.

●●○
●○●
wave aside   dismiss or refuse to consider a comment, remark, suggestion, etc:

☐ She *waved aside* his objections to her plan.

●●
●○●
●●○
wear away   gradually disappear or cause something to disappear, because of use or friction:

☐ This staircase is so old that some of the steps have almost *worn away*.

☐ Over the centuries, the sea has *worn away* the rocks.

●●○
●○●
●●
wear down   **1** gradually become or cause something to become lower, thinner or reduced because of use or friction:

☐ You must buy a new tyre. This one has been *worn* right *down*.

2 weaken or cause somebody or something to be weakened gradually by continuous pressure or opposition:
   ☐ He was sure he would eventually *wear down* her objections to marrying him.

●●   **wear off**   become less intense or no longer felt, especially of a pain or drug:
   ☐ Now that you have taken a pill your headache will soon *wear off.*

●●   **wear on**   pass tediously or slowly, especially of time:
   ☐ She became more and more tired as the evening *wore on.*

●●
●○●
●●○   **wear out¹**   become or cause something to become unusable because of continuous use or wear:
   ☐ Her little boy *wears* his shoes *out* every two months.
   ☐ His shoes *wear out* very quickly.

●○●
●●○   **wear out²**   tire or exhaust somebody or something:
   ☐ Looking after four children *wears* her *out.*

●●○
●○●   **weed out**   get rid of the weakest, worst, etc, in a group or collection:
   ☐ He looked through the applications for the job and *weeded out* the most unsuitable ones.

●●○   **weigh against**   cause people to judge or regard somebody unsympathetically:
   ☐ His years in prison will *weigh against* him when he tries to get a job.

●○●
●●○   **weigh down**   **1** cause somebody or something to bend, especially of a heavy load:
   ☐ She was *weighed down* by her shopping.
   ☐ The snow *weighed down* the branches of the trees.
   2 make somebody feel sad and depressed:
   ☐ Problems of money *weighed* her *down.*

●●○   **weigh on**   cause worry and anxiety to somebody:
   ☐ The pressures of her job *weighed* heavily *on* her and she decided to find a new one.
   ☐ You can tell that something is *weighing on* his mind.

●●○
●○●   **weigh up**   **1** consider something carefully, especially before reaching a decision, making a judgement, etc:
   ☐ He *weighed up* the situation and decided he was unlikely to be successful.
   2 form an opinion about somebody's character:
   ☐ My wife is very quick at *weighing* people *up.*

●●○   **welch/welsh on**   *Informal* fail to pay a debt, keep a promise or agreement, etc:
   ☐ He *welched on* his debts.

☐ She *welshed on* her employer and the promises she had made him.

● ○ ● ● ○   **wheedle out of**   obtain something from somebody by using persuasion and flattery:
☐ She *wheedled* a new car *out of* her father.

● ● ○   **while away**   pass time lazily and pleasantly:
● ○ ●   ☐ He *whiled away* his holiday reading and listening to music.

● ● ○   **whip up   1** prepare something quickly, especially food:
☐ It won't take her long to *whip up* a meal.
2 arouse interest or feelings:
☐ He tried to *whip up* some support for his plan.
☐ I can't *whip up* any enthusiasm for going out this evening.

● ○ ●   **whisk away/off**   suddenly remove somebody or
● ● ○   something, especially in a vehicle:
☐ The police *whisked* the politician *away* as soon as the crowd became violent.

● ● ○   **whistle for**   *Informal* ask for something, especially payment, with no hope of getting it:
☐ We won't be able to pay them until next year. They'll just have to *whistle for* their money.

● ● ○   **whittle away**   reduce something gradually:
● ○ ●   ☐ The high cost of living has been *whittling away* our savings for a long time now.

● ● ○   **whittle down**   reduce something in stages, especially the
● ○ ●   size of a group, collection, list, etc:
☐ Eventually they *whittled down* the number of applicants to three.

● ○ ●   **win back**   regain something, especially affection or suport:
● ● ○   ☐ What can I do to *win* my girlfriend *back*?

● ○ ●(● ○)   **win over (to)**   succeed in getting somebody's support,
● ● ○   agreement, etc, especially by persuasion:
☐ She soon *won* him *over to* her way of thinking.

● ●   **win through/out**   succeed, especially after a difficult period:
☐ He had a long fight against illness but eventually he *won through*.

● ●   **wind down¹   1** work, move or take place with less and less speed, energy, frequency, etc, especially before stopping completely:
☐ School activities start *winding down* about two weeks before the end of term.
2 relax and become calmer:
☐ It took her a week to *wind down* after her exams.

●●○
●○●
    wind down²   gradually reduce the activity or intensity of something, especially before final closure or termination:
□ The company *wound down* its affairs in South Africa.

●●
●●○
●○●
    wind up¹   end or bring something to an end, especially a meeting or business operation:
□ He *wound up* the afternoon by thanking everybody for coming.
□ What will happen to all our jobs if the company *winds up*?

●○●
●●○
    wind up²   cause somebody to become tense or excited:
□ If there's any bad news nowadays, I simply don't tell him. It only *winds* him *up*.

●●
●●○
    wind up³   find yourself in a certain place or state, as the result of a previous action:
□ If you insist on working so hard, you'll *wind up* in hospital.

●●○
●○●
    wipe down   clean a table, wall, car, etc, with a slightly wet cloth:
□ Before you paint a room you should *wipe down* the walls and ceiling.

●●○
●○●
    wipe off/out   cancel a debt:
□ You've helped me so much that I'm willing to *wipe off* the £20 you owe me.

●●○
●○●
    wipe out   **1** clean the inside of something by using a cloth:
□ Don't forget to *wipe out* the bath after you've used it.
2 kill, destroy or get rid of somebody or something, especially in great numbers:
□ A whole regiment was *wiped out* in the battle.
□ Doctors hope that they will be able to *wipe out* malaria very soon.

●●○
●○●
    wipe up¹   remove something which has been dropped or spilled by using a cloth:
□ Please *wipe up* the coffee you have just poured all over my carpet.

●●○
●○●
●●
N
    wipe up²   dry dishes, glasses, cutlery, etc, that have just been washed:
□ Whose turn is it to *wipe up*?
□ I dropped the glass while I was *wiping* it *up*.
□ You can help me do the *wiping-up* if you like.

●○●○
    wish on/onto   want somebody or something to become somebody else's responsibility or property, usually used with *would* and a negative:
□ The child gets naughtier every day. I wouldn't *wish* him *on* my worst enemy.

●●○   **wolf down**   eat something quickly and greedily like a
●○●   wolf:
      □ If you *wolf down* your food like that, you'll be sick.

●●○   **wonder at**   be very surprised by something; usually used
      with a negative:
      □ You can hardly *wonder at* her leaving home. She
      should have done it years ago.

●●○   **work against**   hinder or impede something:
      □ His laziness *works against* his basic intelligence.

●○●   **work in/into**   include something in a story, conversation,
●●○/ etc, especially in a deliberate or contrived way:
●○●○ □ He always manages to *work in* a reference to the
      money I still owe him.

●●○   **work off**   get rid of weight, tension, emotions, etc,
●○●   especially by work or physical activity:
      □ He *worked off* his anger by concentrating on all the
      letters he had to write.
      □ He hoped to *work off* his extra weight by swimming
      and playing tennis.

●○●(●○) **work off (on)**   get rid of an unpleasant feeling or emotion
●●○(●○) by making somebody else suffer:
      □ You needn't think you can *work* your frustration *off*
      on me!

●●○   **work out¹**   **1** calculate or solve something:
●○●   □ Can you *work out* how much money we will need for
      our holiday?
      2 plan, invent or devise something:
      □ He *worked out* all the details of the attack.
      □ They decided to *work out* new rules for the game.
      3 understand somebody's character or reasons; usually
      used with a negative:
      □ I can't *work out* why he behaves as he does.
      □ He's a strange child. I can't *work* him *out*.

●●   **work out²**   **1** have a definite answer:
      □ Surely your maths teacher wouldn't give you a sum
      that didn't *work out*?
      2 have a favourable or happy outcome:
      □ I hope your plans for the future *work out*.
      □ Things do not seem to be *working out* for them as they
      had hoped.
      3 do physical exercises, especially of a boxer, dancer, etc:
      □ He spent the morning *working out* at the gym.
N   □ He had a long *work-out* before his fight.
●●●○ **work out at/to**   have a final cost or total after all
      calculations have been done:
      □ His salary *works out at* £10,000 a year.

☐ The whole journey *worked out to* 310 miles.

●○● **work over** *Informal* beat somebody in a deliberate and calculated way, especially as a punishment or to extract information:
☐ The gang *worked* him *over* until he told them where the money was hidden.

N ☐ They gave him a *working-over*.

●●○ **work towards** try to achieve something:
☐ All the teachers were *working towards* the introduction of new syllabuses.

●●○ **work under** do a job under the guidance or supervision of somebody:
☐ He was lucky to *work under* a professor who was always willing to help young members of staff.

●●○
●○● **work up** 1 gradually develop something, especially a business:
☐ It's amazing how he has managed to *work up* the business from almost nothing.
2 arouse feelings, interest, appetite, etc:
☐ I can't *work up* any enthusiasm for studying today.
☐ He walked twenty kilometres and *worked up* a good appetite for dinner.

●○●(●○) **work up (into/to)** get or cause somebody to get very excited or upset about something:
☐ If you want the men to agree to strike action, you'll have to *work* them *up* a bit first.
☐ She *worked* herself *up into* a terrible state of panic.

●●●○ **work up to** gradually approach or prepare to mention a subject, especially an important or embarrassing one:
☐ I haven't asked her if she can lend me the money yet, but I'm *working up to* it.

●○●●○ **worm out of** get information, a secret, etc, from somebody by using persuasion and cunning:
☐ It took me a long time to *worm* the truth *out of* him.

●● **wrap up¹** 1 put on warm clothes:
☐ It's cold outside, so make sure you *wrap up* well.
2 *Informal* stop talking; often used in the imperative to express anger or irritation:
☐ *Wrap up*, Mary, for goodness' sake! I'm trying to work.

●●○
●●○ **wrap up²** 1 conclude a meeting, discussion, investigation, etc:
☐ His instructions were to *wrap up* the meeting by three o'clock.
2 finalise an agreement, business deal, etc:

□ To *wrap up* the deal, their sales team offered us a £1000 reduction on each model.

●●●○ **wriggle out of**   *Informal* avoid a duty or difficult situation, especially by being cunning or by making excuses:

□ You promised that you would cut the grass today, so don't try *wriggling out of* it.

□ How does he always manage to *wriggle out of* his share of the work?

●●(●○) **write away/off (for)**   send an order for something, especially for a free gift or something that you cannot buy locally:

□ I have *written away for* a copy of the new English dictionary.

□ If you *write off* within two weeks, we'll send you a free record.

●●(●○) **write in (to)**   send a letter to a magazine, newspaper, radio station, etc, to complain, make a request or express an opinion:

□ He *wrote in to* the newspaper to complain about the previous day's headline.

□ The presenter of the programme asked listeners to *write in* with their suggestions.

●○●/
●●○ **write in/into**   include something deliberately in a legal or official document:

□ Make sure that the clause about medical expenses is *written into* the contract.

●○●
●●○ **write off**   **1** accept or decide that somebody or something is no good:

□ He *wrote off* the team without giving them a proper chance.

□ The critics *wrote* him *off* as a conductor after just one concert.

2 damage something badly, especially a car:

□ You're lucky to have *written off* the old car and not the new one.

N □ His car was a complete *write-off*.

3 accept that something, especially an amount of money, is lost and cannot be recovered:

□ The firm had to *write off* the man's debt when they heard that he was bankrupt.

●○●○ **write off as**   form a certain judgement or opinion about somebody or something, especially one that reveals your disappointment or displeasure:

□ Within days she had *written* him *off as* an idiot.

●●(●○)   **write off (for)** see **write away/off (for)**.

●○●(●○)   **write out (of)** remove a character from a television or

●●○   radio series:

       □ She was eventually *written out of* the serial after
       playing the part for ten years.

●○●   **write up** produce a full written account of something,

●●○   especially on the basis of a set of notes:

       □ I've got to stay in tonight and *write up* this afternoon's
       experiment.

       □ If I don't *write up* my notes almost immediately, I
       simply can't understand them.

Z, z

●●(●○)　**zero in (on)** **1** approach or discover the exact position of something, especially of guns:
□ The tanks *zeroed in on* our defences with the most deadly accuracy.
2 concentrate your efforts or focus your attention on something:
□ We should *zero in on* this opportunity to win public approval before it's too late.

●○●
●●○
●●　　　**zip up** help somebody dress by fastening the zip on their clothing; fasten by means of a zip:
□ 'Will you *zip* me *up*, please?' she asked.
□ She hates dresses that *zip up* at the back.

●●(●○)　**zoom in (on)** make the subject of a photograph appear to come closer by the use of a zoom lens:
□ Occasionally the camera would *zoom in on* the old lady's hands.